ABNORMAL PSYCHOLOGY

Richard Gross and Rob McIlveen

Reference Only

Hodder & Stoughton

A MEMBER OF THE HODDER HEADLINE GROUP

PICTURE CREDITS

The authors and publisher would like to thank the following copyright holders for their permission to reproduce illustrative materials in this book:

Associated Press/Kathy Willens for Figure 1.2 (p. 2); **Big Pictures/© Jamie Budge** for Figure 1.3 (p.4); **The Bridgeman Art Library** for Figure 4.1 (p. 38) The Garden of Earthly Delights: Hell, right wing of triptych, detail of 'Tree Man', c. 1500, panel by Hieronymus Bosch (c.1450–1516), Prado, Madrid/ Bridgeman Art Library, London; **Colorific!/ Mark Richards/ Dot Pictures** for Figure 10.1 (p. 108); **Mary Evans Picture Library** for Figure 2.1 (p. 11); **The Freud Museum, Vienna** for Figure 2.2 (p. 13); **Steve Goldberg/ Monkmeyer Press Photo Service** for Figure 5.2 (p. 58); **HarperCollins Publishers** for Figures 2.3 (p. 14) and 3.2 (p. 30); **Johns Hopkins University Press** for Figure 13.1 (p. 141) from Smith, M. L., Glass, G. V. & Miller, T. I. *The Benefits of Psychotherapy* © 1980. Reprinted by permission of the Johns Hopkins University Press; **Lifefile** for Figures 2.5 © Barry Mayes (p. 16) and 6.1 © Mike Maidment (p. 65); **The Kobal Collection** for Figures 3.1 (p. 27) and 10.2 (p. 110); **Rex Features, London** for Figures 1.4 by Charles Ommanney (p. 7), 6.4 © SIPA-PRESS (p. 70), 7.1 by Robin Palmer (p. 77) and 7.2 (p. 78, left); **The Science Museum/ Science and Society Picture Library** for Figure 8.1 (p. 88, left); **The Science Photo Library** for Figures 6.2 (p. 66) and 8.1 Will and Deni Mcintyre (p. 88, right); **The Shakespeare Centre Library, Stratford-upon-Avon** for Figure 6.3 (p. 67); **The Telegraph Colour Library** for Figure 9.1 (p. 97); **John Wiley & Sons** for Figure 5.1 (p. 53) from Lewinsohn, P. M. A behavioural approach to depression. In R. Friedman and M. Katz (eds) *The Psychology of Depression: Contemporary Theory and Research*. Washington DC: Winston/Wiley; **Yes Magazine** for Figure 7.2 (p. 78, right).

Every effort has been made to obtain necessary permission with reference to copyright material. The publishers apologise if inadvertently any sources remain unacknowledged and will be glad to make the necessary arrangements at the earliest opportunity.

Index prepared by Frank Merrett, Cheltenham, Gloucs.

British Library Cataloguing in Publication Data
A catalogue record for this title is available from the British Library

ISBN 0 340 67950 6

First published 1996
Impression number   10   9   8   7   6   5   4   3   2   1
Year   1999   1998   1997   1996

Copyright © 1996 Richard Gross and Rob McIlveen

Hodder Headline Plc, 338 Euston Road, London NW1 3BH by Redwood

CONTENTS

Part 2: Psychopathology

Part 3: Therapeutic approaches

Contents

PREFACE

Our aim in this book is to provide an introduction to the area of abnormal psychology. In order to do this, we have divided the book into three parts. The first, *Conceptions and models of abnormality*, consists of three chapters. In Chapter 1, we look at some of the alternative approaches to defining abnormality and examine some of the problems associated with these. In Chapter 2, we introduce five alternative models or paradigms in abnormal psychology. These are the medical, psychodynamic, behavioural, cognitive and humanistic models. As well as outlining their views on the causes of abnormal behaviour, we also consider some of the implications they have for the treatment of abnormality. Chapter 3 considers two approaches to the classification of abnormal behaviours and examines some of the problems that surround their use.

Part 2 of this book, *Psychopathology*, takes a detailed look at the characteristics of four mental disorders. In Chapters 4 and 5, we look at schizophrenia and depression respectively, and in Chapters 6 and 7, we look at anxiety disorders and eating disorders respectively. For each of the disorders we describe, we also look critically at the explanations that have been advanced to explain their origins.

The third part of this book, *Therapeutic approaches*, consists of six chapters. Each of the models we introduced in Chapter 2 advocates a particular approach to the treatment of mental disorders. In Chapters 8 to 12, we critically consider therapies based on the medical, psychodynamic, behavioural, cognitive and humanistic models. Our final chapter examines the issue of how the effectiveness of therapies can be assessed.

We believe that this book covers the major aspects of abnormal psychology as it would be taught on most courses, including A level and undergraduate courses. While the sequence of chapters and some of the content is based on the revised AEB A level syllabus, the general issues and major models that are discussed, including explanations of disorders and approaches to treatment, represent the core of this important and exciting area of psychology. For the purposes of revision, we have included detailed summaries of the material that is presented in each chapter. Although we have not included a separate glossary, the *Index* contains page numbers in **bold** which refer to definitions and main explanations of particular concepts for easy reference.

DEDICATION

To Jan, Tanya and Jo. Who else! With my love, as always. R.G.

To Gill, William and Katie, with love. R.M.

ACKNOWLEDGEMENTS

As usual, it is a pleasure to acknowledge the help and guidance given to us by Tim Gregson-Williams and Julie Hill at Hodder & Stoughton.

PART 1
Conceptions and models of abnormality

1

WHAT IS ABNORMALITY?

Introduction and overview

Whilst much psychological theory and research deals with normal psychological processes and development, the area of interest of this book is *abnormal* psychology. The twelve chapters which follow are concerned with the classificaton of abnormal behaviour, the causes of certain types of abnormal behaviour, and the ways in which abnormality can be treated. The themes of these chapters assume that it is both possible and meaningful to draw the line between normal and abnormal. Our aim in this chapter is to look at some of the ways in which abnormality has been defined and to consider some of the practical and ethical issues that arise from these definitions.

'Abnormality': two illustrative examples?

William Buckland (1784–1856) was an interesting man. He was Oxford University's inaugural Professor of Geology and the first person in England to recognise that glaciers had once covered much of the northern part of the United Kingdom. Buckland supervised the laying of the first pipe drains in London and was responsible for introducing gas lighting to Oxford. He also ate bluebottles, moles and, having been shown it by a friend, the embalmed heart of the executed King Louis XIV of France.

Figure 1.1 William Buckland: a connoisseur of fine cuisine?

In 1994, a male passenger on a train on the London to Sidcup line was also interesting, at least to other travellers sharing the carriage. Indeed, one of them was moved to write to *The Daily Telegraph* to describe what took place:

'Opposite sat an ordinary-looking, well-dressed man in his mid-thirties who was reading a book called *Railway Systems of North Africa*. The man closed his book and wedged it between himself and another passenger. Bending down, he untied the laces of his right shoe, removed it and placed it on the carriage floor. He then removed his right sock and placed it on his lap. Oblivious to the stares of fellow passengers, he then undid his left shoe lace, removed the shoe, placed it on the floor beside its companion, transferred his left sock to his right foot and put the sock from his right foot onto his left foot. For half a minute he inspected his handiwork and, presumably satisfied, donned his shoes, tied up their laces, retrieved his book and continued reading' (Davies, 1994).

Quite possibly, the consumption of bluebottles and moles, washed down with some bats' urine (a behaviour for which William Buckland was also known) might strike you as being a little 'odd'. Swapping over socks in a crowded railway carriage might also appear 'a little bit strange'. Perhaps you might even go so far as to say that both Buckland and the train passenger were 'abnormal' and you could probably suggest why this was the case. However, and as we will show in the remainder of this chapter, the intuitive definitions we have about the nature of abnormality do not always stand up to rigorous scrutiny!

Defining abnormality as a 'deviation from statistical norms'

By definition, abnormality means 'deviating from the norm or average'. Perhaps the most obvious way to define abnormality is in terms of characteristics or behaviours which are *statistically infrequent*. This definition is an intuitively appealing one. For example, if we know that the average height of a population of adults is 5' 8", we would probably describe an adult who was 7' or 3' as being 'abnormally' tall or short respectively. When people behave in the way that the vast majority of people do not, or do not behave in the way that the vast majority of people do, we have a tendency to label them as being 'abnormal'.

You might have used this definition of abnormality as you read about William Buckland and the passenger on the train. Most people in our culture do not eat flies and moles and so, by this definition of abnormality, William Buckland would be 'abnormal'. So too would the passenger on the train, since transferring one's socks from one foot to another on a crowded train is not something the vast majority of people do.

Unfortunately, there are drawbacks to using a purely statistical approach to defining abnormality. One of these is that it does not take into account the *desirabil-*

ity of a behaviour or characteristic. Eating moles and flies is statistically infrequent *and* probably undesirable. But what about having a Biology degree at the age of 13 and, at age 17, being the youngest doctor in the world? Balamurali Ambati, who completed a six-year medical course in less than four years and can now operate on life and limb (even though he may not be able to drive himself to work), has abilities that we can only marvel at. But he would still be defined as 'abnormal' according to the statistical definition (as indeed would Mozart, who performed his own concerto at the age of three).

Figure 1.2   Balamurali Ambati: a graduate in Biology at the age of 13, a doctor at 17, but abnormal by the deviation from statistical norms definition of abnormality

Another drawback to using a statistical approach to defining abnormality is that, in all cultures, there are people involved in a range of undesirable behaviours. Hassett & White (1989) have suggested that: 'Americans are involved in a wide variety of socially undesirable behaviour patterns from mild depression to child abuse' and that if it were possible to add up all the numbers, 'it would become clear that as many as one out of every two people would fall into at least one of these categories'. These behaviour patterns, which characterise half the American population, would be 'normal' in a statistical sense, but they are also regarded as constituting mental disorders (see Chapter 3).

There is at least one other drawback to the statistical definition of abnormality and that is in deciding just how *far* from the average a person must deviate before being considered 'abnormal'. If the average height of a population is 5' 8", exactly *when* does a person become abnormally tall or short? As Miller & Morley (1986) have remarked, any chosen cut-off point is necessarily an *arbitrary* one.

From what we have said, it seems clear that it is not sufficient to define abnormality *solely* in terms of a deviation from statistical norms. We would, however, accept that it can sometimes be a helpful way of looking at abnormality. In our culture, we consider people who see or hear things that are not there to be 'abnormal', and *most* people in our society do not experience such hallucinations. Nonetheless, a useful definition of abnormality needs to take more into account than just the statistical frequency of behaviours.

Defining abnormality as a 'deviation from ideal mental health'

A second approach to defining abnormality is to identify the characteristics and abilities (which may or may not be statistically frequent) that people *should* possess in order to be considered 'normal'. Abnormality is then defined as deviating from these characteristics. A number of 'ideals' have been proposed. Jahoda (1958), for example, identified *individual choice, resistance to stress, an accurate perception of reality* and *self-actualisation* as

being, amongst others, characteristics of ideal mental health.

This approach is also an appealing one, since the ideals identified above seem to have some sort of validity. However, like the statistical definition, there are also a number of drawbacks to defining abnormality in this way. First, the ideals are so demanding that almost everybody would be considered abnormal to some degree, depending on how many of the ideals they failed to satisfy. According to Abraham Maslow (1968), only a few people achieve *self-actualisation*. As a result, most of us would therefore be considered abnormal as far as this definition was concerned (and dare we suggest that, if most of us are abnormal and therefore in the majority, then by the statistical definition we outlined earlier, being abnormal is normal?).

Second, lists of ideals defining ideal mental health are *value judgements*, that is, judgements reflecting the beliefs of those who construct the lists. A person who hears voices when nobody is there may well be unhealthy as far as some people are concerned. But the person who hears the voices, and welcomes them, would define him- or herself as being perfectly healthy and normal. A culture that emphasised *group cooperation* might reject Jahoda's view that *individual choice* is part of *ideal mental health*. It is important for us to remember that this problem does not arise when judgements are made about *physical health*, since such judgements are neither moral nor philosophical. As Szasz (1960) has observed: 'what (physical) health is can be stated in anatomical and physical terms'. If there are no abnormalities present, then a person is considered to be in 'ideal' health.

A third reason for questioning this approach to abnormality is that it is *bound by culture*. We have occasionally qualified some of our earlier comments with the phrase *in our culture* or *at least as far as our culture is concerned*. Whilst different cultures have some shared ideals about what constitutes mental health, there are some ideals that are not shared. In one culture, the Sambia of New Guinea, male youths are taught that females are poison, and the males engage in prescribed unlimited fellatio. Such behaviour is considered healthy and, indeed, desirable. To give another example, soccer is popular on the island of Java, although the game is not played in quite the same way as it is in Britain. The Javan game is a necessarily quick-passing one, since the ball is first soaked in petrol and then set alight.

Figure 1.3   Football the Javan way: mentally healthy behaviour or not?

ties within a society? Murder is a popular activity among Baltimore youth. Shall we say that, in that city, murder is healthy?'

Even if we accept the point made by Chance, the deviation from ideal mental health definition is also *era-dependent*, that is, it changes over time *within* a particular culture. As Wade & Tavris (1993) have noted, seeing visions was a sign of healthy religious fervour in thirteenth-century Europe, but in twentieth-century Europe, seeing such visions might be a sign of the mental disorder *schizophrenia* (see Chapter 4).

A fifth problem with this approach to defining abnormality is that it is limited by the *context* in which a behaviour occurs. For example, it is 'healthy' to walk around wearing a steel helmet if one works on a building site, but it is less healthy to engage in this behaviour if one is a waiter in a restaurant. Faced with the choice between a plate of highly nutritious salad and a plate of mole with flies, the former would be a healthier choice. In the absence of an alternative, however, a plate of mole with flies might be better than nothing at all!

Defining abnormality as a deviation from ideal mental health can sometimes be helpful. On its own, however, it has sufficient drawbacks for us to conclude that it is less than satisfactory.

Defining abnormality as a 'failure to function adequately'

According to this approach to defining abnormality, which overlaps with the definition we have just discussed, every human being should achieve some sense of personal well-being and make some contribution to a larger social group. Any individual who fails to function adequately in this way is seen as being 'abnormal'. Sue *et al.* (1994) use the terms *practical* or *clinical criteria* to describe the ways in which people fail to function adequately since, as Buss (1966) has noted, they are often the basis on which people come to the attention of psychologists or other interested professionals.

One way in which people can come to the attention of a professional is if they are experiencing *personal distress*

Provided that the game is played near water and that the legs are shaved, Javans consider playing soccer in this way to be 'healthy'. It is unlikely that this view would be shared in Britain, although it might make Arsenal marginally more interesting to watch!

We should acknowledge, however, that those who subscribe to the definition of abnormality as a deviation from ideal mental health would argue that there ought to be some sort of *universal standard* to which we should all, irrespective of culture, aspire. As Chance (1984) has observed:

'Would it really make sense to say that murder and cannibalism are healthy just because some cultures believed them to be, and if it does, then why not apply the same standards to communi-

or *discomfort*. Echoing Buss, (1966), Miller & Morley (1986) have remarked that:

> 'People do not come to clinics because they have some abstract definition of abnormality. For the most part, they come because their feelings or behaviours cause them distress'.

Such feelings or behaviours might not be obvious to other people, but may take the form of intense anxiety, depression, a loss of appetite and many other things.

Unfortunately, whilst such psychological states might cause personal distress, we could not use personal distress by itself as a definition of abnormality, since certain psychological states giving rise to personal distress might be *appropriate responses* in certain situations. Examples here would include experiencing anxiety in response to the presence of a real threat and experiencing depression as a response to the death of a loved one. In such cases, we would not consider these to be abnormal unless they persisted long after the source of them was removed or after most people had adjusted to them.

Moreover, there are some major forms of mental disorders that are not necessarily accompanied by personal distress. *Antisocial personality disorder*, for example, involves repeated acts of crime and violence *without* the person who commits them experiencing feelings of guilt or remorse. With *substance-related disorders*, the consequences of excessive use of, say, alcohol, may be strenuously denied by the user.

Although certain psychological states might not cause personal distress, they may be *distressing to others*. For example, a person who tried to assassinate the Prime Minister might not experience any personal distress at all. However, the fact that this person is a threat to others also constitutes a failure to function adequately. Even a person who does not experience personal distress or is not distressing to others would be failing to function adequately if the behaviour was *maladaptive*, either for the individual concerned or society. By maladaptive, we mean being prevented from efficiently satisfying social and occupational roles. Some mental disorders, such as the substance-related disorders we mentioned earlier, are actually defined in terms of how the (ab)use of the substance produces social and occupational difficulty, such as marital problems and poor performance at work.

We could also include Davison & Neale's (1994) term *unexpected behaviour* as a failure to function adequately. By this, Davison and Neale mean reacting to a situation or an event in ways that could not be predicted or reasonably expected from what we know about human behaviour. If a person behaves in a way which is 'out of all proportion to the situation', then we might say that he or she was failing to function adequately. A person who reacted to the relegation of his or her favourite soccer team by attempting to commit suicide would, for example, be failing to function adequately.

If we have generalised expectations about how people will typically react in certain situations, then behaviour is predictable to the extent that we know about the situation. However, since different situations have more (or less) powerful effects on behaviour, we cannot say that all situations are equal in terms of our ability to predict how a person will behave. There will be some situations in which differences between people will determine what behaviours will occur, which, of course, makes it more difficult to predict what will happen. As a result, we could argue that a person was functioning adequately if behaviour was *partially predictable* and was failing to function adequately if his or her behaviour was *always* extremely predictable or *always* extremely unpredictable. For example, a person who, for whatever reason, was very unpredictable would be difficult to interact with since, when we interact with one another, we need to make assumptions and have expectations about what responses will occur. A person who acted so consistently that he or she seemed to be unaffected by any situation would also strike us as being 'odd', and may give us the impression that we were interacting with a machine rather than another human being.

Finally, we could also include the *bizarreness* of behaviour as an example of a failure to function adequately. Unless it is the case that the Martians, in collusion with the CIA, *are* trying to extract information from a person, it would be hard to deny that a person making such claims was behaving bizarrely. It would be equally hard to deny that such a person was failing to function adequately.

So how do William Buckland and the man on the London to Sidcup line fare as far as this definition of abnormality is concerned? Although Buckland's behaviour might not have caused him distress, it is reasonable to assume that it was distressing to others. However, given his prominent position at Oxford University and other things we know about him from the brief description we gave at the beginning of this chapter, we would probably not call his behaviour maladaptive. His eating of Louis XIV's heart was unexpected, at least to the friend who had shown him it (and who had, incidentally, paid a large sum of money to a grave robber for it). Whether Buckland was partially or extremely predictable/unpredictable is hard to gauge from what historical documents tell us about him. As far as bizarreness is concerned, we would have to question whether his eating and drinking behaviours constituted adequate functioning.

We would assume that the man on the train was not distressed by his own behaviour, nor does it seem from the letter writer's account that other people were. More contentious, perhaps, is whether such behaviour was maladaptive. As was the case with Buckland, it is hard to make an assessment about predictability, but we would probably accept that the behaviour was bizarre. You, of course, may well disagree with us and, in so doing, are gaining first-hand experience of the difficulties involved in defining abnormality!

For at least some psychologists and other interested professionals, the *failure to function adequately* definition of abnormality is the most useful single approach and one which is closest to 'common sense'. However, as is the case with the other definitions we have described, there are problems with defining abnormality in this way. As Gross (1995) has remarked, using the distress of others as a failure to function adequately is a double-edged sword. In some cases, it can be a 'blessing' in that the distress one person experiences as a result of the behaviour of another can, on some occasions, literally be a 'life saver'. On other occasions, it can be a curse, as would be the case when, say, a parent experienced distress over a son or daughter's sexuality, whilst the son or daughter felt perfectly comfortable with it.

We could also question the phrase *out of all proportion to the situation*, which we used when we described unexpected behaviour as a failure to function adequately, since it is not clear who will decide what *out of all proportion* means. It also seems that Davison and Neale considered unexpected behaviours to be those which involve an *over-reaction*. It must surely be the case that a behaviour which is out of all proportion can equally refer to an *under-reaction* as well.

Finally, we might also question what is meant by the term *bizarreness*. As Houston *et al.* (1991) have observed, there are certain behaviours which *in general* would be considered bizarre, but which have occurred under conditions and in contexts such that the perpetrators were able to justify them in terms of survival, political or religious meanings. Whether or not we agree with the justifications, we must accept that, in some contexts, seemingly bizarre behaviours might not be described as 'abnormal' because they allow an individual to function adequately. Dressing up in clothes of the opposite sex, for example, may, depending on the context, be entertaining for others and profitable for the person engaging in the behaviour.

Defining abnormality as a 'deviation from social norms'

In all societies, standards or *norms* for appropriate behaviours and beliefs exist. Put another way, all societies have expectations about how people should behave as well as what they should think. Gross (1995) has proposed that it is useful to think of these in terms of a *continuum of normative behaviour* ranging from behaviours which are *unacceptable, tolerable, acceptable/permissible, desirable*, and ending up with those that are *required/obligatory*. A fourth way of attempting to define abnormality is in terms of the breaking of society's standards or norms.

Consider, for example, homosexuality. At least some people consider homosexuality to be abnormal because it represents a deviation from the 'natural' form of sexual behaviour in humans. Despite the fact that, in Britain, homosexuality is legal between consenting adults over the age of 18, it is still seen by some people as behaviour which violates societal norms or expectations.

It is certainly sometimes the case that behaviour which deviates from social norms is also statistically infrequent. In Britain, drinking bats' urine and swapping over one's socks on a crowded train would be examples. However, some behaviours which are considered to be socially unacceptable in our culture are actually statistically frequent. Various studies (e.g. Gibson, 1967) have

Figure 1.4   Homosexuality is judged by many to be abnormal, because it deviates from heterosexuality, which is defined as the norm. But who defines the norm and can there be more than one (sexual) norm within the same society/culture? And can norms change over time within the same society/culture?

shown high 'confession rates' amongst people asked if they had engaged in a prosecutable offence without actually being convicted for it. As far as the deviation from social norms definition is concerned, most people would be defined as 'abnormal' (and as far as the deviation from statistical norms definition is concerned, criminal behaviour, at least that found in various studies, would be considered 'normal'!).

Like the deviation from ideal mental health definition of abnormality, the deviation from social norms definition is also bound by culture. In Western culture, we consider anyone who assumes that a stranger will try to take advantage of us and be hostile towards us to be overly suspicious. We might even use the label *paranoid* to describe such a person. However, when the anthropologist Mead (1935) studied the Mundugumor people, she found that perpetual suspicion was the norm, since strangers (and even male members of the same household) actually *were* hostile.

In Western culture, the sons of a deceased father are not expected to clean his bones and distribute them to relatives to wear as ornaments. Amongst the Trobriand islanders studied by Malinowski (1929), however, such behaviour was expected and hence 'normal'. Indeed, a widow who did not wear her former husband's jawbone on a necklace was failing to behave in accordance with her culture's expectations and was considered abnormal. Perhaps it is possible that a culture exists in

which William Buckland's eating and drinking habits would fail to raise an eyebrow.

The deviation from social norms approach to defining abnormality is further weakened by the fact that it, too, is era-dependent. As values change, so particular behaviours move from being considered abnormal to normal to abnormal again and so on. As Atkinson *et al.* (1993) have noted, some behaviours today tend to be viewed as differences in lifestyle rather than signs of abnormality, the smoking of marijuana being, perhaps, one such example.

As was the case with other definitions of abnormality, it can be helpful to use the idea of violating societal norms or expectations as an approach to defining abnormality. By itself, however, it cannot serve as a complete and acceptable definition.

Conclusions

It is clear that all the definitions of abnormality we have discussed have both good and bad points. All are helpful as ways of conceptualising abnormality, but none on its own is sufficient as a definition of abnormality. As we will see elsewhere in this book, not all of the characteristics we have used in our description of approaches to abnormality are necessarily evident in those behaviours which are *classified* as being mental disorders. Indeed, any of the behaviours classified as being mental disorders may reflect only one, or a combination, of the characteristics. As Sue *et al.* (1994) have noted, different definitions of abnormality carry different implications, and there is certainly no consensus on a 'best definition'.

Drawing on research conducted by Strupp & Hadley (1977) and Wakefield (1992), Sue and his colleagues have suggested that a *multiple perspectives* (or *multiple definitions*) view is, perhaps, one way of approaching the very difficult task of defining abnormality. As they note, a truly adequate understanding of abnormality can probably only be achieved through a comprehensive evaluation of all points of view.

SUMMARY

- Perhaps the most obvious way to define abnormality is in terms of characteristics/behaviours which are **statistically infrequent (deviation from statistical norms)**. However, while this might be intuitively appealing, it does not take into account the **desirability** of a characteristic/behaviour. It also fails to recognise that in all cultures large numbers of people (perhaps as many as half the population) engage in behaviours that may be regarded as constituting mental disorders.

- The statistical definition also raises the crucial issue of deciding how **far** from the average a person must deviate before being considered 'abnormal'; any chosen cut-off point is necessarily **arbitrary.** Although this definition of abnormality can sometimes be helpful, it is not sufficient **on its own**.

- The **deviation from ideal mental health** definition first requires us to identify the characteristics/behaviours that people **should** possess in order to be considered 'normal' (i.e. 'ideal mental health'). Jahoda's proposals are appealing but they are so demanding that almost everyone would fall short on at least some criteria, such as self-actualisation, and would be considered abnormal to that extent. Lists of ideals about mental health are also **value judgements** couched in moral/philosophical terms, unlike judgements about **physical health**, which can be defined in anatomical/physical terms.

- Defining abnormality in terms of deviation from ideal mental health is **bound by culture**. While different cultures share some ideals, there are others that are not shared, as illustrated by the unlimited fellatio practised by male youths among the Sambia of New Guinea and the Javan way of playing football.

- Those who subscribe to the deviation from ideal mental health definition, would argue that there **ought** to be some sort of 'universal standard', regardless of culture, such as murder being abnormal. However, even if this argument is accepted, the definition is still **era-dependent** and limited by the **context** in which a behaviour occurs.

- According to the definition of abnormality as a **failure to function adequately**, every human being should achieve some sense of personal well-being and make some contribution to a larger social group. People often come to the attention of psychologists and other professionals when they fail to function adequately according to 'practical' or 'clinical criteria'.

- People may also come to the attention of psychologists and other professionals if they are experiencing **personal distress/discomfort.** Such feelings may not be apparent to others, but may take the form of intense anxiety/depression/loss of appetite and so on. However, certain psychological states giving rise to personal distress might be **appropriate responses** in certain situations, as when experiencing depression in response to the death of a loved one. Only if these responses persisited long after their source was removed or after most people had adjusted to them would they be considered abnormal.

- There are also some major forms of mental disorders that may not be accompanied by personal distress, such as **antisocial personality.** However, certain psychological states may be **distressing to others**, as when being a threat to others constitutes a failure to function adequately. Another form taken by failure to function adequately is behaviour that is **maladaptive**, i.e. which prevents the individual from efficiently satisfying social and occupational roles (as in the definition of **substance-related disorders**).

- Failure to function adequately may also take the form of **unexpected behaviour**, as when a person reacts 'out of all proportion to the situation'.

- If a person's behaviour was **always** highly unpredictable or **always** highly predictable, then we should consider that person not to be functioning adequately. Similarly, **bizarre** behaviour is evidence of not functioning adequately.
- While the 'failure to function adequately' definition is considered by many to be the most useful single approach, and the one which comes closest to 'common sense', there are also problems with it. The distress of others can be both a 'blessing' and a 'curse' as far as the person whose behaviour is causing the distress is concerned, while 'acting out of all proportion to the situation' seems to beg the question of what a normal reaction is and must include **under-** as well as **over-reaction.** In some contexts, otherwise bizarre behaviour might actually help a person to function adequately.
- In all societies there are **norms** for appropriate behaviours and beliefs; these can be thought of in terms of a 'continuum of normative behaviour', ranging from 'unacceptable', 'tolerable', 'acceptable/permissible', 'desirable', to 'required/obligatory'. Abnormality can be defined in terms of the breaking of society's standards/norms.
- While certain behaviours that deviate from social norms are also statistically infrequent, others are actually quite common, as when people are asked if they have engaged in a prosecutable offence without actually being convicted for it. So, according to the **deviation from social norms** definition, most people would be defined as abnormal, while according to the deviation from statistical norms definition, they would be defined as normal.
- The deviation from social norms definition is culture-bound, as demonstrated by the normal suspiciousness of the Mundugumor people and the wearing by widows of their late husband's jawbone among the Trobriand islanders. It is also era-dependent, so that as values change, the same behaviours may be judged differently, in terms of normality/abnormality; some present-day behaviours may be viewed as differences in **lifestyle** rather than signs of abnormality.
- Clearly, no one definition of abnormality on its own is adequate. Behaviours that are **classified** as being mental disorders will not necessarily reflect all these various definitions, but may only reflect one or some combination of these definitions. A truly adequate understanding of abnormality can probably only be achieved through a 'multiple perspectives'/'multiple definitions' approach.

2

AN INTRODUCTION TO MODELS IN ABNORMAL PSYCHOLOGY

Introduction and overview

In the previous chapter we looked at several ways in which psychological abnormality has been defined and we noted that there is no single way of defining abnormality which satisfies everyone. In the same way, psychologists do not agree on what *causes* abnormality (whatever it is) and how it can best be *treated*. There are at least five models (or *paradigms*) in abnormal psychology which place distinct interpretations on the causes of abnormality, the focus or goals of therapy, and the methods used to treat disturbed individuals. Our aim in this chapter is to outline the assumptions made by the *medical, psychodynamic, behavioural, cognitive* and *humanistic* models of abnormality and their implications for treatment. In a way, this chapter will provide an orienting function for the remainder of this book. In part 2, we will look at four mental disorders and discuss the attempts made by the models presented here to explain them. In part 3, we will look at the therapeutic approaches that derive from the models outlined in this chapter. Before we look at the five models, we will try to place them in context by taking a brief look at historical models of abnormality.

A brief history of models of abnormality

Throughout most of our history, we appear to have considered abnormality to be a sign of 'possession' by demons or evil spirits. Skeletons from the Stone Age, for example, have been discovered with egg-shaped holes in the skull. Although we cannot be certain, it is possible that these holes were drilled into the skull (a procedure called *trephining*) in order to 'release' the spirits that were presumably responsible for a person's abnormal behaviour. Whether trephining was effective is debatable. However, the fact that the skulls of some skeletons show evidence that the holes had begun to grow over suggests that the 'operation' did not inevitably lead to immediate death.

The so-called '*demonological*' model of abnormality was especially popular in the Middle Ages. Hundreds of thousands of people (mostly women) were convicted of being 'witches' and were executed for their 'crimes'. The *Hammer of the Witches*, a manual produced by two Dominican monks, contained information about how witches could be identified. For example, a birthmark, scar or mole on a woman's skin was interpreted as an indication that she had signed a pact with the devil. In order to establish whether they were possessed, those

Figure 2.1   Etching of a witch ducking stool, one of the tests used in the Middle Ages to establish whether someone was a witch. A 'pure' person would sink to the bottom (and drown), while an 'impure' person would be able to keep her head above water. The survivors, by definition, were witches, who were in league with the devil and were therefore burned at the stake (or executed in some other way)

accused underwent various tests. Based on the fact that pure metals sink to the bottom of a melting pot whereas impurities float to the surface, it was 'reasoned' that pure people would sink to the bottom when placed in water whilst impure people (who were in league with the devil) would be able to keep their heads above water. 'Pure' people would, of course, die by drowning, and 'impure' people would suffer some other fate (such as being burned at the stake). It is from this 'diagnostic test', incidentially, that the phrase *damned if I do and damned if I don't* comes.

The medical model of abnormality

Although some physicians in the Middle Ages called for a more rational approach to abnormality, it was not until the 18th century (the *age of enlightenment*) that the demonological model began to lose its appeal, and a different model or perspective emerged. Phillipe Pinel (1745–1826) in Europe and Dorothea Dix (1802–1887) in America were the pioneers of change. Rather than seeing abnormal behaviour as some sort of supernatural possession, they argued that it should be seen as a kind of *illness* which could be treated with appropriate *medical* techniques.

Whilst this viewpoint was different, it was not, in fact, new. In the fourth century BC, the Greek physician Hippocrates proposed that in what we now call *epilepsy*:

'If you cut open the head, you will find the brain humid, full of sweat and smelling badly. And in this way you may see that it is not a god which injured the body, but disease' (quoted in Zilboorg & Henry, 1941).

In the eighteenth century, the view that mental disorders are illnesses based on the pathology of an organ, namely the brain, was emphasised by Albrecht von Haller in his book *Elements of Physiology*. Von Haller believed that the brain played a central role in psychic functions and that considerable understanding could be gained by studying the brains of the 'insane' through post-mortem dissection. Nearly one hundred years later, William Griesinger in his book *The Pathology and Therapy of Psychic Disorders* insisted that *all* forms of psychological disorder could be explained in terms of brain pathology. The discovery that *general paresis of the insane*, a disorder characterised by a deterioration in thought processes and memory, was caused by a micro-organism (the *syphilis spirochete*), coupled with findings relating to the adverse effects exerted by toxins, infections and so on, gave the medical model immense prestige.

The early successes for the medical (or *biomedical*) model were largely based on showing that mental disorders could be linked to the gross destruction of brain tissue. In more recent times, the medical model has turned its attention to the role played by *genetics* and *neurotransmitters* in the development of mental disorders whilst retaining its interest in the role played by brain damage in such disorders. Genes act by directing biochemical events, and neurotransmitters are the chemicals that send 'messages' from neuron to neuron. *Biochemical theories* of mental disorders explain their development in terms of some sort of *imbalance* in the concentration of these chemicals. *Genetic theories* derive from the observation that at least some psychological disorders have a tendency to run in families. By means of DNA, the material that contains our genetic codes, some disorders may be transmitted from generation to generation. The methodology involved in studying the role of genetic factors will be explored in more detail in Chapter 4.

Because the medical model sees mental disorders as having physical causes, the therapeutic approaches favoured by it are *physical* and are known collectively as *somatic therapy*. Three somatic approaches currently in use are *chemotherapy* (the use of drugs), *electroconvulsive therapy* (the use of electricity) and *psychosurgery* (the use of surgical procedures). As we will see in Chapter 8, these therapies have had some success in the treatment of various disorders. However, they have also been subject to extensive criticism. For example, the drugs used in chemotherapy all have unpleasant, and in some cases permanent, side-effects. Moreover, such drugs do not offer a 'cure' for a disorder but merely *alleviate* the symptoms of it for as long as the drug remains active in the nervous system. More disturbingly, what Kovel (1978) calls *biological directives* have been used as *agents of social control*. Critics see the zombie-like state that some *psychotherapeutic* drugs produce as 'pharmacological strait-jackets', exerting the same effects as the actual strait-jackets they were hoped to replace. As we will see in Chapter 8, electroconvulsive therapy and psychosurgery lack a convincing scientific rationale to explain the effects they exert. For some critics, this is reason enough for their use to be discontinued.

The psychodynamic model of abnormality

The view that mental disorders have physical origins was challenged in the late nineteenth century by Sigmund Freud (1856–1939). Whilst Freud believed that mental disorders were caused by internal factors, he saw these as being psychological rather than physical in nature. He first made this claim as a way of explaining *hysteria*, a condition in which physical symptoms (such as deafness) are experienced, but for which no underlying physical cause can be found. Freud, who was a qualified physician, astonished his medical colleagues by suggesting that hysteria's cause stemmed from unresolved and unconscious conflicts that had their origins in childhood.

The psychodynamic perspective has been both influential and controversial. Freud believed that personality is comprised of three structures and that all behaviour is a product of their interaction. The structure present at birth is the *id*, which is the impulsive, subjective and pleasure-seeking part of personality. The id operates on the *pleasure principle*, that is, the immediate gratification of instinctual needs without any regard for how

this gratification is achieved. The *ego*, the second structure, develops from the id in order to help us cope with the external world, which is necessary for survival. It operates on the *reality principle*, that is, the gratification of the id's needs in socially acceptable ways. The third part of the personality, the *superego*, is the last to develop and is concerned with moral judgements and moralistic considerations. Freud saw these as representing society's ideals and values as interpreted by our parents. The *conscience* part of the superego instils guilt feelings in us when we engage in immoral or unethical behaviour. The *ego-ideal* part of the superego rewards moral or ethical behaviour with feelings of pride.

When these structures are 'in balance', psychological normality is maintained. However, Freud saw conflict between them as always being present to some degree. When the conflict cannot be managed, disorders arise. Freud saw early childhood experiences as shaping both normal and abnormal behaviour. As we noted earlier, he believed hysteria stemmed from unresolved and unconscious sexual conflicts that originated in childhood. He also believed that all psychological disorders could be explained in this way.

Freud also saw human development as passing through a series of *psychosexual stages*. These are shown in Box 2.1.

Box 2.1   Freudian psychosexual stages of development

The oral stage: The principal erogenous zone during the first two years of life is the mouth, and the infant's greatest source of gratification is sucking.

The anal stage: Between two and three years of age, the membranes of the anal region provide the major source of pleasurable stimulation.

The phallic stage: From three to five or six years of age, self-manipulation of the genitals provides the major source of pleasurable sensation.

The latency stage: Until the age of 12, the child's sexual motivations recede in importance as a preoccupation with developing skills and other activities occurs.

The genital stage: After puberty, the deepest feelings of pleasure come from heterosexual relations.

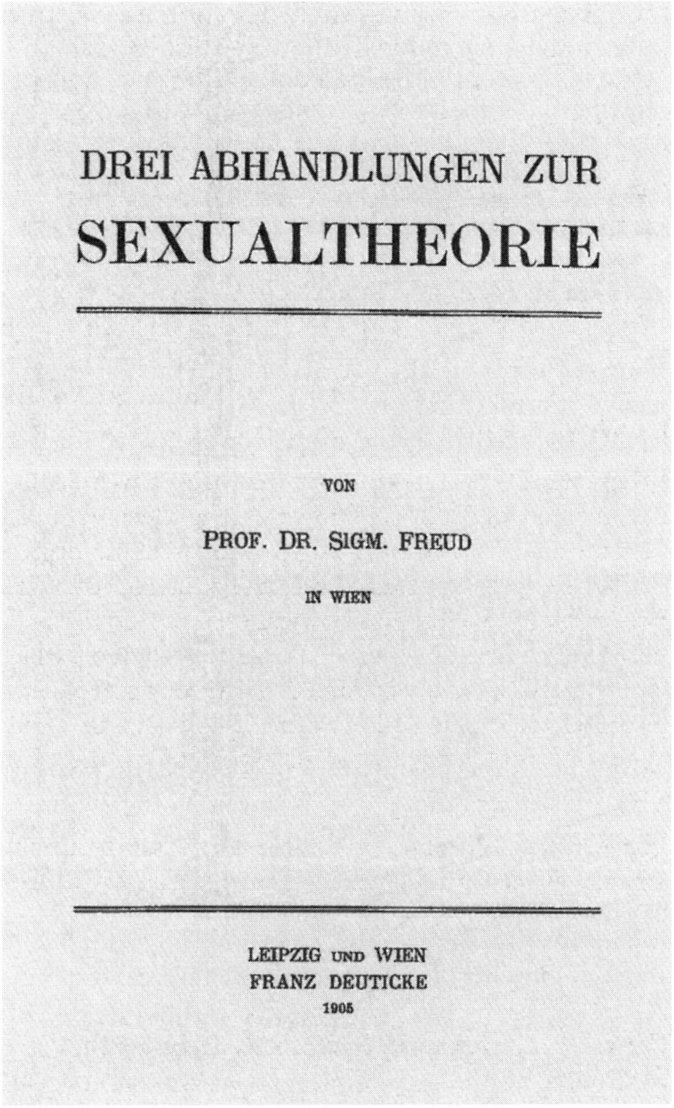

DREI ABHANDLUNGEN ZUR

SEXUALTHEORIE

VON

PROF. DR. SIGM. FREUD

IN WIEN

LEIPZIG UND WIEN
FRANZ DEUTICKE
1905

Figure 2.2 *Three Essays on the Theory of Sexuality* **by Prof. Dr. Sigm. Freud, the cover of the first edition, published by Franz Deuticke, Vienna, 1905**

The nature of the conflicts and the ways that they are expressed are held to reflect the stage of development the child was in at the time the conflict occurred. In order to avoid the pain caused by the conflict, Freud proposed the existence of *defence mechanisms* as a way of preventing anxiety-arousing impulses and thoughts from reaching consciousness. All of these unconsciously operating mechanisms serve to protect us by distorting reality. Some of the mechanisms are described in Box 2.2.

> **Box 2.2   Some defence mechanisms**
>
> **Repression**: Unacceptable thoughts or impulses are 'forgotten' by being pushed from consciousness into unconsciousness. An example would be a woman failing to recognise her attraction to her handsome new son-in-law.
>
> **Reaction formation**: In this, the opposite of an unacceptable wish or impulse is expressed. For example, a person strongly drawn to gambling may express the view that gambling is repulsive.
>
> **Rationalisation**: This involves socially acceptable reasons being given for thoughts or actions that are based on unacceptable motives. An example would be eating an entire chocolate cake because we 'didn't want it to spoil in the summer heat'.
>
> **Displacement**: This is when an emotional response is redirected from a dangerous object to a safe one. For example, anger towards one's boss might be redirected towards the family dog.
>
> **Projection**: In this, unacceptable motives or impulses are transferred to others. A man who is sexually attracted to a neighbour perceives the neighbour as being sexually attracted to him.
>
> **Regression**: This involves responding to a threatening situation in a way appropriate to an earlier age or level of development. For example, an adult has a 'temper tantrum' when he or she does not get his or her own way.

In order to treat psychological disorders, Freud developed *psychoanalysis*. As we will see in Chapter 9, the first aim of therapy is to *make the unconscious conscious*.

Through what Winnicott (1958) has termed a *therapeutic regression*, the person receiving psychoanalysis is directed to re-experience *repressed* (or deeply buried) unconscious feelings and wishes which were frustrated in childhood. This takes place in the 'safe' context of the psychoanalyst's consulting room, and the person is encouraged to experience the feelings and wishes in a more appropriate way with what Alexander (1946) termed *a new ending*. Providing disturbed people with *insight* (that is, self-knowledge and self-understanding) is held to enable them to adjust successfully to their deep-rooted conflicts and deal with them in a 'more mature' way. We will discuss the psychodynamic approach to therapy in detail in Chapter 9.

The assumptions made by the psychodynamic model

and the therapies that derive from it have been subject to much criticism. As we will see in Part 2, despite the psychodynamic model's claims to have explanatory power, the experimental support for it is weak. Freud's lack of scientific rigour in developing the model (most notably his dependence on inference rather than objective evidence) has also attracted criticism. Freud's model was based on data derived largely from his studies of upper-middle-class Viennese women between the ages of 20 and 44. Despite this restricted sample, Freud was able to develop a model of personality development in children! Even though the women studied by Freud had serious emotional problems, Freud was still able to develop a theory of normal psychological development. And, although the women lived in a time and place when all forms of sexual expression, especially in women, were universally frowned upon, Freud concluded that their sexual preoccupations were typical of all people.

The psychodynamic model has also been criticised for its *reductionist* interpretation of life. In its purest form, the model sees people as being driven by 'animal instincts' which are beyond our control. Because, as Bootzin & Acocella (1984) have put it, 'the die is cast early in life', we are seen as being helpless to change ourselves. Although weaker versions of Freud's original theory have attempted to overcome these criticisms, Freud (1915) seemed unmoved by at least some of them:

> 'One can only characterise as simple-minded, the fear that . . . all the highest goods of humanity, as they are called – research, art, love, ethical and

social sense – will lose their dignity because (the psychodynamic model) is in a position to demonstrate their origins in elementary and animal instinctual impulses'.

The behavioural model of abnormality

Both the medical and psychodynamic models explain mental disorders in terms of *internal* factors, their difference being that in the former disorders are seen as having an underlying physical cause whilst in the latter the cause is held to be psychological. By contrast, the behavioural model sees disorders as *maladaptive behaviours* which are learned and maintained in the same way as adaptive behaviours. According to supporters of the behavioural model, the best way of explaining mental disorders is to look at the *environmental conditions* in which a particular behaviour is displayed.

At the beginning of this century, Ivan Pavlov discovered a learning process that is now known as *classical conditioning* (it is also sometimes referred to as *respondent* or *Pavlovian conditioning*). In this, a stimulus which does not normally elicit a particular response will eventually come to do so if it is reliably paired with another stimulus that does normally elicit the response. For example, if a hungry dog is shown food it will salivate (and the response occurs reflexively because it is controlled by the autonomic nervous system). Pavlov called a stimulus which automatically elicits a response

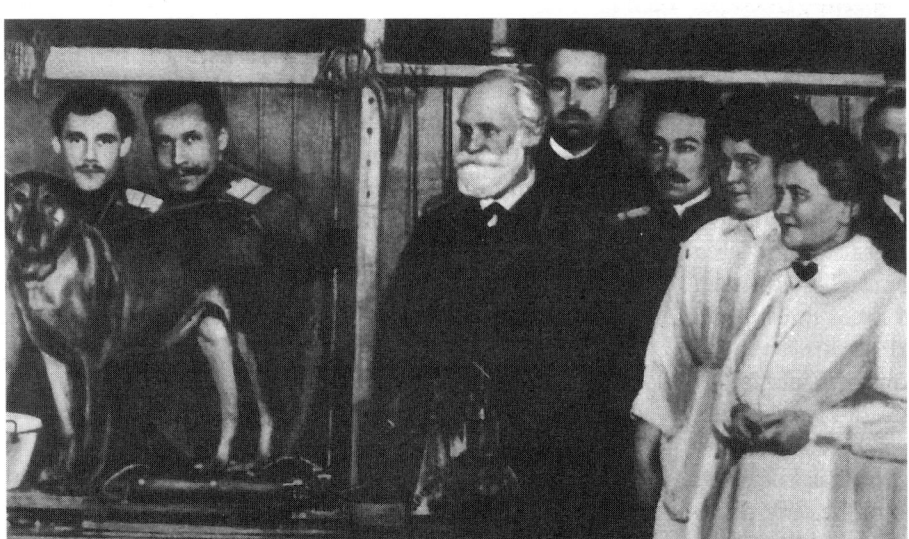

Figure 2.3   Ivan Pavlov and his assistants accidentally discovered classical conditioning while collecting saliva from dogs

an *unconditional stimulus* (or *UCS*). The response it elicits is called an *unconditional response* (or *UCR*). A stimulus that does not normally elicit a given unconditional response is called a *neutral stimulus* (or *NS*). If such a stimulus is repeatedly paired with an unconditional stimulus, then it will, through a process of association, acquire some of the properties of the unconditional stimulus. When the previously neutral stimulus is capable of eliciting an unconditional response in the absence of the unconditional stimulus, it has become a *conditioned stimulus* (or *CS*), and the response it elicits is termed a *conditioned response* (or *CR*).

The role of this form of learning in humans was taken up by J. B. Watson, who is credited with recognising its importance in potentially explaining the development of psychological disorders. In one of psychology's most famous (or infamous) experiments, Watson and Rayner (1920) used Pavlovian principles to classically condition a fear response in a young child called Albert. According to Jones (1925):

> 'Albert, eleven months of age, was an infant with a phlegmatic disposition, afraid of nothing "under the sun" except a loud noise made by striking a steel bar. This made him cry. By striking the bar at the same time that Albert touched a white rat, the fear was transferred to the white rat. After seven combined stimulations, rat and sound, Albert not only became greatly disturbed at the sight of a rat, but this fear had spread to include a white rabbit, cotton wool, a fur coat and the experimenter's (white) hair. It did not transfer to wooden blocks and other objects very dissimilar to the rat.'

Watson and Rayner's study demonstrated that it was possible for a *phobia* to be acquired through classical conditioning. For some psychologists, classical conditioning explains the acquisition of *all* abnormal fears. According to Wolpe & Rachman (1960):

> 'any neutral stimulus, simple or complex, that happens to make an impact on an individual at about the same time a fear reaction is evoked, acquires the ability to evoke fear subsequently ... there will be generalisation of fear reactions to stimuli resembling the conditioned stimulus'.

According to the learning model, when we fear something, we tend to avoid it, and this avoidance reduces

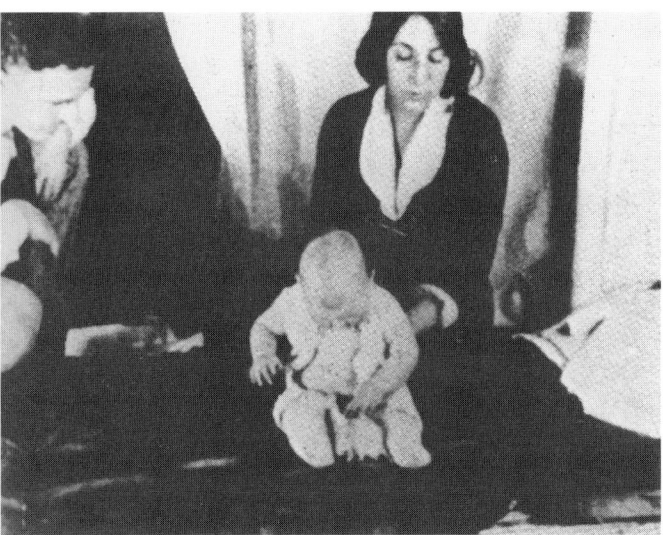

Figure 2.4   A very rare photograph of John Watson and Rosalie Rayner during the conditioning of Little Albert

our fear. This, says the model, is how certain behaviours are *maintained* (see Chapter 6).

At the same time that Pavlov was researching classical conditioning, an American psychologist, Edward Thorndike, observed that animals would tend to repeat behaviours when they were associated with positive consequences, but would tend not to produce behaviours that were associated with unpleasant consequences. Thorndike's work was taken up by B. F. Skinner who coined the term *operant conditioning*. An *operant behaviour* is a voluntary and controllable one. In a situation in which we find our physiological activity changing in an uncomfortable way, we cannot 'will' it to return to normal. However, we can *operate* on our environment by removing ourselves from the situation in which the unpleasant physiological activity is occurring.

Skinner used the term *reinforcer* to describe anything that increases the frequency or magnitude of a particular behaviour. *Positive reinforcers* are those which provide a wanted or pleasant consequence (which may be tangible or social). It is also possible to increase a behaviour's frequency by removing an unpleasant stimulus. Anything which does this is a *negative reinforcer*. Things which decrease the frequency of a behaviour are termed *punishers*. In *positive punishment*, an unpleasant stimulus is given when an unwanted behaviour occurs. In *negative punishment* (or *omission*), a positive reinforcer is removed when an unwanted behaviour occurs. As we will see in Parts 2 and 3, both classical and

Figure 2.5   Gambling represents an important example of how positive reinforcement ('rewards') can influence behaviour. People will go on feeding money into a fruit machine, despite 'hitting the jackpot' only very occasionally – and unpredictably. In fact, the more intermittent the reward, the more resistant the behaviour is to extinction

operant conditioning principles can be used to explain the development and maintenance of at least some mental disorders and to treat those disorders.

Classical and operant conditioning differ in two main ways. First, the former involves the development of involuntary behaviours (such as fear), whereas the latter is related to voluntary behaviours. Second, behaviours based on *classical conditioning* are controlled by stimuli (e.g. food) which *precede* the response (salivation, for example). Behaviours based on *operant conditioning* are controlled by events (e.g. the presentation of food) that *follow* particular responses (pressing a lever, for example).

Therapeutic approaches based on the behavioural model have been extremely influential, and all have at least three things in common. First, they focus on maladaptive behaviours and, rather than speculating as to the cause of these behaviours and the historical reasons for their development, the behaviour itself is seen as being the problem. As a result, therapies based on the behavioural model attempt to change behaviour by whatever means are most effective. Such approaches therefore attempt to induce behavioural change by means of a systematic application of learning principles. Second, the success or failure of a treatment is based on changes in specific and observable changes in behaviour. Third, all behaviourally oriented therapists are committed to the idea that the value claimed for any treatment must be documented by evidence from controlled experimental studies (see Chapter 13). We will discuss behavioural approaches to therapy in Chapter 10.

The cognitive model of abnormality

Both classical and operant conditioning require that people actually perform behaviours in order for those behaviours to be learned. However, whilst accepting the principles of conditioning, *social learning theorists* such as Bandura (1969) have pointed out that certain behaviours can be acquired simply by watching them being performed. Bandura calls this *observational learning*, and his approach to understanding and treating mental disorders represents a link between the behavioural and cognitive models of abnormality.

Like the psychodynamic model, the cognitive model of abnormality is concerned with internal processes. However, instead of emphasising the role played by unconscious conflicts, the cognitive model focuses on internal events such as thoughts, expectations and attitudes that accompany and, in some cases, are believed to be the cause of, mental disorders. At least in part, the cognitive model developed as a result of a growing dissatisfaction with some of the weaknesses of a strict behavioural approach and its concentration on overt behaviours, to the neglect of our thoughts and interpretations of the way we behave.

Instead of examining literal environmental contingencies as the origins of mental disorders, supporters of the cognitive model suggest that it is the *mediating processes*, such as our interpretations, the way we think about and perceive ourselves, others and the environment, that are important factors. Although the cognitive model became influential in the 1950s, the view that cognitive factors play an important role in emotional and behavioural problems is not new. Over 2,000 years ago, the Greek philosopher Epictetus wrote that: 'men are not disturbed by things but by the view they take of them'. In *Hamlet*, Shakespeare expresses a similar point when Hamlet says: 'there is nothing either good or bad but thinking makes it so'.

One cognitive approach to understanding behaviour sees people as *information processors*. The information-processing approach likens the human mind to a computer. As with computers, information (based on our perceptions) is put into the system, stored, retrieved, manipulated and, at some point in the future, taken out of the system. According to this view, disorders occur when the input-output sequence is disturbed in some way. For example, the faulty storage or manipulation of information may lead to a distorted output or a lack of output. For information-processing theorists, at least some disorders might be explained in terms of the faulty manipulation of information.

Other supporters of the cognitive model see certain mental disorders as stemming from irrational and maladaptive assumptions and thoughts. Ellis (1962) calls these *irrational assumptions*, whilst Beck (1967) calls them *cognitive errors* and Meichenbaum (1976) uses the term *counter-productive self-statements*. Since the cognitive model sees mental disorders arising as a result of 'faulty thinking' and since, to a large degree, our behaviour is controlled by the way we think, supporters of the cognitive model see the most logical and effective way to change maladaptive behaviour as the changing of the maladaptive thinking that underlies it.

Wessler (1986) sees therapies based on the cognitive model as being a collection of assumptions about psychological disorders and a set of treatment interventions in which human cognitions are assigned a central role. Beck & Weishaar (1989) summarise cognitive approaches to therapy in the following way:

'Cognitive therapy consists of highly specific learning experiences designed to teach patients (1) to monitor their negative, automatic thoughts (cognitions); (2) to recognise the connection between cognition, affect and behaviour; (3) to examine the evidence for and against distorted automatic thoughts; (4) to substitute more reality-oriented interpretations for these biased cognitions; and (5) to learn to identify and alter the beliefs that predispose them to distort their experiences.'

There are several types of cognitive therapy, and we will consider some of these in Chapter 11. One of the most important contributors has been Aaron Beck (e.g. 1974). Beck argues that disorders like depression are often 'rooted' in the maladaptive ways in which people think about themselves and the world they live in. Depressed people characteristically think in a negative way and are likely to view minor (or even neutral) events as self-devaluing or hopeless. Some of the kinds of illogical thinking that can contribute to depression are illustrated in Box 2.3. Beck believes that such thoughts deepen the depression and lower a person's motivation to take constructive action.

Box 2.3   Some examples of illogical thinking that can contribute to depression (after Beck, 1974)

Magnification and minimisation: Some people magnify difficulties and failures whilst minimising their accomplishments and successes. For example, a student who gets a low grade on one essay might magnify that and minimise his or her high-grade achievements on previous essays.

Selective abstraction: People sometimes arrive at a conclusion which is based on only one rather than several factors that could have made a contribution. For example, the goalkeeper of a football team that is beaten may blame himself, despite the fact that other team members also played badly.

Arbitrary inference: A person arrives at a conclusion about him- or herself despite the absence of any supporting evidence for that conclusion. For example, a student who misses a lecture might see him- or herself as incompetent, despite the fact that the bus taking him or her to college was late.

Overgeneralisation: Some people arrive at a sweeping conclusion based on a single and sometimes trivial event. For example, a student might conclude that he or she is unworthy of a place at a college because an application form contained a minor mistake.

The aim of Beck's therapy is to try and alter the way in which depressed people think about their situations and to take steps to challenge beliefs about their worthlessness, inadequacy and ability to change their circumstances. This *cognitive restructuring* approach is characteristic of all the therapeutic approaches derived from the cognitive model.

By attempting to identify maladaptive thoughts and beliefs that occur in many different situations and with many different disorders, the cognitive model and its therapeutic approaches are less mechanical and more 'in tune' with people's conscious experiences than are approaches based on the behavioural model. Not surprisingly, supporters of the behavioural model have been the most critical of the cognitive model. Skinner (1990), for example, saw the cognitive model as a return to *unscientific mentalism* and warned that, because cognitive phenomena are not observable, they cannot possibly form the foundations of empiricism (Sue *et al.* 1994). Arguing from a humanistic perspective (see below), Corey (1991) has argued that human behaviour is more than thoughts and beliefs and that, in a sense, the cognitive model is as mechanistic as the behavioural model in reducing human beings to 'the sum of their cognitive parts'.

Despite these reservations, the current emphasis in psychology on the role of cognition suggests that the cognitive model will continue to be influential as a way of both explaining and treating psychological disorders.

The humanistic model of abnormality

As we noted earlier, one of the criticisms made of the psychodynamic model is that it is both deterministic and pessimistic in seeing people as being inevitably bound in a struggle against the selfish desires of the id. Rather than emphasising the unconscious sexual and aggressive impulses of 'sick' people, humanistic psychologists take a very different view of human nature and assume that people are *sets of potentials* who are basically good and strive for growth, dignity and self-determination. Instead of the mechanistic approach adopted by the behavioural model which, in its strictest form, reduces subjective experiences to a chain of conditioned responses, humanists see the whole of personality (including our experiences of sorrow and joy, frustration and fulfilment, and alienation and intimacy) as worthy of study. This emphasis on positive human potential and seeing the world through a person's rather than an experimenter's eyes has been championed by Abraham Maslow and Carl Rogers.

For humanists, what makes us different from non-human animals is our possession of *free will* and our desire to achieve *self-actualisation*. It is these that makes each of us unique, free, rational and self-determining. Humanists see psychological normality as the ability to accept ourselves, to realise our potential, to achieve intimacy with others and to find meaning in life. The humanistic model sees mental disorders as arising not because of 'unresolved inner conflicts' (as the psychodynamic model proposes), but because external factors somehow block personal growth. For example, instead of providing us with what Rogers (1951) terms *unconditional positive regard*, that is, the assurance that we will be loved and accepted despite our shortcomings, our acceptance by others is often *conditional* on us acting in certain ways or meeting specific standards. Instead of sharing feelings with us and recognising our own feelings, some people hide their emotions behind a 'social mask' and pay little or no attention to the emotions we are experiencing. The result of this is a *distorted self-concept*, that is, a view of the self that does not match our feelings or experiences. This causes us to deny our true feelings, narrows our awareness of our own uniqueness and blocks our potential for growth.

Humanistic therapies evolved relatively recently and, although they peaked in popularity in the 1960s and 1970s, they continue to be influential today. The goals of humanistic therapy are to remove the blocks to self-development, to put people in touch with the true self and to promote continued growth rather than allowing external factors to determine behaviour. People undergoing humanistic therapy are called *clients* rather than *patients* and they are treated as *partners* in the endeavour of therapy. Indeed, responsibility for the success of the therapy is placed more with the client than the therapist (or *facilitator*). Therapy takes place in special, supportive environments that will allow a client to achieve self-awareness, self-acceptance, personal fulfilment and self-actualisation. Rather than making the past the focus of attention, humanistic therapies *tend* to focus on the present or the 'here and now' and on conscious thoughts and feelings rather than repressed conflicts. In addition, the therapist consciously avoids giving advice or assuming the role of an 'expert', since this would serve to impose the therapist's own views on the client.

There are many different forms of humanistic therapy. Some of these are considered to be on the 'fringe', but others have been particularly influential. The best known and most widely practised humanistic therapy is Carl Rogers' *client-centred therapy*. Another widely practised and influential therapy is *Gestalt therapy*, which was devised by Frederick Perls. The procedures used in these two types of humanistic therapy along with several others will be discussed in detail in Chapter 12.

Conclusions

In this chapter we have outlined several models which attempt to explain the causes of abnormal behaviour and identify ways in which abnormal behaviour can be treated. In their different ways, each of the models has made a significant contribution to the understanding and treatment of abnormal behaviour, although there are important issues that arise from them.

SUMMARY

- Psychologists disagree about the causes of **abnormality** and the best way of treating it. Five major models are the **medical, psychodynamic, behavioural, cognitive** and **humanistic models.**
- For much of human history, abnormality has been seen as a sign of possession by demons or evil spirits. This **demonological** model was particularly popular in the Middle Ages, when witches were believed to be in league with the devil and were killed in large numbers.
- By the 18th century, the demonological model began to lose its appeal. Pinel in Europe and Dix in America pioneered the alternative view (originally proposed by Hippocrates in the fourth century BC) that abnormality should be seen as a kind of **illness**, based on the pathology of the brain, and treatable by appropriate **medical** techniques.
- Von Haller believed the brain played a central role in psychic functions and advocated post-mortems of the brains of the 'insane'. Griesinger claimed that all forms of psychological disorder are caused by **brain pathology**. The medical model was supported by the discovery that 'general paresis of the insane' is caused by syphilis.
- More recently, the medical model has turned towards the role of **genetics** and **neurotransmitters** in the development of mental disorders. **Genetic theories** are based on the observation that certain disorders tend to run in families, while **biochemical theories** focus on imbalances in the concentration of neurotransmitters.
- The therapeutic approaches favoured by the medical model are collectively known as **somatic therapy**, in particular **chemotherapy, electroconvulsive therapy** and **psychosurgery**. While these have all had some success in treating various disorders, they have also all been criticised; for example, **psychotherapeutic** drugs have undesirable side-effects and have been used as agents of social control and pharmacological strait-jackets.
- Freud's **psychodynamic model** sees mental disorders (such as hysteria) as caused by internal, psychological factors, namely unresolved, unconscious childhood conflicts.
- Freud views all behaviour as the product of interaction between the **id**, which operates according to the **pleasure principle**, the **ego**, which operates according to the **reality principle**, and the **superego**, which comprises the **conscience** and the **ego-ideal** and represents the moral part of personality. Disorders arise when conflict between these structures becomes unmanageable.
- Personality development passes through five **psychosexual stages**, namely the **oral, anal, phallic, latency** and **genital.** The nature of the conflicts and how they are expressed reflect the

developmental stage of the child when the conflict occurs.

- **Defence mechanisms** prevent anxiety-arousing impulses and thoughts from reaching consciousness; they include **repression, reaction formation, rationalisation, displacement, projection** and **regression.**
- **Psychoanalysis** involves the re-experience of repressed childhood feelings and wishes, through a **therapeutic regression**, in the safety of the consulting room. The disturbed person is provided with **insight** which makes possible a more mature way of coping with deep-rooted conflicts.
- Freud's model has been criticised for its lack of scientific rigour and experimental evidence; he proposed a theory of normal psychological development based on a very unrepresentative sample of adults. His emphasis on animal instincts as the source of all human behaviour has been criticised for being **reductionist**.
- According to the **behavioural model**, disorders are **learned maladaptive behaviours**. The learning process involved is either **classical** or **operant** conditioning.
- **Classical** (respondent/Pavlovian) **conditioning** involves an initially neutral stimulus coming to elicit a response previously elicited only by an unconditioned stimulus, through pairing the two stimuli.
- Watson was the first to suggest that psychological disorders, such as phobias, could be explained in terms of classical conditioning; this was demonstrated in Watson and Rayner's study involving Albert.
- Wolpe & Rachman believe that all phobias can be explained in terms of classical conditioning. Avoiding the object of our fears reduces our fear, which helps to explain how certain behaviours are **maintained**.
- Based on Thorndike's work, Skinner investigated **operant conditioning**, based on voluntary/controllable (i.e. operant) behaviour (in contrast with the involuntary behaviour involved in classical conditioning). **Positive** and **negative reinforcers** both **increase** a behaviour's frequency, while **positive** and **negative punishers** both **decrease** a behaviour's frequency.
- While respondent behaviours are controlled by stimuli which **precede** them, operant behaviours are controlled by events that **follow** them.
- Therapeutic approaches based on the behavioural model focus on maladaptive behaviours and try to change them without trying to establish their causes and history. Success is measured in terms of

changes in specific and observable behaviours which must be documented through controlled experimental studies.

- According to **social learning theorists**, such as Bandura, certain behaviours can be acquired simply through **observational learning**. This approach stresses the role of thoughts, interpretations of our behaviour and other cognitions as **mediating processes** between the individual and environmental contingencies.
- The **information-processing approach** compares the human mind to a computer; disorders occur when the input-output sequence is disturbed in some way, i.e. there is faulty manipulation of information.
- According to other cognitive approaches, mental disorders are seen as stemming from 'irrational assumptions' (Ellis), 'cognitive errors' (Beck) or 'counter-productive self-statements' (Meichenbaum). The most logical and effective way of changing maladaptive behaviour is to change the 'faulty thinking' underlying it.
- Beck argues that depressed people typically think in a negative way, such that minor events are seen as self-devaluing or hopeless. Some of the illogical kinds of thinking that can contribute to depression include **magnification** and **minimisation, selective abstraction, arbitrary inference** and **overgeneralisation.**
- All therapeutic approaches derived from the cognitive model involve **cognitive restructuring**, i.e. challenging depressed people's beliefs about their worthlessness, inadequacy and ability to change their circumstances.
- Despite criticisms from both behaviourists and humanistic psychologists, the cognitive model and its therapeutic approaches may be seen as less mechanical and more 'in tune' with people's conscious experience than the behavioural model and its approaches, and are currently very influential.
- According to the **humanistic model**, people are basically good, striving for growth, dignity and self-determination. The whole range of human emotional experience is worthy of study and what makes us distinctive as a species is our possession of **free will** and the desire to achieve **self-actualisation.**
- Mental disorders are seen as arising because external factors prevent personal growth. For example, instead of receiving **unconditional positive regard**, acceptance by others may be **conditional** or they may ignore our emotions. The result is a **distorted self-concept.**
- The goals of humanistic therapy are to remove

the blocks to personal growth in the client, who has greater responsibility for the success of the therapy than the therapist/facilitator. The focus is on present, conscious thoughts and feelings within a supportive environment.

- The best known and most widely practised humanistic therapy is Rogers' **client-centred therapy**; another is Perls' **Gestalt therapy**.

3

CLASSIFYING ABNORMAL BEHAVIOUR

Introduction and overview

Of all the models presented in the previous chapter, by far the most influential has been the medical model of abnormality. An integral part of this model is its view that it is possible to *classify* mental disorders and, by virtue of this, to *diagnose* people according to the disorders identified by *classificatory systems*. The two classificatory systems currently in use both derive from the work of Emil Kraepelin (1913). The classificatory system currently used in Britain and most other parts of the world is called ICD-10. The system currently in use in North America is called DSM-IV. Our aim in this chapter is to describe these two classificatory systems and examine some of the practical and other issues that surround their use. We will begin by briefly looking at the history of attempts to classify abnormal behaviour.

A brief history of classificatory systems

The sorting of people into categories so that their behaviour may be predicted is not new. The first person to attempt a unified classification of abnormal mental states was the Ancient Greek physician Hippocrates (see Chapter 2, page 11). Hippocrates identified three categories of abnormal behaviour:

mania (abnormal excitement), *melancholia* (abnormal dejection) and *phrenitis* (brain fever). In the first century AD, Asclepiades, a Greek physician practising in Rome, described differences between hallucinations, delusions and illusions, and explained how each of these could be used as a diagnostic sign. Attempts at beginning a classificatory system were made by the pioneer reformer Philip Pinel (see page 11), who grouped disorders he believed were psychological or mental in nature into a category he called *neurosis* (defined as functional diseases of the nervous system) and divided these into several types.

The first comprehensive attempt to classify abnormal behaviours was developed by Emil Kraepelin who, in 1913, published a classificatory system that brought together earlier systems and at the same time elaborated on them in important ways. After carefully observing hospitalised patients and examining their records, Kraepelin suggested that there were eighteen distinct types of mental disorder, each of which had a characteristic pattern of *symptoms* (which Kraepelin termed a *syndrome*), a distinct course of development, particular underlying physical causes and a characteristic outcome. Kraepelin's work was important in the development of two classificatory systems which were introduced after the Second World War. In 1948, the *World Health Organisation* (WHO) was created and, shortly afterwards, published the *International Standard Classification of Diseases, Injuries and Causes of Death* (ICD). The ICD was a manual that provided a classification of all diseases and disorders, including those the WHO considered to be *psychological* in nature. Independently, and at around the same time, the *American Psychiatric Association* (1952) published the first edition of its *Diagnostic and Statistical Manual of Mental Disorders* (DSM), which contained a classification of mental disorders based on a scheme developed by the US Army in World War II.

Both the ICD and DSM classificatory systems have undergone several revisions since their introduction. The most recent revision of the ICD is the tenth (*ICD-10*). The *Clinical Descriptions and Diagnostic Guidelines of the ICD-10 Classification of Mental and Behavioural Disorders* (CDDG) was published in 1991 and the *Diagnostic Criteria for Research* (DCR) in 1993. The version of DSM currently in use is *DSM-IV* which was published in 1994 (American Psychiatric Association, 1994), and has 912 pages, of which 650 are devoted to the descriptions and the diagnostic criteria of the disorders in the classificatory system.

Kraepelin's system is also embodied in the 1983 Mental Health Act (England and Wales) which identifies three categories of *mental disturbance* or *mental disorder*. These are *mental illness* (neurosis, organic psychosis and functional psychosis), *personality disorder* and *mental impairment*.

The ICD-10 and DSM-IV classificatory systems

ICD-10 identifies eleven major categories of mental disorder. These are shown in Box 3.1, along with some examples of disorders that appear in each category.

> **Box 3.1   Major categories in ICD-10 and some specific examples of disorders included in those categories**
>
> **1   Organic, including symptomatic, mental disorders**: dementia in Alzheimer's disease; organic amnestic syndrome; personality and behavioural disorders due to brain disease, damage and dysfunction.
>
> **2   Mental and behavioural disorders due to psychoactive substance use**: substances include alcohol, cannabinoids, cocaine and hallucinogens.
>
> **3   Schizophrenia, schizotypal and delusional disorders**: schizophrenia (paranoid, hebephrenic, catatonic, undifferentiated, residual, simple, other and unspecified types); schizotypal disorder; persistent delusional disorders.
>
> **4   Mood (affective) disorders**: manic episode (including hypomania); bipolar affective disorder; depressive episode; recurrent depressive disorder; persistent mood (affective) disorders (including cyclothymia and dysthymia).
>
> **5   Neurotic, stress-related and somatoform disorders**: phobic anxiety disorders (including agoraphobia, social phobias and specific (isolated) phobias); anxiety disorders (including panic disorder, generalised anxiety disorder); obsessive-compulsive disorder; reaction to severe stress and adjustment disorders (including post-traumatic stress disorder); dissociative (conversion) disorders (including dissociative amnesia, fugue and multiple personality disorder); somatoform disorders (including hypochondriacal disorders); other neurotic disorders (including neurasthenia).
>
> **6   Behavioural syndromes associated with physiological disturbances and physical factors**: eating disorders (including anorexia nervosa and bulimia nervosa); non-organic sleep disorders (including sleep-walking, night terrors); sexual dysfunction not caused by organic disorder or disease (including lack or loss of sexual desire, premature ejaculation); mental and behavioural disorders associated with the puerperium, not elsewhere classified.
>
> **7   Disorders of adult personality and behaviour**: specific personality disorders (including paranoid, schizoid, dissocial, emotionally unstable, histrionic, anankastic, anxious or avoidant, and dependent disorders); habit and impulse disorders (including pathological gambling, fire-setting and stealing); gender and identity disorders (including transsexualism); disorders of sexual preference (including fetishism, voyeurism and paedophilia).
>
> **8   Mental retardation**: mental retardation which is mild, moderate, severe or profound.
>
> **9   Disorders of psychological development**: specific disorders of speech and language (including expressive, specific speech articulation and receptive language disorders); specific developmental disorders of scholastic skills (including

disorders of reading, spelling, arithmetic and scholastic skills); pervasive developmental disorder (including childhood autism, atypical autism, Rett's syndrome, Asperger's syndrome).

10   Behavioural and emotional disorders wth onset usually occurring in childhood and adolescence: hyperkinetic disorder (including disorders of activity and attention, hyperkinetic conduct disorder); conduct disorders; mixed disorders of conduct and emotion; tic disorders; other behavioural and emotional disorders with onset usually occurring in childhood and adolescence (including non-organic enuresis; non-organic encopresis; feeding disorder of infancy and childhood; pica of infancy and childhood; stereotyped movement disorders); stuttering and cluttering.

11   Unspecified mental disorder: mental disorder not otherwise specified.

Box 3.2 describes the major categories and some specific examples of disorders recognised in DSM-IV.

Box 3.2   Major categories in DSM-IV and some specific examples of disorders included in those categories

1   Delirium, dementia, amnestic and other cognitive disorders: deliria; dementias (e.g. of Alzheimer's type); amnestic disorders.

2   Schizophrenic and other psychotic disorders: schizophrenia (paranoid, disorganised, catatonic, undifferentiated and residual types); schizophreniform disorder; schizoaffective disorder; delusional disorder; brief psychotic disorder; shared psychotic disorder.

3   Substance-related disorders: alcohol-use disorders; amphetamine- (or related substance) use disorders; caffeine-use disorders; cannabis-use disorders; hallucinogen-use disorders; inhalant-use disorders; nicotine-use disorders; opioid-use disorders; phencyclidine- (or related substance) use disorders; sedative, hypnotic or anxiolytic substance-use disorders.

4   Mood disorders: depressive disorders (e.g. major depressive disorder); bipolar disorders (e.g. bipolar I disorder [such as single manic episode] and bipolar II disorder [recurrent major depressive episodes with hypomania]); cyclothymic disorder.

5   Anxiety disorders: panic disorder (with or without agoraphobia); agoraphobia; specific or simple phobia; social phobia; obsessive-compulsive disorder; post-traumatic stress disorder.

6   Somatoform disorders: somatisation disorder; conversion disorder; hypochondriasis; body dysmorphic disorder; pain disorder.

7   Dissociative disorders: dissociative disorder; dissociative fugue; dissociative identity disorder or multiple personality disorder; depersonalisation disorder.

8   Adjustment disorders: adjustment disorder (with anxiety, depressed mood, disturbance of conduct, mixed disturbance of emotions and conduct, or mixed anxiety and depressed mood).

9   Disorders first diagnosed in infancy, childhood or adolescence: mental retardation (mild, moderate, severe, profound); learning disorders (reading disorder, mathematic disorder, disorder of written expression).

10   Personality disorders: paranoid; schizoid; schizotypal; antisocial; borderline; histrionic; narcissistic; avoidant; dependent; obsessive-compulsive.

11   Sexual and gender identity disorders: sexual desire disorders (e.g. hyperactive sexual desire disorder); sexual arousal disorders (e.g. female sexual arousal disorder); orgasm disorders (e.g. premature ejaculation); sexual pain disorders (e.g. vaginismus); paraphilias (e.g. exhibitionism, fetishism, voyeurism); gender identity disorders (in children or in adolescents and adults).

12   Impulse control disorders not elsewhere classified: intermittent explosive disorder; kleptomania; pyromania; pathological gambling; trichotillomania.

13   Factitious disorders: factitious disorder with predominantly psychological or physical signs and symptoms.

14   Sleep disorders: dyssomnias (e.g. primary insomnia, narcolepsy); parasomnias (e.g. sleep terror disorder, sleepwalking disorder).

15   Eating disorders: anorexia nervosa; bulimia nervosa.

16   Mental disorders due to a general medical condition not elsewehere classified: catatonic disorder due to a general medical condition; personality change due to a general medical condition.

17   Other conditions that may be a focus of clinical attention: medication induced movement disorders (e.g. neuroleptic induced Parkinsonism); relational problems (e.g. partner or sibling relational problem); problems related to abuse or neglect (e.g. physical and/or sexual abuse of child); additional conditions that may be a focus of clinical attention (e.g. bereavement, occupational problem, phase of life problem).

COMPARING DSM AND ICD

A comparison of DSM-IV and ICD-10 indicates that the two systems overlap quite considerably, and for many categories, the two systems are virtually identical (Cooper, 1995). Given the extensive meetings involving the World Health Organisation and the Alcohol, Drug Abuse and Mental Health Administration of the USA that took place between 1988 and 1992, this is hardly surprising. For example, what ICD-10 calls *Mental and behavioural disorders due to psychoactive substance use* is referred to as *Substance-related disorders* in DSM-IV.

From Boxes 3.1 and 3.2 it is also clear, however, that each system uses a different number of major categories, and that most of these differences arise because of the larger number of discrete categories used in DSM-IV to classify disorders that appear under a smaller number of more general categories in ICD. For example, *neurotic, stress-related* and *somatoform* disorders appear as a single category in ICD-10 and include disorders which appear under four headings in DSM-IV (*anxiety disorders, somatoform disorders, dissociative disorders* and *adjustment disorders*). In the same way, what ICD-10 terms *disorders of adult personality and behaviour* appears in DSM under four headings (*personality disorders, sexual and gender identity disorders, impulse control disorders not elsewhere classified* and *factitious disorders*). It is also the case that a general DSM-IV category can incorporate more than one ICD-10 category. For example, what DSM calls *disorders usually first diagnosed in infancy, childhood or adolescence* is categorised by ICD-10 as *behavioural and emotional disorders with onset usually occurring in childhood or adolescence, disorders of psychological development* and *mental retardation*.

PSYCHOSIS AND NEUROSIS

One of the oldest distinctions in abnormal psychology has been between *psychosis* and *neurosis*. As a psychiatrist's joke has it, the psychotic believes that 2 + 2 = 5, whilst the neurotic knows that 2 + 2 = 4 but is really bothered by the fact. Of course, the distinction is much more complex than the joke would have us believe. Box 3.3 illustrates the traditional distinctions that are made between psychosis and neurosis.

> **Box 3.3   The traditional distinctions made between neurosis and psychosis**
>
> **Effects on personality**: Only a part of personality is affected in neurosis, whereas in psychosis, the whole of personality is affected.
>
> **Contact with reality**: The neurotic maintains contact with reality, whereas the psychotic loses contact. Hallucinations and delusions, for example, represent the inability to distinguish between subjective experience and external reality.
>
> **Insight**: The neurotic has insight, that is, recognises that he or she has a problem. The psychotic lacks this insight.
>
> **Relationship of disorder with 'normal' behaviour**: Neurotic behaviours are viewed as an exaggeration of normal behaviour, whereas psychotic behaviours are *discontinuous* with normal behaviour.
>
> **Relationship of disorder with pre-morbid personality**: Neurotic disturbances are related to the individual's personality prior to the disorder (the pre-morbid personality). Psychotic disorders are not related to the pre-morbid personality.

Although the traditional distinction between psychosis and neurosis has been dropped in present classificatory systems, ICD-10 still uses the term *neurotic* and DSM-IV the term *psychotic*. Gelder *et al.* (1989) have identified four major reasons for abolishing the distinction between psychosis and neurosis. First, disorders that were included under the broad categories of neurosis and psychosis actually had little in common. Thus, diverse conditions were grouped together under these broad headings. Second, it is less informative to classify a disorder as neurotic or psychotic than to classify it as a disorder within those very broad categories. For example, the label *schizophrenic* is much more informative than the label *psychotic*. Third, the criteria used to distinguish neurosis and psychosis are all liable to exceptions. Finally, the neuroses were grouped because of the view that they shared common origins (which were heavily influenced by the psychodynamic model), rather than on the basis of observable commonalities between them.

Yet despite moves to remove the distinction between psychosis and neurosis, the terms are still used in every-day psychiatric practice, as they are convenient terms for disorders that cannot be given a more precise diagnosis. The terms are also still in general use as, for example, is the case with the term *antipsychotic drugs* to describe a group of drugs commonly used in the treatment of schizophrenia (see Chapter 8, page 84). As Lewis (1975) has observed, it is sometimes the case that psychiatric concepts outlive their obituarists!

Classificatory systems and the concept of mental illness

Although neither DSM-IV nor ICD-10 uses the term *mental illness*, much of the vocabulary that is used to refer to abnormal behaviour comes from medicine. For example, abnormal behaviour is referred to as *psychopathology* and is classified on the basis of its *symptoms*, the classification being called a *diagnosis*. The term *therapy* refers to methods used to change behaviour, and the location in which such therapies are conducted are often termed *mental hospitals*. Indeed, the individual is usually referred to as a *patient* and is considered *cured* when the abnormal behaviour is no longer displayed.

The tendency to think about abnormal behaviour as though it were indicative of some underlying illness has been defended by Blaney (1975) on the grounds that it is more *humane* to regard the disturbed individual as *ill* or *mad* rather than simply *bad*. However, critics have argued that the label *mentally ill* removes *responsibility* for behaviour, and a person so described is seen as being a 'victim' to whom something has happened and who needs 'care'. However, it has been argued that the label *mentally ill* is more stigmatising than the label *bad* or *morally defective*, since illness is something over

which a person has no control, whilst 'being bad' implies an element of choice.

Szasz (1974, 1994) has argued that stigmatising labels are used for political purposes by those in power to exclude people who have upset the social order. Of course, carrying out behaviours that society does not approve of can result in imprisonment. The imprisoned person, however, is still seen as being responsible for his or her behaviour. Yet in the former Soviet Union, for example, political dissidents were diagnosed as schizophrenic for expressing views that only a person whom the authorities saw as 'not being in their right mind' would express. Since those views were expressed, dissidents were obviously not 'in their right minds'.

Labelling has many other negative consequences. For example, Farina (1982) has shown that people described as 'former mental patients' are reacted to more negatively than people with exactly the same symptoms who are not so labelled. Labelling also denies people's uniqueness if they are pigeon-holed and stereotyped in terms of a diagnostic category. A label may even become *self-fulfilling*, that is, a person might respond to being labelled by behaving in a way that is consistent with the label, thus *confirming* the label that was originally applied.

In his book *The Myth of Mental Illness*, Szasz (1962) argued that psychiatry assumes that mental illness is caused by diseases or disorders of the nervous system, particularly the brain, and that these manifest themselves in terms of abnormal thinking and behaviour. Szasz argued that, if this is so, then they should be called *diseases of the brain* or *neurophysiological disorders*. This would remove the confusion between disorders with a physical or organic basis and so-called 'problems in living' the person might have. The former, of course, must be seen in an anatomical and physiological context, whereas the latter must be seen in an ethical and social context. Szasz argued that the vast majority of 'mental illnesses' are actually 'problems in living' and that it was the exception rather than the rule to come across an individual suffering from some organic brain disorder, who would be considered 'mentally ill'. As Bailey (1979) has noted, this fact is recognised by at least some psychiatrists who distinguish between *organic psychoses* (which do have an underlying physical cause) and *functional psychoses* (which either do not or have yet to be shown to have an underlying physical cause: see below for a further discussion of this point).

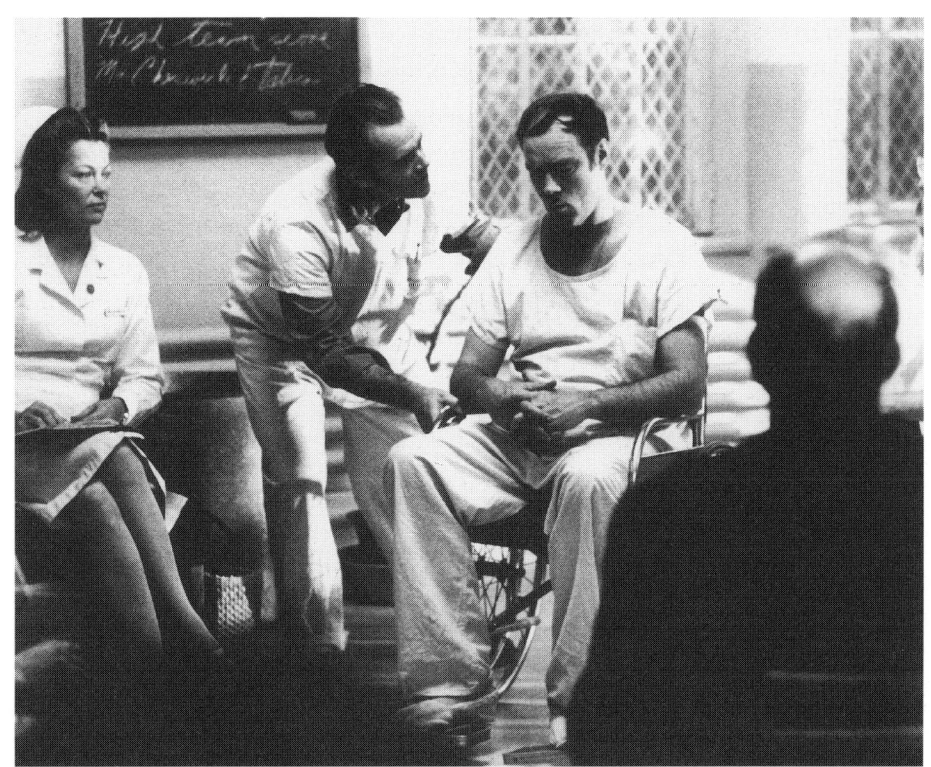

Figure 3.1   A still from the 1975 film, *One Flew Over the Cuckoo's Nest,* **based on Ken Kesey's 1962 novel of the same title. McMurphy (Jack Nicholson) is trying to persuade an unresponsive member of the ward therapy group to vote for a change in the ward routine at the state mental hospital where both are patients. McMurphy is an anti-conformist, a charming, but manipulative rebel, who gets involved in a power struggle with 'Big Nurse' Ratched (Louise Fletcher); she succeeds in preventing the desired change. Eventually, McMurphy is crushed by the system, which labels his rebellious behaviour as indicative of mental illness and 'treats' it, initially by ECT and finally by lobotomy. In this way, not only is his rebelliousness stopped, but his entire personality is destroyed**

Indeed, as Heather (1976) has argued, even if the functional psychoses could be shown to be organic in nature, there would still be a large number of disorders which even organic psychiatrists would admit cannot be conceived of as bodily diseases.

Furthermore, if an illness does not affect the brain, then how can something like the mind (a non-spatial, non-physical entity) be conceived of as suffering from a disorder of a physico-chemical nature? Like Szasz, Bailey has argued that organic mental illnesses are not actually mental illnesses at all. Rather, they are *physical illnesses* in which mental symptoms are manifested, and these aid diagnosis and treatment. Additionally, so-called functional mental illnesses are also not illnesses at all but are disorders of *psychosocial or interpersonal functioning* (Szasz's 'problems in living') in which the mental symptoms that occur are important in determining the most appropriate form of therapy. As a result of this debate, neither DSM-IV nor ICD-10 uses the term *mental illness*. Instead, they use the term *mental disorder* which DSM-IV defines as:

'a clinically significant behaviour or psychological syndrome or pattern that occurs in a person and that is associated with present distress (a painful symptom), disability (impairment of one or more important areas of functioning), a significant increased risk of suffering death, pain, disability or an important loss of freedom. In addition, this syndrome or pattern must not be merely an expectable response to a particular event such as, for example, the death of a loved one'.

ICD-10 uses the term *mental disorder* to imply the existence of a clinically recognisable set of symptoms or behaviours associated in most cases with distress and interference with personal functions.

In connection with the above, it should also be noted that DSM-IV has removed the category *organic mental disorders* and replaced it with the category *delirium, dementia, amnestic and other cognitive disorders,* 'because it implies that other disorders in the manual do not have an organic component'. According to Henderson *et al.* (1994), because research has shown that biological factors do have an influence through a whole range of disorders, it is now considered misleading to use the term *organic*. Consequently, the concept of psychological abnormality has become even more 'medicalised' than it has ever been. Although ICD-10 retains a separate category for *organic* disorders, the use of the word organic has been challenged as 'a neuropsychiatrist's nightmare' (Lewis, 1994), although Henderson and his colleagues (1994) argue that DSM-IV's preference for *cognitive* instead of *organic* may be seen as undervaluing the frequent behavioural component in many cognitive (or organic) disorders.

The goals of classification

Whatever their differences and similarities, both DSM-IV and ICD-10 have certain goals. Three main goals associated with the use of classificatory systems can be identified. The first is *to provide a common shorthand language*, that is, a common set of terms with agreed-on meanings. Diagnostic categories summarise large amounts of information about characteristic symptoms and the typical cause of a disorder, along with its typical age of onset, predisposing factors, course, prevalence, sex ratio and associated problems. This allows effective communication to take place between professionals, research to be conducted on different aspects of disorders, and an evaluation of treatment to be undertaken (see below).

The second goal concerns *the understanding of the origins of disorders*. If disorders have different origins, then it might be possible to uncover them by grouping people according to similarities in behaviour and then looking for other ways in which they may be similar. For example, a group of people displaying a particular behaviour might show, say, a certain structural abnormality in the brain or have had similar experiences early in life. The accurate diagnosis of disorders is necessary to enable research to be carried out into their origins. Any conclusions reached are likely to be biased if people have been assigned to the wrong grouping. Additionally, misdiagnoses give rise to inaccurate estimates about the *incidence* and *prevalence* of psychological disorders, as well as misleading information about their causes and correlates. Fewer mistakes would be made if more was known about the causes and natural history of disorders.

The third goal concerns *treatment plans*. Since there are a wide variety of therapies (see Chapters 8 to 12), accurate diagnosis is necessary to match a disorder to the treatment in order to ensure maximum benefit for the individual. By treating everybody as new and unique, it is difficult to predict how to treat any one. Therefore, knowing that a person's symptoms are similar to those of another person whose progress followed a particular course or who benefitted from a certain kind of treatment can also be helpful.

The goals of classification can only be achieved if the classification of abnormal behaviour is both *reliable* and *valid*. It is to these issues that we will now turn.

SOME PROBLEMS WITH THE CLASSIFICATION OF MENTAL DISORDERS

In one of psychology's most famous published investigations (entitled *On Being Sane in Insane Places*), Rosenhan (1973) reported what happened when 8 psychiatrically normal people from various backgrounds presented themselves at the admissions offices of different psychiatric hospitals in the USA complaining of hearing bizarre and disembodied voices saying 'empty', 'hollow' and 'thud'. All of the *pseudopatients* were admitted to the hospitals, most being diagnosed as schizophrenic. Once admitted, they behaved normally. However, the diagnoses given to them seemed to bias the staff's interpretation of their behaviour. For example, pacing a corridor out of boredom was interpreted as 'anxiety' by the staff. When one of the pseudopatients began to make notes, a nurse recorded this behaviour as 'patient engages in writing behaviour'. Shortly after admission, the pseudopatients stopped claiming to hear voices, and all were eventually discharged with a diagnosis of 'schizophrenia in remission', that is, a lessening in the degree of schizophrenic symptoms. It seems that the only people who were suspicious of the pseudopatients were their 'fellow' patients, one of whom commented, 'You're not crazy, you're a journalist or a professor. You're checking up on the hospital'. It took between 7 and 52 days (the average being 19) for staff to be convinced that the pseudopatients were 'well enough' to be discharged.

In a second investigation, members of a teaching hospital were told about the findings that had been obtained and were informed that more pseudopatients would try to gain admission to the hospital during a particular 3-month period. Each member of staff was asked to rate every new patient as an impostor or not. During the period, 193 patients were admitted, of whom 41 were confidently alleged to be impostors by at least one member of staff. 23 were suspected by one psychiatrist, and a further 19 were suspected by one psychiatrist *and* one other staff member. However, Rosenhan did not send *any* pseudopatients. All of those who presented themselves for admission were genuine.

The reliability of classificatory systems

In the context of classificatory systems of abnormal behaviour, reliability refers to the *consistency* of a diagnosis across repeated measurements. Clearly, no system of classification is of any value unless users of it can agree with one another when trying to reach a diagnosis. A study conducted by Zigler & Phillips (1961) reported a range of 54–84% agreement in studies assessing reliability for broad categories of disorders. However, Kendell (1975) showed that when more differentiated categories were used (such as specific types of anxiety), reliability ranged from 32–57%. Other research (Davison & Neale, 1994) has reported reliability coefficients of 0.92 for psychosexual disorders (the highest agreement rate) and 0.54 for somatoform disorders (the lowest agreement rate). Although the degree of agreement for some disorders is low, it has been argued that they are as good as those observed in some medical diagnoses. For example, research has shown an agreement rate of only 66% for cause of death when death certificates were compared with post-mortem reports, and agreement between doctors regarding angina, emphysema and tonsillitis (diagnosed without a definitive laboratory test) was no better, and sometimes worse, than that for schizophrenia (Falek and Moser, 1975).

There have been several attempts to improve the reliability of diagnosis. The *US-UK diagnostic project* (Cooper *et al.*, 1972) was designed to improve reliability and arose from the observation that schizophrenia was much more likely to be diagnosed by American psychiatrists than British psychiatrists, whereas for manic depression the reverse was true. Cooper and his colleagues found that when specific criteria for the two disorders were established and the two groups of clinicians trained in these, the level of agreement was significantly higher. Research also shows that agreement can be improved if psychiatrists use standardised interview schedules such as Wing *et al.*'s (1974) *Present State Examination* (e.g. Okasha *et al.*, 1993).

In DSM-III (published in 1980), a system of *multiaxial classification*, was introduced. DSM-II (published in 1968) required only a so-called 'diagnostic label' (such as schizophrenia) to be used. However, DSM-III and DSM-IV make use of five different axes which represent different areas of functioning. These are shown in Box 3.4.

> ### Box 3.4   The five axes used in DSM-IV
>
> **Axis I: Clinical syndromes and other conditions that may be a focus of clinical attention**: This lists all the mental disorders (except personality disorders and mental retardation). A person with more than one disorder has all listed, with the principal disorder being listed first. 'Other conditions' may include problems related to abuse or neglect, academic problems and 'phase of life' problems.
>
> **Axis II: Personality disorders**: These are life-long, deeply ingrained, inflexible and maladaptive traits and behaviours which may occur quite independently of Axis I clinical disorders. These are likely to affect an individual's ability to be treated.
>
> **Axis III: General medical conditions**: This lists any medical conditions that could potentially affect a person's mental state and hence would be relevant to understanding and treating a disorder.
>
> **Axis IV: Psychosocial and environmental problems**: These are problems that might affect the diagnosis, treatment and prognosis of a diagnosed disorder. For example, a person may have experienced a stressful event such as divorce or the death of a loved one. Ratings are made from 1 to 7, with 7 indicating a *catastrophic* event or events.
>
> **Axis V: Global assessment of functioning**: On this, the clinician provides a rating of the person's psychological, social and occupational functioning. Using the *Global Assessment of Functioning Scale*, 0 denotes *persistent danger* and 100 *superior functioning* with no symptoms.

Rather than being assigned to a single category (such as schizophrenia), people are assessed more broadly, giving a more global and in-depth picture. Axes 1, 2 and 3 are compulsory in terms of making a diagnosis, but Axes 4 and 5 are optional. Although ICD-10 does not have separate axes in the way that DSM-IV does, built into its groupings of disorders are broad types of aetiology or causes (such as organic causes, substance use and stress).

During ICD-10's construction, it was agreed that the incomplete and controversial state of knowledge about the causes of mental disorders meant that classification

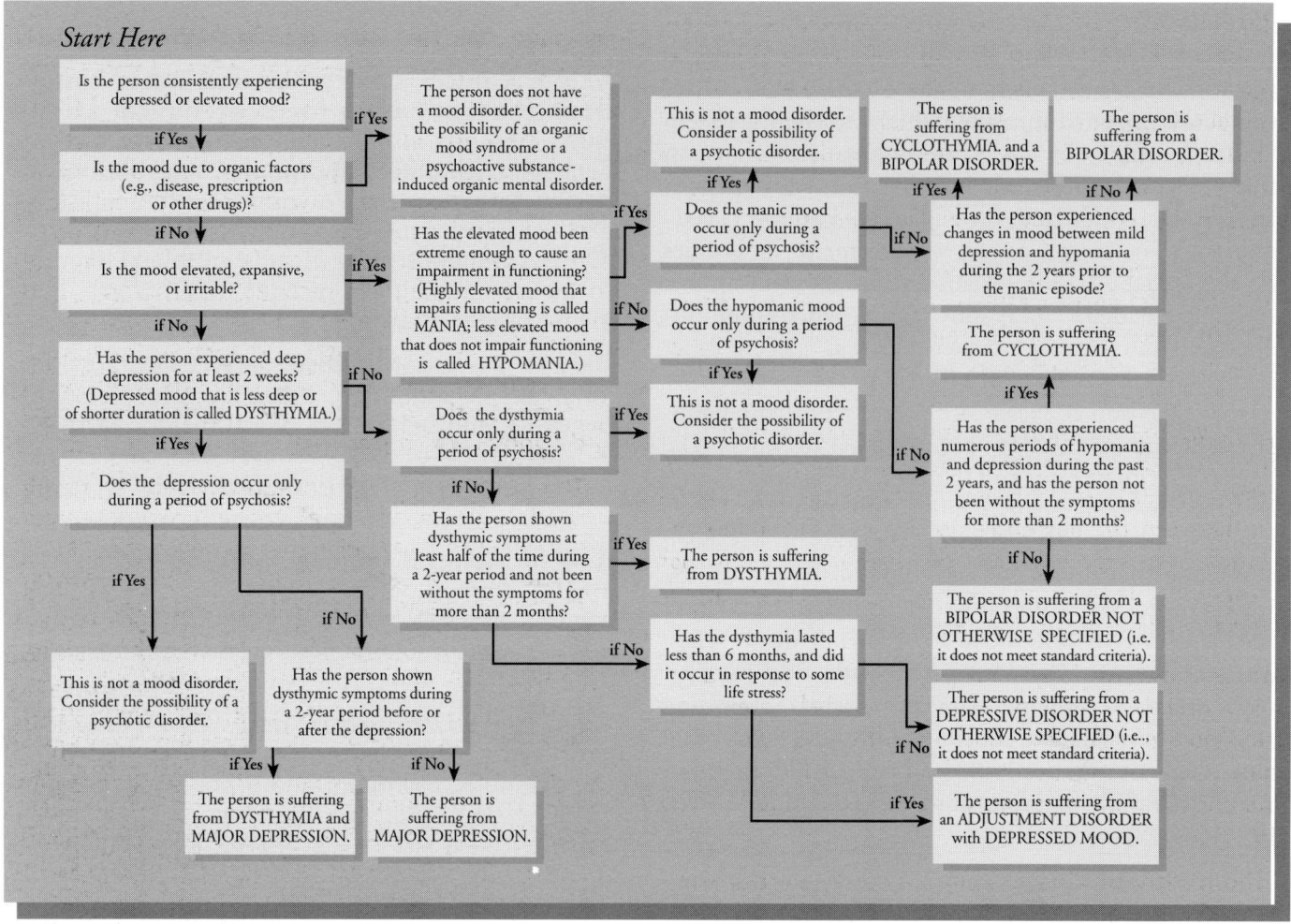

Figure 3.2   Decision tree for mood disorder. Note that cyclothymia (or cyclothymic disorder) is defined as numerous periods of hypomania and depression during the past two years but absent for more than two months. Dysthymia (or dysthymic disorder) refers to a depressed mood that is less severe or shorter lasting than major depression

should be worked out on a *descriptive* basis. This implied that the disorders should be grouped according to similarities and differences of symptoms and signs so that a particular disorder should appear only in one diagnostic category. Unfortunately, this did not appeal to clinicians, who like to give prominence to aetiology wherever possible. As a result, ICD-10 includes broad types of aetiology within its various categories. Cooper (1995) has argued that whilst ICD-10 is 'impure' from a classificatory view, it is much more likely to be used by clinicians. DSM, by contrast, makes no assumptions about causation when a diagnosis is made, that is, it is *atheoretical.*

Both DSM-IV and ICD-10 appear to be much more reliable than their predecessors, and as far as ICD-10 is concerned, Sartorius *et al.* (1993) have concluded that

its clinical guidelines are suitable for widespread international use because of their high reliability. Holmes (1994) reports that the use of *decision trees*, as shown in Figure 3.2, and *computer programs* to aid diagnosis has also increased reliability. Even so, there is still room for subjective intepretation to play a role in the diagnostic process. For example, in *mania* (see Chapter 5, page 51), the elevated mood must be 'abnormally and persistently elevated', and the assessment on Axis V requires comparison between the individual 'and an average person' which, as Davison & Neale (1994) have noted, begs the question of what an average person actually is!

The validity of classificatory systems

Validity refers to an estimation of the accuracy of a particular measure. In this context, validity is the extent to which a diagnosis reflects an actual disorder. Clearly, reliability is a precondition for validity. If a disorder cannot be agreed upon, the different views expressed cannot all be correct. Because, for most disorders, there is no absolute standard against which a diagnosis can be compared, validity is much more difficult to assess. As Holmes (1994) has observed, there is no guarantee that a person has received the 'correct' diagnosis.

At least one of the purposes of making a diagnosis is to enable a suitable program of treatment to be chosen (the third goal of classification we identified above). However, Heather (1976) has argued that there is only a 50% chance of correctly predicting what treatment people will receive on the basis of the diagnosis they are given. Indeed, in a study conducted by Bannister *et al.* (1964) of 1,000 cases, there was no clear-cut relationship between the diagnoses people were given and the treatment they received (and one reason for this is that factors other than diagnosis may be equally important in deciding on a particular treatment).

Critics of diagnostic systems have argued that the diagnostic process cannot be valid if the label a person is given does not allow a clinician to make a judgement about the cause of the disorder or a prediction about prognosis and likely response to treatment. As Mackay (1975) has observed:

'The notion of illness implies a relatively discrete disease entity with associated signs and symptoms, which has a specific cause, a certain probability of recovery and its own treatments. The various states of unhappiness, anxiety and confusion which we term "mental illness" fall far short of these criteria in most cases.'

Defenders of classificatory systems have countered their critics by comparing psychiatric diagnosis with medical diagnosis. As we noted earlier (see page 29), medical diagnosis is not without its problems. Moreover, whilst Rosenhan's study is widely interpreted as a damning indictment of psychiatric diagnosis, the claims made by Rosenhan can be disputed, as illustrated in Box 3.5.

Box 3.5   Some challenges to Rosenhan's study, *On Being Sane in Insane Places* **(1973)**

As the clinicians in the Rosenhan study were not required to distinguish between the normal and the abnormal, the study tells us nothing about the accuracy of diagnosis per se. Rather, the study was really assessing whether people pretending to have mental disorders could be detected. Spitzer (1975) has made the following observations:

- On the basis of the data the clinicians had, no other diagnoses than those given were justified. Each pseudopatient *insisted* on admission, which itself is an important symptom of emotional disturbance. As Kety (1974) has remarked, a person who swallowed a quart of blood and then went to hospital vomiting blood would probably be diagnosed as having a peptic ulcer. Just because the physician failed to notice the deception would not imply that diagnosis was impossible.

- The behaviour of the pseudopatients after admission was *not* normal. Normal people would say, 'I'm not crazy, I just pretended to be. Now I want to be released'. At least at first, however, the pseudopatients remained impassive.

- The label *in remission* (which the pseudopatients were released with) is very rarely used and implies that the psychiatrists knew there was something different about the pseudopatients. Fleischman (1973) notes that all of the non-psychotic people observed by the psychiatrists were, by virtue of being given the label *in remission*, diagnosed as non-psychotic. This, of course, is a 100% record of accuracy!

- The use of the word 'insane', whilst catchy, is inaccurate. Insane is not a psychiatric diagnostic category, but a legal term decided in a court of law. As such, Rosenhan used the term incorrectly.

SOME OTHER ISSUES SURROUNDING CLASSIFICATORY SYSTEMS

When Kraepelin visited south-east Asia at the turn of the century, he noted that there were cultural variations in mental disorders. Despite this, Kraepelin considered mental disorder to be universal. As he noted:

'Mental illness in Java showed broadly the same clinical picture as we see in our country ... The overall similarity far outweighed the deviant features' (cited in Dein, 1994).

Until fairly recently, Western diagnostic categories were viewed as universal, and non-Western patterns of unusual or undesired behaviour were seen as variants of these Western categories. According to Dein (1994), *transcultural psychiatry* was preoccupied with the pursuit of *culture-bound syndromes* and the systematic attempt to fit them into Western psychiatric categories. As Littlewood (1992) has observed, the view was taken that, whilst the expression of a disorder might be culturally variable, there was a *core* hidden within the disorder which is common to all cultures. Unfortunately, the difficulty with this model is that the *biological core* remained elusive.

Transcultural psychiatry is 'now synonymous with the psychiatry of ethnic minorities' (Dein, 1994). Rather than looking at the pathological aspects of the culture of immigrant groups, emphasis has changed to a preoccupation with race and racism. In Britain, markedly increased rates of schizophrenia among Afro-Caribbean immigrants and overdoses among British Asian women have been the themes that have attracted most attention. Although black people account for only 5% of the total British population, 25% of patients on psychiatric wards are black (Banyard, 1996: see Figure 3.3). According to Littlewood & Lipsedge (1989), black patients in psychiatric hospitals are more likely than white patients to see a junior doctor rather than a consultant or senior doctor and are more likely to receive some types of therapy than others.

A number of explanations have been advanced to explain the higher incidence of diagnosed schizophrenia in immigrant groups (see, for example, Eagles, 1991, and Gaines, 1992). One of these concerns the misinterpretation by white, middle-class psychiatrists of

behaviour which is perfectly ordinary within Afro-Caribbean culture. For white people, the game of dominoes is a quiet affair, the silence being broken only when a player 'knocks' to indicate a domino cannot be played. The way in which Caribbean men play dominoes, however, could be seen as 'aggressive' and 'threatening' by a white observer, who might consider such behaviour to be indicative of a psychological problem (Banyard, 1996).

Another explanation derives from the observation that of those people from Caribbean backgrounds who had been diagnosed as schizophrenic, only 15% showed the classic diagnostic indicators. The other 85% had a distinctive pattern of symptoms which some psychiatrists referred to as *West Indian psychosis* (Littlewood & Lipsedge, 1989). Littlewood and Lipsedge have argued that mental illness in ethnic minorities is often an intelligible response to disadvantage and racism.

One of the major 'symptoms' displayed by members of ethnic minorities is the feeling of being persecuted (which is a *delusion of persecution*: see Chapter 4, page 37). Delusions are false beliefs about things. If a person believes that someone is 'out to get me', when this is not the case, he or she is deluded. But if someone really *is* persecuting a person, the belief is an accurate perception of the world rather than a delusion. Grier & Cobbs (1968) use the term *adaptive paranoid response* to describe a mental disorder brought about by a hostile environment. In a society which is intolerant of minority groups, survival depends at least in part on a 'healthy' cultural paranoia, which is a demanding requirement. As Grier and Cobbs have remarked, 'not everyone can manage it with grace'.

Several other issues have also interested transcultural psychiatrists. Littlewood (1992), for example, has challenged the international validity of DSM-IV on the grounds that the assumptions Axis V (see Box 3.4) makes about nuclear family life, occupation and education are *ethnocentric*. Further discussion of the political implications of psychiatric diagnosis and the way that psychiatric diagnoses may function as ideologies, which mystify reality, obscure relations of power and domination and prevent people from grasping their situation in the world, has been addressed by Scheper-Hughes (1991). Scheper-Hughes points out that in Brazil, hunger is medicalised into a diagnosis of *nervos* and treated by medication, an example of psychosocial stress being misidentified in biological terms.

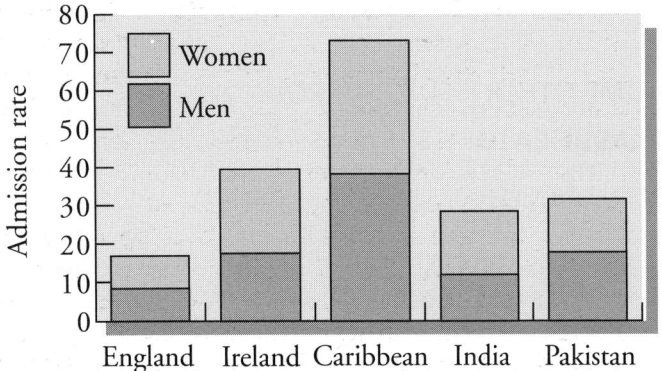

Figure 3.3   Country of birth and hospital admission for schizophrenia (after Banyard, 1996)

Do we need ICD and DSM?

Since ICD-10 and DSM-IV are so similar, the need for both of them has been questioned. Cooper (1995) points out that from the perspective of the World Health Organisation, there is a statutory obligation to the member states of the United Nations Organisation to update the ICD at regular intervals (which, until recently, has been every ten years). The American Psychiatric Association has no such obligation, but Cooper believes that they would argue along the lines that national classifications are able to reflect national traditions and usage, and that national pride suggests there should be a worthy successor to DSM-IV.

Conclusions

The focus of this chapter has been on the classificatory systems that are currently used in the diagnosis of abnormal behaviour. Two classificatory systems are currently in use: ICD-10 and DSM-IV. Although these systems are generally accepted as being useful, there are important practical and other issues that surround their use.

SUMMARY

- The most influential model of abnormality is the medical model, central to which is the **classification** of mental disorders and the **diagnosis** of people accordingly.
- Hippocrates identified three categories of abnormal behaviour: **mania, melancholia** and **phrenitis**. Asclepiades distinguished between hallucinations, delusions and illusions. Pinel grouped psychological disorders together as **neurosis**.
- The first comprehensive attempt to classify abnormal behaviours was Kraepelin's **classificatory system**. He proposed 18 distinct types of disorder, each with its own characteristic pattern of **symptoms (syndrome)**, distinct course of development, underlying physical causes and outcome.
- The World Health Organisation's (WHO) **International Classification of Diseases (ICD)** includes psychological disorders, while the American Psychiatric Association's **Diagnostic and Statistical Manual of Mental Disorders (DSM)** is exclusively concerned with mental disorders.
- Both classificatory systems derive from the work of Kraepelin. Both have been revised several times, the latest versions being ICD-10 (used in Britain and other parts of the world) and DSM-IV (used in North America). Kraepelin's system is also embodied in the 1983 Mental Health Act, which identifies three categories of **mental disturbance/disorder**, i.e. **mental illness, personality disorder** and **mental impairment**.
- ICD-10 identifies 11 major categories of mental disorder: **organic**, including **symptomatic, mental disorders; mental and behavioural disorders due to psychoactive substance use; schizophrenia, schizotypal and delusional disorders; mood (affective) disorders; neurotic, stress-related and somatoform disorders; behavioural syndromes associated with physiological disturbances and physical factors; disorders of adult personality and behaviour; mental retardation; disorders of psychological development; behavioural and emotional disorders with onset usually occurring in childhood and adolescence; unspecified mental disorder.**
- DSM-IV identifies 17 major categories: **delirium, amnestic and other cognitive disorders; schizophrenic and other psychotic disorders; substance-related disorders; mood disorders; anxiety disorders; somatoform disorders; dissociative disorders; adjustment disorders; disorders first diagnosed in infancy, childhood or adolescence; personality disorders; sexual and gender identity disorders; impulse control disorders not elsewhere classified; factitious disorders; sleep disorders; eating disorders; mental disorders due to a general medical condition not elsewhere classified; other conditions that may be a focus of clinical attention.**
- Although there is considerable overlap between the two systems, DSM-IV uses a larger number of categories to classify disorders that appear under a smaller number of more general ICD categories. However, a general DSM category sometimes incorporates more than one ICD category.
- Traditionally, psychiatrists have distinguished

between **neurosis** and **psychosis**. Compared with psychosis, neurosis is seen as affecting only a part of the personality, being an exaggeration of normal behaviour and as related to the pre-morbid personality. Neurotics also maintain contact with reality and have insight.

- Neither system any longer makes the distinction between neurosis and psychosis, one of the reasons being that there are exceptions to all the criteria used to make it. However, ICD-10 still uses the term 'neurotic' and DSM-IV the term 'psychotic', and psychiatrists find it convenient to use them in everyday practice.

- Although neither system uses the term 'mental illness', the vocabulary used to refer to abnormal behaviour comes from medicine, such as **psychopathology, symptoms, diagnosis, therapy, mental hospitals, patients** and **cured**.

- It has been argued that it is more humane to regard abnormality as indicating 'illness/madness' rather than 'badness'. But it also removes responsibility from the person and is a more stigmatising label which can be used for political purposes, as in the former Soviet Union.

- Labelling someone in terms of mental disorder can bias other people's reactions, denies a person's uniqueness and may become **self-fulfilling**.

- According to Szasz, diseases/disorders of the nervous system, particularly the brain, which manifest themselves as abnormal thinking and behaviour, should be called 'neurophysiological disorders'; these must be seen in an anatomical/physiological context, while 'problems in living' (or disorders of psychosocial/interpersonal functioning), which is what most 'mental illnesses' are, must be seen in an ethical and social context.

- This distinction corresponds to the distinction between **organic** and **functional psychoses** respectively. Because of the debate about the meaning of 'mental illness', both DSM-IV and ICD-10 use the term 'mental disorder' instead. DSM-IV has dropped the category 'organic mental disorders' because this, misleadingly, implies that other disorders are not influenced by biological factors. This serves to make the concept of abnormality more medical than it has ever been.

- Three main goals of classificatory systems are a common shorthand language concerning all relevant aspects of a particular disorder, the understanding of the origins of disorders, which is closely tied to accurate diagnosis, and the setting-up of treatment plans. These goals can only be achieved if the classification systems are both **reliable** and **valid**.

- In the context of classificatory systems, **reliability** refers to the **consistency** with which different users can reach the same diagnosis. The degree of agreement varies, depending on how broad or specific the category is and between different disorders. Overall, reliability is as good as in some medical diagnoses.

- The **US-UK diagnostic project** was designed to improve the reliability of diagnosis of schizophrenia and manic-depression between American and British psychiatrists by training them to apply specific criteria. The **Present State Examination** has also helped to increase reliability.

- DSM-III introduced **multiaxial classification**, whereby the patient is evaluated on five different areas of functioning: **clinical syndromes, personality disorders/mental retardation, general medical conditions, psychosocial/environmental problems** and **global assessment of functioning**. This provides a more global and in-depth assessment than just applying a single 'diagnostic label'.

- While ICD-10 does not have separate axes, broad types of causes, such as organic, substance use and stress, are built into its groupings of disorders. This makes it less 'pure' from a classificatory point of view than DSM, which is more atheoretical and descriptive, but it is more attractive to clinicians, who prefer highlighting aetiology.

- Despite the improved reliability of both DSM-IV and ICD-10, aided by the use of decision trees and computer programs, there is still room for subjective interpretation in diagnosis, as when comparison is made with 'an average person' on Axis V of DSM.

- **Validity** refers to the extent to which a diagnosis reflects an actual disorder. While reliability is a precondition for validity, there is no absolute standard against which a diagnosis can be matched, making validity very difficult to assess.

- Studies showing the low predictability of treatment based on patients' diagnosis suggest that classificatory systems have low validity. Similarly, validity requires that clinicians should be able to make judgements about the cause of a disorder or about prognosis.

- Rosenhan's famous experiment involving pseudo-patients gaining admission into various psychiatric hospitals in the USA, and the subsequent study in which staff at a teaching hospital were told the results of the first study and led to expect that pseudopatients would try to gain admission, are widely interpreted as exposing psychiatric diagnosis' lack of reliability and validity. However,

Rosenhan is not without his own critics.

- Until recently, Western diagnostic categories were seen as universal, with a biological 'core' sometimes hidden by cultural variations. **Transcultural psychiatry** was concerned with these variations or **culture-bound syndromes**.
- Transcultural psychiatry no longer concentrates on the pathological aspects of the culture of immigrant groups, but is concerned with the incidence of different disorders among different cultural/ethnic groups, different hospitalisation rates and issues of race and racism within psychiatry.
- One explanation for the higher incidence of diagnosed schizophrenia in immigrant groups is the misinterpretation by white psychiatrists of behaviour which is perfectly normal within Afro-Caribbean culture. Mental illness in ethnic minorities is often an intelligible response to disadvantage and racism, as in **adaptive paranoid response** (in contrast with a **delusion of persecution**).
- Axis V on DSM-IV has been accused of being **ethnocentric**, and psychiatric diagnoses may function as ideologies and prevent people from appreciating the power relationships in their society.
- While the World Health Organisation is obliged to update the ICD at regular intervals, the American Psychiatric Association would probably argue that DSM reflects national traditions and usage and improving it is a matter of national pride.

PART 2
Psychopathology

4

SCHIZOPHRENIA

Introduction and overview

Of all the disorders identified in the ICD-10 and DSM-IV classificatory systems, schizophrenia is the most serious. The disorder was originally called *dementia praecox* (or *senility of youth*) by Kraepelin, who believed that it occurred early in adult life and was characterised by a progressive deterioration or dementia. However, Bleuler (1911) observed that the disorder often begins later than Kraepelin believed and is not always characterised by a progressive deterioration. Bleuler coined the word *schizophrenia* to refer to a *splitting* of the various functions of the mind and a disorder in which *the personality loses its unity*. Our first aim in this chapter is to examine the nature of schizophrenia, the characteristics that are associated with it, the subtypes that have been identified, and the course of the disorder. Perhaps because of its nature, the causes of schizophrenia have received more attention than any other mental disorder. Given the large number of characteristics associated with schizophrenia, it will not be surprising to learn that a large number of theories have been advanced to explain it. Our second aim in this chapter is to examine the plausibility of the various explanations of schizophrenia that have been proposed.

The characteristics of schizophrenia

As we have just noted, schizophrenia refers to a disorder in which the personality loses its unity. It is important not to confuse schizophrenia with *multiple personality disorder*, a disorder in which the personality splits into two or more separate *identities*. The confusion probably arises because the word *schizophrenia* derives from the Greek words *schizein* (to split) and *phren* (the mind). As we will see, schizophrenia results in a 'splitting' between thoughts and feelings, the consequences being bizarre behaviour which is maladaptive.

In Britain, the diagnosis of schizophrenia relies on what Schneider (1959) has called *first-rank symptoms*. The presence of one or more of these symptoms in the absence of any form of brain disease is likely to result in a diagnosis of schizophrenia being made. There are three first rank symptoms. These are *passivity experiences and thought disturbances, hallucinations* and *primary delusions*.

PASSIVITY EXPERIENCES AND THOUGHT DISTURBANCES

These include *thought insertion* (the belief that thoughts are being inserted into the mind from outside, under the control of external forces), *thought withdrawal* (the belief that thoughts are being removed from the mind under the control of external forces) and *thought broadcasting* (the belief that thoughts are being broadcast or otherwise made known to others). External forces may include 'the Martians', 'the Communists' and 'the Government', and the mechanism by which thoughts are affected is often a 'special ray' or a radio transmitter. Thought broadcasting is also an example of a *delusion* (see below).

HALLUCINATIONS

Hallucinations are perceptions of stimuli that are not actually present. They may occur in any sense modality, but the most common are *auditory*. Typically, voices are heard coming from outside the individual's head and offer a 'running commentary' on behaviour in the third person (such as 'He is washing his hands. Now he'll go and dry them'). Often, the voices will comment on the individual's character, usually in an insulting way, or give commands.

Somatosensory hallucinations involve changes in how the body feels. It may, for example, be described as 'burning' or 'numb'. *Depersonalisation*, in which the person reports feeling separated from his or her body, may also occur. For example, parts of the body are often perceived as being 'different'. Bick & Kinsbourne (1987) have suggested that at least some auditory hallucinations may be projections of the individual's *own* thoughts.

Friston (cited in Highfield, 1995) has shown that there is a breakdown in 'dialogue' between the frontal regions of the brain (which deal with intentions) and the temporal lobes (which are responsible for language processing and which register the consequences of our actions). This results in a failure to integrate our behaviours in the world with our perception of the consequences of those behaviours. In the case of auditory hallucinations, it has been hypothesised that normal thoughts progress via internal language into a form in which they can be articulated and, if desired, spoken. This progression involves a *feedback loop* which warns the next stage of the process what is happening, that is, the loop tells us that the inner speech is our own. In auditory hallucinations, the feedback loop is held to be broken. According to Friston, then, schizophrenics talk to themselves but do not realise it.

PRIMARY DELUSIONS

Delusions are false beliefs which persist even in the presence of evidence which disconfirms the belief. A *delusion of grandeur* is the belief that one is somebody who is or was important or powerful (such as Jesus Christ, Queen Victoria or Napoleon). A *delusion of persecution* is the belief that one is being plotted or conspired against or being interfered with by certain people or organised groups. A *delusion of reference* is the belief that objects, events and so on have a (typically negative) significance. For example, a person may believe that the words of a song specifically refer to him or her. A *delusion of nihilism* is the belief that nothing really exists and that all things are simply shadows. The belief that one has really been dead for years and is observing the world from afar is also common. All of these delusions are held with extraordinary conviction, and the deluded individual may be so convinced of their truth that he or she acts on them, even if this involves murder. A particularly interesting class of delusions is described in Box 4.1.

Box 4.1   Rock and roll delusions

Case 1: A 25-year-old single man, whose mother suffered from schizophrenia, believed that Hank Marvin (guitarist with The Shadows) owed him a large sum of money. This idea took seed some years earlier when he had been at a Hank Marvin concert and the star had given him a special look. He refused treatment. When last seen, he intended to go to the next local Hank Marvin concert and he expected that Hank would make a sign to invite him for a drink.

Case 2: A 20-year-old single man had a history of delinquency, multiple drug abuse and overdose in his teens. Schizophrenia was diagnosed when he was 21 and he has required continuous in-patient treatment since the age of 22. He has experienced voices coming from the television which say that he is the double of David Cassidy (a teen idol of the early 1970s). At times he has been convinced that he is David Cassidy, Elvis Presley or David Essex. He believed that John Lennon was trying to get him out of hospital and blamed hospital staff for killing Lennon and Presley.

Case 3: A 30-year-old single girl, diagnosed as schizophrenic, had a past history of alcohol and multiple drug abuse. In 1980, she burnt her wrist with a cigarette after hearing Linda McCartney's voice telling her to do it. She also heard Paul McCartney's voice telling her to wait for him. Recently, she relapsed nine months after stopping treatment and has heard several voices, including those of Boy George and Sting, commenting on her actions.

(adapted from Robinson, 1984)

The first-rank symptoms are subjective experiences which can only be inferred on the basis of the individual's verbal reports. According to Slater & Roth (1969), hallucinations are the least important of the first-rank symptoms because they are not exclusive to schizophrenia (and this is also true of delusions: see, for example, Chapter 5). Slater and Roth have identified four different characteristics of schizophrenia that are directly observable from the individual's behaviour. These are *thought process disorder, disturbances of affect, psychomotor disorders* and *lack of volition*.

THOUGHT PROCESS DISORDER

Although we are constantly bombarded by sensory information, we are ordinarily able to selectively attend to some and exclude other sources of information. In schizophrenia, however, this ability is impaired and leads to overwhelming and unintegrated ideas and sensations, which affect the ability to concentrate. Thus, schizophrenics are distracted by anything and everything. The schizophrenic's failure to maintain an attentional focus is reflected in the inability to maintain a focus of thought. In turn, this is reflected in the inability to maintain a focus in language.

The classic disturbance in the *form* of schizophrenic thought (as opposed to its *content*) involves *loose associations* in which the individual shifts from one topic to another as new associations come up and fails to form coherent and logical thoughts. As a result, language is often rambling and disjointed. Very often, one idea seems to trigger an association with another. When associations become too loose, the result is incoherence

Figure 4.1 There is a great deal of similarity between the paintings produced by psychotic patients and this section of a picture of Hell, painted by the 16th-century Dutch painter Hieronymus Bosch. Notice the mutilated bodies of people and animals, the tightly packed canvas, and the apparent association between eroticism and filth, decay, and mutilation

or what is termed a *word salad*. Box 4.2 illustrates this. Note how the first example also shows *poverty of content*, in which words may be used in a grammatically correct way, but little is conveyed or communicated.

Box 4.2   Loose associations

Example 1

Dear Mother,

I am writing on paper. The pen which I am using is from a factory called 'Perry & Co'. This factory is in England. I assume this. Behind the name Perry & Co, the city of London is inscribed, but not the city. The city of London is in England. I know this from my schooldays. Then, I always liked geography. My last teacher in that subject was Professor August A. He was a man with black eyes. I also like black eyes. There are also blue and grey eyes and other sorts, too. I have heard it said that snakes have green eyes. All people have eyes. There are some, too, who are blind. These blind people are led about by a boy.

Example 2

I am the nun. If that's enough, you are still his. That is a brave cavalier, take him as your husband, Karoline, you well know, though you are my Lord, you were just a dream. If you are the dove-cote, Mrs K. is still beset by fear. Otherwise I am not so exact in eating. Handle the gravy carefully. Where is the paint brush? Where are you, Herman?

(taken from Bleuler, 1911)

The sound of a word may also trigger an association with a similar sounding word, a phenomenon known as *clang associations*, as in 'The King of Spain feels no pain in the drain of the crane. I'm lame, you're tame: with fame, I'll be the same'. Schizophrenic thought is also reflected in *neologisms*, that is, the invention of new words (such as *glump* and *wooger*) or the combination of common words in a unique fashion such as 'belly bad luck and brutal and outrageous' to describe stomach ache. Other characteristics include *thought blocking*, in which the individual stops in the middle of a sentence or word, and *literal interpretation*, in which communication is overly concrete in form.

DISTURBANCES OF AFFECT

Thought process disorder may be brief and intermittent, at least in some cases of schizophrenia. However, disturbances of affect (or *emotional disturbances*) and the other symptoms we will describe tend to be fairly stable. The three main types of emotional disturbance are *blunting*, *flattened affect* and *inappropriate affect*.

Blunting

This refers to an apparent lack of emotional sensitivity in which the individual remains impassive in response to events that would ordinarily evoke a strong emotional reaction. For example, when told that a close relative had died, a schizophrenic might respond in a monotonic voice: 'Really? Is that so?'

Flattened affect

This refers to a more pervasive and general absence of emotional expression in which the person appears devoid of any sort of emotional tone. According to some researchers (e.g. Mednick, 1958), these phenomena reflect the schizophrenic's 'turning off' from stimuli they are incapable of dealing with in order to protect themselves.

Inappropriate affect

This is the displaying of an emotion which is incongruous with its context. For example, when asked if a meal was enjoyable or when offered a gift, a schizophrenic may become agitated and violent. Similarly, the receipt of bad news may be followed by uncontrolled giggling.

PSYCHOMOTOR DISTURBANCES

In some schizophrenics, motor behaviour is affected. This might involve the individual assuming an unusual posture which is maintained for hours or even days, a phenomenon known as *catatonia*. Efforts to alter the position are usually met with resistance and sometimes violence. In *stereotypy*, the person engages in purposeless, repetitive movements, such as rocking back and forth or knitting an imaginary sweater. Instead of being mute and unmoving, the individual may be wild and excited, showing frenetically high levels of motor activity.

LACK OF VOLITION

This refers to the tendency of the individual to withdraw from interactions with other people. This sometimes involves living an asocial and secluded life, because the individual loses drive, interest in the environment, and so on. More disturbed individuals appear to be oblivious to the presence of others and completely unresponsive, when others (such as friends and relatives) attempt contact.

Types of schizophrenia

As illustrated in Boxes 3.1 and 3.2 (see pages 23–25), both ICD-10 and DSM-IV distinguish between different types of schizophrenia. This is because the characteristics of the disorder are so variable.

HEBEPHRENIC SCHIZOPHRENIA

The most severe type of schizophrenia is *disorganised* or *hebephrenic schizophrenia* (*hebephrenic* means 'silly mind'). The disorder is most often diagnosed in adolescence and young adulthood and is usually progressive and irreversible. Its main characteristics are incoherence of language, disorganised behaviour, disorganised delusions, vivid hallucinations (which are often sexual or religious) and a loosening of associations. It is also characterised by flattened or inappropriate affect and accompanied by extreme social withdrawal and impairment.

SIMPLE SCHIZOPHRENIA

This usually appears during late adolescence and has a slow, gradual onset. Principally, the simple schizophrenic gradually withdraws from reality and has difficulty in making or maintaining friends, is aimless and lacks drive, and shows a decline in academic or occupational performance. Male simple schizophrenics often become drifters or tramps, whilst females often become prostitutes. This type of schizophrenia is only recognised by ICD and, although acknowledging it to be controversial, retains it because it is still used in some countries.

CATATONIC SCHIZOPHRENIA

The word *catatonia* comes from the Greek *katateinein* meaning 'to stretch or draw tight'. The major characteristic of catatonic schizophrenia is a striking impairment of motor activity. The individual may hold unusual and difficult positions for hours or even days, even as their limbs grow swollen, stiff and blue from lack of movement. A particularly striking characteristic is *waxy flexibility,* in which the individual maintains a position into which he or she has been manipulated by others.

Immobility is not the only motor disorder. Catatonic schizophrenics may engage in *agitated catatonia,* that is, bouts of wild, excited movement, and they may become dangerous and unpredictable. *Mutism* is another characteristic. In this, the person appears to be totally unresponsive to external stimuli. However, catatonic schizophrenics often *are* aware of what others were saying or doing during the catatonic episode, as evidenced by the reports they give after the episode has subsided. One other characteristic is *negativism,* in which the individual sits either motionless and resistant to instructions or does the opposite of what has been requested.

PARANOID SCHIZOPHRENIA

This has the presence of well-organised, delusional thoughts as its dominant characteristic. Paranoid schizophrenics show the highest level of awareness and least impairment of the ability to carry out daily functions. Thus, language and behaviour appear relatively normal in this type of schizophrenia. However, the delusions are usually accompanied by hallucinations, which may be auditory, visual or olfactory, and these are typically consistent with the delusions. Paranoid schizophrenia tends to have a later onset than the other schizophrenias, and the disorder is the most homogenous type (that is, paranoid schizophrenics are more alike than simple, catatonic and hebephrenic schizophrenics).

UNDIFFERENTIATED (OR ATYPICAL) SCHIZOPHRENIA

This is a 'catch-all' category in which people who either fit the criteria for more than one type or do not appear to be of any clear type are placed. For example, people who demonstrate disorders of thought, perception and emotion, but do not exhibit features particular to the types we described above, would be labelled as undifferentiated.

As well as the types described above, several others have been identified. *Schizophreniform psychosis* is a syndrome similar to schizophrenia, but lasts for less than 6 months. *Schizotypal disorder* refers to eccentric behaviour and unusual thoughts and emotions which resemble those seen in schizophrenia, but without definite and characteristic schizophrenic abnormalities. *Schizo-*

affective disorder involves episodes in which both schizophrenic and affective characteristics are prominent, but which do not justify a diagnosis of either schizophrenia or an affective disorder (see Chapter 3).

The course of schizophrenia

The characteristics of schizophrenia we have described very rarely appear in 'full-blown' form. Typically, there are three phases in the development of schizophrenia. The *prodromal phase* usually occurs in early adolescence (in which case the term *process schizophrenia* is sometimes used) or in relatively well-adjusted people in early adulthood (in which case the term *reactive schizophrenia* is used). The individual becomes less interested in work, school, leisure activities and so on. Typically, the individual becomes increasingly withdrawn, eccentric, emotionally flat, cares little for health and appearance, and shows lowered productivity at either work or school. This phase may last from a few weeks to years.

In the second or *active phase*, the major characteristics of schizophrenia appear. This phase varies in the length of its duration. In some people, it lasts for only a few months, whereas in others it lasts for a lifetime. If and when this phase subsides (as, for example, is usually the case when therapy is given), the person enters the *residual phase*. This is characterised by a lessening of the major characteristics and a more-or-less return to the prodromal phase. According to Bleuler (1978), around 25% of schizophrenics regain the capacity to function normally, 10% remain permanently in the active phase and 50–65% alternate between the residual and active phases.

The concept of schizophrenia

Whether schizophrenia is a single disorder which has several types or whether each type is a distinct disorder has been hotly debated. Gelder *et al.* (1989) believe that, with the possible exception of paranoid schizophrenia, the other types that are recognised are actually of doubtful validity and they point to evidence suggesting that the types are difficult to distinguish between in clinical practice (which relates to the issues of reliability and validity of classificatory systems that were discussed in Chapter 3). Because of the lack of reliability, Carson (1989) and Sarbin (1992), amongst others, have argued

that the concept of schizophrenia is 'almost hopelessly in tatters' and that there is no such entity as schizophrenia.

Space does not permit us to explore this issue in any detail. However, it is clearly the case that the origins of the variety of bizarre behaviours we have described need explaining. It is to the explanations that have been proposed that we now turn.

Explanations of schizophrenia

BEHAVIOURAL MODEL

According to the *behavioural model*, schizophrenia can be explained in terms of conditioning and observational learning. Supporters of the behavioural model argue that people show schizophrenic behaviour when it is more likely than normal behaviour to receive reinforcement. Ullman & Krasner (1969), for example, have suggested that in psychiatric institutions hospital staff may unintentionally reinforce schizophrenic behaviour by paying more attention to those who display the characteristics of the disorder. Other patients can 'acquire' the characteristics by observational learning, that is, by observing others being reinforced for behaving bizarrely in the same way that children who disrupt classes tend to receive more attention from teachers than do non-disruptive children. Alternatively, schizophrenia may be acquired through the *absence* of reinforcement for attending to appropriate objects.

Certainly, as we will see in Chapter 10, schizophrenic behaviour can be modified through conditioning, although there is little evidence to suggest that such techniques can make major changes to the expression of thought disorders. Moreover, it is difficult to see how schizophrenic behaviour patterns can be *acquired* when people have had no opportunity to observe such patterns. For these reasons at least, it is generally accepted that the behavioural model has little contribution to make to the understanding of the causes of schizophrenia.

PSYCHODYNAMIC MODEL

One *psychodynamic* explanation of schizophrenia suggests that the disorder results from an ego that has difficulty in distinguishing between the self and the external world. However, the major psychodynamic account of schizophrenia attributes the disorder to a *regression* to an infantile stage of functioning (the *oral* stage of development). Freud believed that schizophrenia occurred when a person's ego either became overwhelmed by the demands of the id or was besieged by unbearable guilt from the superego (see Chapter 2).

Rather than attempting to deal with the intense *intrapsychic conflict*, the ego retreats to the oral stage of psychosexual development, a stage in which the infant has not yet learned that it and the world are separate. Initially, *regressive symptoms* occur, and the individual may experience delusions of self-importance. Fantasies become confused with reality, which gives rise to hallucinations and delusions (which Freud called *restitutional symptoms*), as the ego attempts to regain reality.

It has been suggested that the incoherent delusions and bizarre speech patterns displayed in schizophrenia may make sense when preceded by the phrase 'I dreamed ...'. However, the fact that schizophrenic behaviour is not that similar to infantile behaviour and the fact that the psychodynamic model is unable to predict schizophrenic outcome on the basis of theoretically predisposing early experiences, has resulted in little credence being given to such an account.

THE ROLE OF SOCIAL AND FAMILY RELATIONSHIPS

The role of *social and family relationships* in the development of schizophrenia has been investigated by a number of researchers. According to Bateson *et al.* (1956), parents predispose children to schizophrenia by communicating with them in ways that place the children in a 'no-win' situation. A father might, for example, complain about the lack of affection shown by his daughter, whilst at the same time telling her that she is too old to hug him when she tries to be affectionate. Bateson and his colleagues used the term *double bind* to describe the multiple verbal and non-verbal messages that are contradictory and cannot all be met. Children who experience such double binds may begin to lose their grip on reality and see their own feelings, perceptions, knowledge and so on as being unreliable indicators of reality.

A similar approach has been taken by Wynne *et al.* (1977), who argue that *deviant communication* within

families may lead to children doubting their own feelings and perceptions. Wynne and his colleagues have proposed that some parents often refuse to recognise the meaning of words that are used by their children and instead substitute words of their own. This can be confusing if the children are young, and may play a role in the development of schizophrenia.

A different view has been advanced by Lidz (1973), who suggests that families of schizophrenics are frequently marked by what he terms *marital schism* or *marital skew*. When both parents are preoccupied with their own severe problems, they threaten the continuity of the household, and marital schism occurs. Marital skew occurs when one disturbed parent dominates the household. For example, Fromm-Reichman (1948) advanced the concept of the *schizophrenogenic* mother (that is, the mother who generates schizophrenic children). Such mothers were seen as being domineering, cold, rejecting and guilt-producing. Fromm-Reichman argued that, in conjunction with a passive and ineffectual father, such mothers 'drove' their children to schizophrenia.

The view that family interactions play a causal role in the development of schizophrenia lacks empirical support, and such approaches have difficulty in explaining why abnormal patterns develop in some rather than all of the children in a family. Klebanoff (1959) has suggested that the family patterns which are correlated with schizophrenia actually constitute a *reasonable* response to an unusual child. Thus, children who were brain-damaged and retarded tended to have mothers that were more possessive and controlling than mothers of non-disturbed children. Although family factors probably do not play a causal role in the development of schizophrenia, Doane *et al.* (1985) have suggested that the way in which the family reacts to offspring when the symptoms have appeared may play a role in influencing an individual's functioning. In support of this, Doane and his colleagues found that the recurrence of schizophrenic symptoms was reduced when parents reduced their hostility, criticism and intrusiveness towards the schizophrenic offspring.

COGNITIVE MODEL

As we noted earlier on in this chapter, the characteristic disorders evident in schizophrenia are those involving thought, perception, attention and language. Supporters of the *cognitive model* see these as being *causes* rather than *consequences* of the disorder. For example, Maher (1968) sees the bizarre use of language in schizophrenia as a result of a fault in the way in which information is processed. Maher identifies certain words, that is, those which have multiple meanings to an individual, as *vulnerable words*. When such words are used, a person may respond in a way which is personally relevant but semantically irrelevant or inappropriate.

The cognitive model proposes that catatonic schizophrenia may be the result of a breakdown in the ability to *selectively attend* to material. Because the human information-processing system is of limited capacity, we need some way of purposefully selecting what information to process. Impairment of the selective attention mechanism would result in the senses being bombarded with information. The cognitive model suggests that the catatonic schizophrenic's lack of interaction with the outside world occurs because it is the only way in which the amount of sensory stimulation can be kept to a manageable level (Pickering, 1981).

MEDICAL MODEL

Genetic influences

It has long been known that there is a tendency for schizophrenia to run in families. The likelihood of a person developing the disorder is estimated to be about 1 in 100. However, if a person has one schizophrenic parent, the likelihood increases to 1 in 5. If both parents are schizophrenic, the likelihood is increased yet further, to about 1 in 2 or 1 in 3. These observations have led some researchers to propose that schizophrenia can best be explained in *genetic* terms.

One important method of studying the inheritance of characteristics involves comparing the *resemblance* of identical and non-identical twins (and, in very rare cases, quadruplets: see Rosenthal, 1963). Where a characteristic is *continuous*, as is the case in intelligence as measured by intelligence test scores, resemblance is defined in terms of the *correlation* between the test scores of the twins. However, schizophrenia is considered to be *discontinuous*, that is, a person either is schizophrenic or is not. With something that is *discontinous*, resemblance is defined in terms of a *concordance rate*. This is the percentage of twins who share the same trait. If two twins are schizophrenic, they are said to be *concordant* for schizophrenia. If one twin is schizo-

phrenic and the other is not, they are *discordant*.

One of the most famous twin studies was carried out by Gottesman & Shields (1972), who looked at the history of 45,000 individuals treated at two London hospitals between 1948 and 1964. Gottesman and Shields identified 57 schizophrenics with twins who could be located and who agreed to participate in the study. Using diagnosis and hospitalisation as the criteria for schizophrenia, the researchers reported a concordance rate of 42% for identical twins and 9% for non-identical twins.

Several other studies have reported concordance rates which, although different from those obtained by Gottesman and Shields, consistently show that the concordance rate is higher for identical than non-identical twins, as shown in Table 4.1 overleaf. Despite the consistently higher concordance rate for identical twins, the concordance rate in *all* studies has always been less than the theoretically expected 100%. However, Heston (1970) showed that if an identical twin has a schizophrenic disorder, there is a 90% chance that the other twin will have *some sort* of psychological disorder.

Of course, there is always the possibility that the *environment* plays an influential role, and given that twins tend to be raised in the same environment, it would be reckless to attribute the findings obtained by Heston and others exclusively to genetic factors. However, the evidence suggests that, when identical twins are separated at birth (and presumably raised in different environments), the concordance rate is as high as that obtained for identical twins raised in the same environment.

Clearly, identical twins who have been reared in different environments represent one way of controlling for the effects of environmental factors. Research has also looked at the effects of genetics when environmental factors are controlled in other ways. One approach is to study children brought up in foster homes or who have been adopted and have schizophrenic mothers. The usual method is to compare the incidence of schizophrenia in the biological and adoptive parents of adopted children with the disorder. In a famous study, Heston (1966) compared 47 children of schizophrenic mothers, the children having been adopted before the age of 1 month, with 50 matched children raised in the home of their biological and non-schizophrenic mothers. The 'blind' testing of the children by psychiatrists

Study	'Narrow' concordance *		'Broad' concordance *	
	% MZs	% DZs	% MZs	% DZs
Rosanoff *et al.* (1934) USA (41 MZs, 53 DZs)	44	9	61	13
Kallmann (1946) USA (174 MZs, 296 DZs)	59	11	69	11–14
Slater (1953) England (37 MZs, 58 DZs)	65	14	65	14
Gottesman and Shields (1966) England (24 MZs, 33 DZs)	42	15	54	18
Kringlen (1968) Norway (55 MZs, 90 DZs)	25	7	38	10
Allen *et al.* (1972) USA (95 MZs, 125 DZs)	14	4	27	5
Fischer (1973) Denmark (21 MZs, 41 DZs)	24	10	48	20

* 'Narrow' based on attempt to apply a relatively strict set of criteria when diagnosing schizophrenia. 'Broad' includes 'borderline schizophrenia', 'schizoaffective psychosis', 'paranoid with schizophrenia-like features'.

Table 4.1   Shows concordance rates for schizophrenia for identical (MZ) and non-identical (DZ) twins (based on Rose et al., 1984)

revealed that 10% of the children with schizophrenic mothers were diagnosed as schizophrenic, whereas none of the children of non-schizophrenic mothers was so diagnosed. Also, children of schizophrenic mothers were more likely than children of non-schizophrenic mothers to be:

'morally defective, sociopathic, neurotic, criminal and to have been discharged from the armed forces on psychiatric grounds' (Heston, 1966).

In another influential study, Kety *et al.* (1968) examined Denmark's *Folkregister*, a lifelong record of Danish citizens. The researchers compiled lists of children who had been adopted and either later developed schizophrenia or did not develop the disorder at all. The incidence of schizophrenia in the adoptive families of those who developed schizophrenia was as low as in the adoptive families of those who did not develop the disorder. However, the incidence of schizophrenia in the biological families was far higher than expected in those who developed the disorder. If the disposition towards schizophrenia is environmental, then the incidence would be expected to be higher among adoptive relatives with whom the adopted child shared an environment. However, if hereditary factors are important, we would expect the incidence to be higher in biological than in adoptive relatives. The data reported by Kety and his colleagues showed that 21% of the biological relatives displayed schizophrenic symptoms compared with only 5% of the adoptive relatives. Recent research has looked at the incidence of schizophrenia in twins *themselves*. The findings from one important study are described in Box 4.3.

Box 4.3 Are twins more at risk from schizophrenia?

The question of whether schizophrenia is more frequent in twins is an important one because identifying population groups at increased risk of a disorder gives clues as to the causes of that disorder. Several studies (e.g. Gottesman & Shields, 1972) have reported that the rate of schizophrenia among twins does not differ from that of non-twins. However, using the *New Danish Twin Register* and the *Danish Psychiatric Case Register* to identify all the twins, Klaning *et al.* (1996) found a 28% increase in the rate of first admissions for schizophrenia in twins as compared with the general Danish population. Indeed, an increased rate of first admissions for *any* psychiatric disorder was found in twins as compared to the total population.

Klaning *et al.* suggest that there are several potential explanations for their findings. For example, the increased rate among twins might be due to their greater exposure to perinatal complications (such as low birth weight) which might lower the 'threshold' for developing schizophrenia. Alternatively, the psychological environment might be different for twins and this provides a greater risk for developing the disorder. Klaning *et al.*'s study is the first to demonstrate an increased occurrence of schizophrenia among twins and provides researchers with new possibilities in the study of risk factors for the disorder.

From what we have seen, it would be reasonable to conclude that genetic factors play at least some role (and perhaps a major one) in the development of schizophrenia. However, attempts to identify the gene or genes responsible have not as yet been successful. Claims have been made about genetic markers on chromosomes 5 and 22, and then quickly retracted when subsequent research has failed to find evidence of the involvement of these genetic markers (Highfield, 1993a). As we have seen, the evidence indicates that even if genes are involved, genetic factors alone cannot be responsible. For that reason, researchers have looked at other possible influences.

Biochemical influences

As we noted in Chapter 2 (see page 11), one of the ways in which genes may influence behaviour is through *biochemical agents in the brain*. According to the *inborn-error of metabolism hypothesis*, some people inherit an error of metabolism which causes the body to break down naturally occurring chemicals into toxic ones. These toxic chemicals are held to be responsible for the characteristics of schizophrenia. Osmond & Smythies (1953) were amongst the first to note that there were similarities between the experiences of people who had taken hallucinogenic drugs (such as LSD) and the experiences of people diagnosed as schizophrenic. There is some evidence to support the view that the brain produces its own *internal hallucinogens*. For example, Smythies (1976) reported small amounts of hallucinogen-like chemicals in the cerebrospinal fluid of schizophrenics, whilst Murray *et al.* (1979) reported that the hallucinogen *dimethyltryptamine* (*DMT*) was present in the urine of schizophrenics. Moreover, when DMT levels decreased, schizophrenic symptoms also decreased. However, later research indicated that the characteristics of schizophrenia were *different* to those produced by the hallucinogenic drugs, and researchers turned their attention to other biochemical agents.

Perhaps because the hallucinogenic drugs were chemically similar to two neurotransmitters which occur naturally in the brain (namely *norepinephrine* and *dopamine*), they became the focus of research. Of these two neurotransmitters, dopamine has received the overwhelming majority of research attention. The earliest theory implicating dopamine proposed that schizophrenia was caused by the *excess* production of this neurotransmitter in the brain, and post-mortem studies of people diagnosed as schizophrenic have shown higher than normal concentrations of dopamine, especially in the limbic system (Iversen, 1979). However, it is generally agreed that, rather than producing more dopamine *per se*, it is more plausible to propose that more dopamine is *utilised* as a result of overly sensitive post-synaptic receptors for the neurotransmitter or because of above normal reactivity to dopamine due to an increased number of receptor sites. For example, Philip Seeman and his colleagues at the University of Toronto have reported that the density of one site, called the D4 receptor, was six times greater in the brain tissue of schizophrenics than non-schizophrenics. As Seeman has observed:

'For every bombardment of dopamine, you get six times as much message transmitted, and that seems to go along with the symptoms of halluci-nations and delusions' (quoted in Highfield, 1993b).

The role of dopamine is supported by several lines of evidence. For example, in non-schizophrenic individuals, the psychoactive drugs cocaine and amphetamine produce characteristics which are very similar to those observed in some types of schizophrenia (e.g. delusions of persecution and hallucinations), and the two drugs are known to cause the stimulation of receptors for dopamine. Additionally, Davis (1974) has reported that in schizophrenic individuals, cocaine and amphetamine *exacerbate* their symptoms. Research has also shown that drugs which are effective in reducing the symptoms of schizophrenia (such as the *phenothiazines*: see Chapter 8) reduce the concentration of dopamine in the brain by blocking dopamine receptors and preventing them from becoming stimulated (Kimble, 1988).

A number of researchers have suggested that genetic factors might create a predisposition towards schizophrenia which interacts with other factors to produce schizophrenic behaviour. Whilst most environments are conducive to normal development, some may trigger disorders such as schizophrenia. The *diathesis-stress model* is one way of explaining an interaction between genetic and biochemical factors, which accounts for the finding that not everybody who might be genetically predisposed to the disorder (by virtue of, say, having a schizophrenic parent) develops it.

The model proposes that schizophrenia occurs as a result of a biological vulnerability (diathesis) to a disorder interacting with personally significant environmental stressors. Genetic vulnerability is believed to put a person at risk, but environmental stressors (such as leaving home or losing a job) must be present for the gene to be 'switched on'. The *vulnerability-stress model* (Nuechterlein & Dawson, 1984) is an extension of the diathesis-stress model which specifies the genetically determined traits that can make a person vulnerable. These include hyperactivity and information-processing deficits.

Yet whilst the evidence linking dopamine to schizophrenia is impressive, researchers have been cautious about uncritically accepting that it plays a causal role. For example, the availability of dopamine could be just *one* factor in the sequence of schizophrenia's develop-ment rather than the *only* factor. More importantly, the drugs used to treat schizophrenia are not always effective in reducing its symptoms.

According to Crow *et al.* (1982), drugs are only helpful in treating what Kraepelin called the *positive symptoms* of schizophrenia (and what are now called *Type 1 symptoms*). These include the classic symptoms of schizophrenia, that is, delusions, hallucinations and thought disorder. The *negative* (or *Type 2*) *symptoms* of decreased speech, lack of drive, diminished social interaction and loss of emotional response do not seem to be affected by drug treatment. This has led to the speculation that the positive symptoms of schizophrenia have one cause (possibly related to dopamine), whereas the negative symptoms might have some other cause.

Neurodevelopmental influences

One cause that might be related to the negative symptoms of schizophrenia is *damage to the brain*. There is now extensive evidence of structural abnormalities in the brains of schizophrenics, which Johnson (1989) has described as 'powerful evidence that schizophrenia is a brain disease'. In one study, Stevens (1982) showed that many people with schizophrenia display symptoms that clearly indicate neurological disease, especially with regard to eye movements. Symptoms included decreased rate of eye blink, staring, lack of blink reflex in response to a tap on the forehead, poor visual pursuit movements and poor pupillary reactions to light. Post-mortems conducted by Stevens suggested a disease that had occurred earlier in life and had partially healed or one that was slowly progressing at the time of death. Certainly, there is evidence to suggest that at least some schizophrenics have undergone difficult births in which the brain might have suffered a lack of oxygen (Harrison, 1995). The apparent decline in the number of cases of schizophrenia appearing might be related to improvements in maternity care. Research using CAT scan and PET and MRI imaging devices to compare schizophrenic and non-schizophrenic brains has been reviewed by Chua & McKenna (1995). Several kinds of structural abnormality have been discovered in the schizophrenic brain, including an unusually small corpus collosum, high densities of white matter in the right frontal and parietal lobes, a smaller volume of temporal lobe grey matter and unusually large ventricles (the hollow spaces in the brain filled with cerebrospinal fluid), indicating the loss of brain tissue elsewhere. However, on the basis of their review, Chua and McKenna have argued that the only well-established structural abnormality in schizophrenia is lateral ventricular enlargement, and even this is modest and shows considerable overlap with the non-schizophrenic population. Whilst they do not believe schizophrenia to be characterised by any simple focal reduction in brain activity, Chua and McKenna believe that complex alterations in the normal reciprocal patterns of activation between anatomically related areas of the cerebral cortex might characterise the disorder.

If schizophrenia (or at least some symptoms of it) is the result of the failure of the brain to develop normally for some reason (which would make schizophrenia a *neurodevelopmental disorder*), it is important to know when this damage occurs. One theory suggests that the damage may be due to a *viral infection*. It is well known that there are seasonal variations in chickenpox and measles, which are known to be caused by viruses. According to Torrey *et al.* (1977), the finding that significantly more people who develop schizophrenia are born in late winter and early spring than at other times of the year is not a statistical quirk. Torrey (1988) believes that schizophrenia may be the result of a virus affecting pre-natal development, especially during the second trimester of pregnancy, when the developing brain is forming crucial interconnections. For example, in normal development, *pre-alpha cells* are formed in the middle of the brain and migrate towards the cortex. In schizophrenic brains, however, the cells get only 85% of the way to their final destination. Support for a viral theory comes from longitudinal studies conducted by Barr *et al.* (1990) and O'Callaghan *et al.* (1991, 1993). These researchers reported an increased risk for schizophrenia for those in the fifth month of foetal development during the 1957 *influenza pandemic.*

Research conducted by Bracha *et al.* (1991) has shown that one identical twin who develops schizophrenia is significantly more likely to have various hand deformities as compared with the other twin. The relevance of this finding is that hands are formed during the second trimester of pregnancy, which might suggest that the same pre-natal trauma or virus which affects the brain also affects the hands. In order to explain schizophrenia's tendency to run in families, Stevens (1982) has proposed that whatever causes the damage affects only people with an *inherited susceptibility* to schizophrenia and does not affect those with non-schizophrenic heredity.

At present, there seems to be no agreement amongst researchers as to the plausibility of viral theories. For example, some researchers have failed to find an association between births during the 1957 influenza epidemic and the later development of schizophrenia. As Crow & Done (1992) have noted, it is ridiculous to suggest that the alleged schizophrenogenic effects of the epidemic were genuine and present in Finland, England, Wales and Edinburgh (as some studies have reported) but absent in the rest of Scotland and the United States (which other studies have found), since the virus that caused the epidemic could not have changed. Other researchers (e.g. O'Callaghan *et al.,* 1994) have failed to find evidence of *any* significant associations between later schizophrenia and maternal exposure to a variety of infectious diseases other than influenza. As Claridge (1987) has remarked, the season of birth effect has many equally plausible explanations, one being that it might reflect the cycles of sexual activity among the parents of future psychotics, a hypothesis which does not seem to have attracted much attention, despite its credibility as an explanation for the data. What does seem likely, though, is that the claim for schizophrenia being a result of a virus caught from domestic cats (which is based on the observation that there is a higher incidence of the disorder in countries where cats are kept as pets) is almost certainly untrue! (Bentall, 1996)

Conclusions

This chapter has looked at the characteristics of schizophrenia and the various explanations for this most serious of mental disorders. Some of these explanations are more plausible than others and have received considerable support from research studies. However, an explanation for the disorder which is accepted by all of those working in the area so far remains elusive.

SUMMARY

- Schizophrenia is the most serious of all the disorders identified in ICD-10 and DSM-IV. Originally called **dementia praecox** by Kraepelin, Bleuler observed that schizophrenia often begins later in life and does not always involve progressive deterioration; the term was coined to refer to a 'splitting' within the personality which 'loses its unity'. Schizophrenia is often confused with **multiple personality disorder**.

- In Britain, the diagnosis of schizophrenia is based on Schneider's **first-rank symptoms**, namely **passivity experiences and thought disorder** (including thought insertion, thought withdrawal and thought broadcasting), **hallucinations** (usually auditory, but also somatosensory, as in depersonalisation) and **primary delusions** (such as delusions of grandeur, persecution, reference and nihilism).

- Auditory hallucinations may be the result of a breakdown in the **feedback loop** which normally informs us that our inner speech is, in fact, our own thoughts being converted into internal language; schizophrenics talk to themselves but do not realise it. This relates to a more general failure to integrate behavioural intentions (controlled by the frontal regions of the brain) and perception of the consequences of behaviour (controlled by the temporal lobes).

- First-rank symptoms are subjective experiences which can only be inferred from verbal reports. Neither hallucinations nor delusions are exclusive to schizophrenia. Slater and Roth identify four different characteristics of schizophrenia that are directly observable from behaviour, namely **thought process disorder** (including loose associations, 'word salads' and poverty of content, clang associations, neologisms, thought blocking and literal interpretation), **disturbances of affect/emotional disturbances** (in particular blunting, flattened affect and inappropriate affect), **psychomotor disturbances** (such as catatonia and stereotypy) and **lack of volition**.

- **Disorganised/hebephrenic** schizophrenia is the most severe type. It is usually diagnosed only in adolescence/young adulthood and is progressive and irreversible. Characteristics include incoherent language, delusions and vivid hallucinations and extreme social withdrawal.

- **Simple schizophrenia** (only recognised by ICD) usually appears gradually during late adolescence. The main characteristics are withdrawal from reality, difficulty with friendships, aimlessness and lack of drive.

- **Catatonic schizophrenia** involves a striking impairment of motor activity, such as waxy flexibility and agitated catatonia. Other characteristics include mutism and negativism.

- **Paranoid schizophrenia** is characterised by delusions, often accompanied by hallucinations; everyday functioning is largely unimpaired. It tends to occur later than other types of schizophrenia and is the most homogeneous type.

- **Undifferentiated/atypical schizophrenia** is a category reserved for those who fit the criteria for more than one type or who do not appear to fit any particular category.

- **Schizophreniform psychosis** is similar to schizophrenia, but lasts for less than six months. **Schizotypal disorder** refers to eccentric behaviour and unusual thoughts and emotions resembling those seen in schizophrenia. **Schizoaffective disorder** involves both schizophrenic and affective episodes.

- Three phases in the development of schizophrenia are the **prodromal phase** (relating to process and reactive schizophrenia, in early adolescence and early adulthood respectively), in which the individual becomes increasingly withdrawn and emotionally flat, the **active phase**, in which the major characteristics of schizophrenia appear, and the **residual phase**, in which there is a return to the prodromal phase.

- There is much debate surrounding the existence of distinct types of schizophrenia, as well as the concept of schizophrenia itself. However, a number of explanations of the bizarre behaviours associated with the disorder have been proposed.

- According to the **behavioural model**, schizophrenia can be explained in terms of conditioning and observational learning. Although schizophrenic behaviour can be modified through techniques based on conditioning, thought disorders seem to be largely unaffected. The behavioural model can account for the maintenance of schizophrenic behaviour much better than for why it appears in the first place.

- The major **psychodynamic** explanation of schizophrenia is that it involves a regression to the oral stage in the face of overwhelming demands by the id or guilt from the superego. Regressive

- symptoms are followed by restitutional symptoms (hallucinations and delusions), as the ego tries to regain contact with reality. The psychodynamic account is a poor predictor of schizophrenic outcome.
- According to Bateson *et al.*, parents predispose children to schizophrenia by presenting them with 'double binds', which make them doubt their own perceptions and feelings as reliable indicators of reality. This is similar to the deviant communication noted by Wynne *et al.*
- According to Lidz, families of schizophrenics are marked by **marital schism/skew**. Fromm-Reichman's **schizophrenogenic** mother is domineering, cold, rejecting and guilt-producing and, in conjunction with a passive and ineffectual father, she drives her child to schizophrenia.
- Family interaction explanations fail to explain why only some children in a family become schizophrenic, and those family patterns may be a response to an unusual child rather than a cause of abnormality. However, the family's response to offspring once the symptoms have appeared may influence that individual's functioning.
- According to the **cognitive model**, schizophrenia is caused by thought, attention and language disorders, as in the bizarre use of language resulting from faulty information-processing. For example, in the case of catatonic schizophrenia, there may be a breakdown in the ability to **selectively attend** to information, resulting in bombardment of the senses. The catatonic schizophrenic's lack of interaction with the outside world may be the only way of keeping the amount of sensory stimulation to a manageable level.
- The observation that schizophrenia tends to run in families and that having one or both schizophrenic parents increases the child's likelihood of becoming so, suggest that there may be **genetic** factors involved.
- With a **continuous** characteristic (such as intelligence), **resemblance** is defined in terms of the **correlation** between test scores of twins (identical and non-identical); with a **discontinuous** characteristic (such as schizophrenia), resemblance is defined in terms of a **concordance rate**.
- A number of studies, including that by Gottesman and Shields, have consistently reported concordance rates that are higher for identical than for non-identical twins. However, the concordance rates are always less than the theoretically expected 100%, implicating the role of environmental factors. Yet when identical twins are separated at birth, the concordance rate is as high as when they are raised together.
- An alternative way of controlling for the effects of environmental factors is through fostering or adoption studies; the usual method is to compare the incidence of schizophrenia in the biological and adoptive parents of adopted children with schizophrenia. In the Kety *et al.* Danish study, 21% of the biological relatives displayed schizophrenic symptoms compared with only 5% of the adoptive relatives.
- Recent research has looked at the increased risk of schizophrenia in twins **themselves**, which provides clues as to the causes of the disorder. While several earlier studies reported that twins are no more at risk than non-twins, Klaning *et al.*'s Danish study found a 28% increase in the rate of first admissions for schizophrenia in twins compared with the general population. One possible explanation is that twins are more exposed to perinatal complications which lower the 'threshold' for developing schizophrenia; another is that the psychological environment might be different for twins.
- While genetic factors seem to play at least some role, attempts to identify the gene/genes responsible for schizophrenia have so far failed.
- One way in which genes may influence behaviour is through **biochemical agents in the brain**. One such biochemical approach is the **inborn-error of metabolism hypothesis**, according to which some people inherit an error of metabolism which causes the body to break down naturally occurring chemicals into toxic ones which produce the symptoms of schizophrenia.
- Another biochemical theory maintains that the brain produces its own 'internal hallucinogens', such as **dimethyltryptamine/DMT**. However, while early research reported similarities between the effects of hallucinogenic drugs and the experiences of schizophrenics, this was later shown not to be the case.
- The neurotransmitter dopamine has received considerable attention. Post-mortems show that schizophrenics have higher concentrations of dopamine than normal people, but rather than schizophrenia being caused by a simple excess of dopamine in the brain, it is how it is **utilised** that matters. Schizophrenics appear to have more numerous or densely packed receptor sites, which could account for hallucinations and delusions.
- Cocaine and amphetamine, known to stimulate dopamine receptors, produce schizophrenia-like

symptoms in non-schizophrenics, as well as exacerbating the symptoms of diagnosed schizophrenics. Conversely, the phenothiazines, which reduce the symptoms of schizophrenia, also block dopamine receptors.

- The **diathesis-stress model** proposes that schizophrenia is the result of an interaction between a biological vulnerability and personally significant environmental stressors. The **vulnerability-stress model** specifies the genetically determined traits that can make a person vulnerable, such as hyperactivity and faulty information-processing.

- It is possible that **positive/Type 1 symptoms** have one cause, possibly related to dopamine, while **negative/Type 2 symptoms** have some other cause, such as brain damage, as revealed through abnormal eye movements. Damage may be caused by oxygen deficits at birth. While a number of structural differences between the brains of schizophrenics and non-schizophrenics have been proposed, these differences are modest and there is considerable overlap between the two populations.

- Schizophrenia might be a **neurodevelopmental disorder** in which the brain fails to develop normally. One cause might be a **viral infection**, especially during the second trimester of pregnancy, when the developing brain is forming crucial interconnections, such as those made by **pre-alpha cells**.

- Although there is some evidence to support viral theories, including the increased risk for schizophrenia for those in the fifth month of foetal development during the 1957 influenza pandemic, overall it is very inconclusive and at times contradictory. Almost certainly, there is no truth in the claim that schizophrenia is the result of a virus caught from domestic cats.

5

DEPRESSION

Introduction and overview

What both DSM-IV and ICD-10 call *mood* (or *affective*) *disorders* involve a prolonged and fundamental disturbance of mood and emotions. Mood refers to a pervasive and sustained emotional state that colours a person's perceptions, thoughts and behaviours. At one extreme of this is *manic disorder* (or *mania*), which is characterised by wild, exuberant and unrealistic activity and a flight of ideas or distracting thoughts. At the other extreme is *depressive disorder*, which represents the complete reverse of mania. Mania usually occurs in conjunction with depression and in such cases is described as *bipolar disorder*. However, in the rare cases in which mania occurs alone, the term bipolar is also used, the term *unipolar* being reserved for the person who experiences episodes of depression alone. The term *manic-depressive* refers to both the unipolar and bipolar forms of affective disorder.

Our aim in this chapter is to describe the characteristics associated with depression and to look at some of the explanations that have been offered to explain what Seligman (1973) has termed 'the common cold' of psychological problems.

The characteristics of depression

By the term 'common cold' of psychological problems, Seligman means that depression is the most common psychological problem people face. If the students questioned by Beck & Young (1978) are a guide, then most of us will, at some time during the coming year, experience some of the symptoms of depression. In the case of the death of a loved one or when a relationship has ended, depression is a normal experience. Indeed, most psychologically healthy people occasionally 'get the blues' or 'feel down'. However, such depression usually passes fairly quickly. In order to be diagnosed as suffering from *clinical depression*, a number of the characteristics shown in Box 5.1 need to have co-occurred for a period of time.

> **Box 5.1   The characteristics of clinical depression**
>
> Clinical depression is defined by persistent low mood for at least two weeks, plus at least five of the following:
>
> - poor appetite or weight loss or increased appetite or weight gain (a change of 1 lb per week over several weeks or 10 lb in a year when not dieting)

- difficulty in sleeping (*insomnia*) or sleeping longer than usual (*hypersomnia*)

- loss of energy or tiredness to the point of being unable to make even the simplest everyday decisions

- an observable slowing down or agitation. In an attempt to discharge feelings of restlessness, people will often wring their hands, pace about or complain (termed *agitated depression*)

- a markedly diminished loss of interest or pleasure in activities that were once enjoyed

- feelings of self-reproach or excessive or inappropriate guilt over real or imagined misdeeds. These may develop into *delusions* (see Chapter 4, page 37). For example, people may believe that God or the devil is punishing them for their sins or that they alone are responsible for the evil in the world

- complaints or evidence of diminished ability to think or concentrate

- recurrent thoughts of death (not just a fear of dying), suicide, suicidal thoughts without a specific plan, or a suicide attempt or a specific plan for committing suicide.

(adapted from Spitzer *et al.*, 1981)

Unipolar depression can occur at any age, and the characteristics may appear gradually or suddenly. It has been estimated that, in the United States, 15% of adults aged between 18 and 74 will experience serious depression. In Britain, the figure has been estimated at 5% (SANE, 1993a). Box 5.2 describes a typical case.

Box 5.2   A typical case of depression

A 55-year-old man has suffered from appetite loss and a 50-pound weight loss over the past six months. His loss of appetite has been accompanied by a burning pain in his chest, back and abdomen, which he is convinced indicates a fatal abdominal cancer. He is withdrawn and isolated, unable to work, uninterested in friends and family, and unresponsive to their attempts to make him feel better. He awakes at 4 a.m. and is unable to fall back asleep. He claims to feel worse in the mornings and to improve slightly as the day wears on. He is markedly agitated and speaks of feelings of extreme unworthiness. He says that he would be better off dead and that he welcomes his impending demise from cancer.

(adapted from Spitzer *et al.*, 1981)

Deeply embedded within psychiatric thinking is the view that a distinction can be made between *endogenous* and *exogenous* (or *reactive*) depression. Endogenous means 'coming from within' and was the term used to describe depression arising from biochemical disturbances in the brain. Exogenous means 'coming from the outside' and was used to describe depression that occurred as a reaction (hence *reactive*) to stressful life experiences. However, as Williams & Hargreaves (1995) have noted, this distinction is controversial and *endogenous* is now used to describe a cluster of symptoms rather than the origins of the depression.

Bipolar disorder is characterised by alternating periods of mania (whose major characteristics we briefly described in the introduction to this chapter) and depression, which seem to be unrelated to external events. The duration and frequency of the periods vary from person to person. In some cases, periods of mania and depression may be separated by long periods of normal functioning. In other cases, manic and depressive episodes quickly follow one another, and these unending cycles can be destructive for the people affected, their families and friends.

As we noted, depression can occur at any age. Bipolar disorder, however, generally appears in the early 20s. Unlike depression (which is more prevalent in women: see pages 58–59), bipolar disorder is equally prevalent in men and women, although the disorder itself is much less common than depression. Interestingly, Jamison (1989) has reported a disproportionately higher incidence of *bipolar* disorder among creative people. For example, among 47 award-winning British writers and artists, 38% were treated for bipolar disorder. In the general population, about 1% will be treated for this disorder. Box 5.3 describes a woman with bipolar disorder.

Box 5.3: A case of bipolar disorder

For four months, Mrs S. has spent most of her time lying in bed. She appears sad and deep in thought and often states, 'I'm no good to anyone; I'm going to be dead soon'. She expresses many feelings of hopelessness and listlessness and has difficulty concentrating. Suddenly, one day, her mood seems to be remarkably better. She is pleasant, verbalises more and appears somewhat cheerful. The following day, however, the rate of her speech is increased, she is moving rapidly, shows a flight of ideas, and intrudes into everyone's activities. Over a couple of days, this activity increases to the point where she is unable to control her actions and attempts to break the furniture.

(adapted from Spitzer *et al*. 1981)

Explanations of depression

THE BEHAVIOURAL MODEL

Behavioural approaches to depression focus on the role played by *reinforcement*. Early theories suggested that depression is a result of a reduction in reinforcement (Ferster, 1965). For example, the death of a loved one is associated with depression and is also associated with a loss of positive reinforcement from the external environment. Ferster's view was expanded by Lewinsohn (1974). Like Ferster, Lewinsohn argues that certain events, such as the loss of a job, induce depression, because they cause a reduction in positive reinforcement.

A depressed person may spend less time in social activities, which, at least initially, leads to concern and attention being paid by that person's friends. Lewinsohn argues that the attention the depressed person receives *reinforces* the depressed behaviour. However, after a while friends become tired of the person and no longer pay him or her any attention. Thus, the reinforcement of attention is reduced and this exacerbates the depression that is experienced. The result of this is that the depressed individual is caught in a cycle from which escape is difficult. Figure 5.1 illustrates Lewinsohn's proposals.

Lewinsohn also sees people who lack social skills as being the prime candidates for depression, because social ineptness is unlikely to bring reinforcement from other people. As a result, the socially unskilled individual may exhibit the form of passive behaviour that characterises depression. MacPhillamy & Lewinsohn (1974) have found that depressed people report having fewer pleasant experiences than non-depressed people, and that greater depression is correlated with fewer

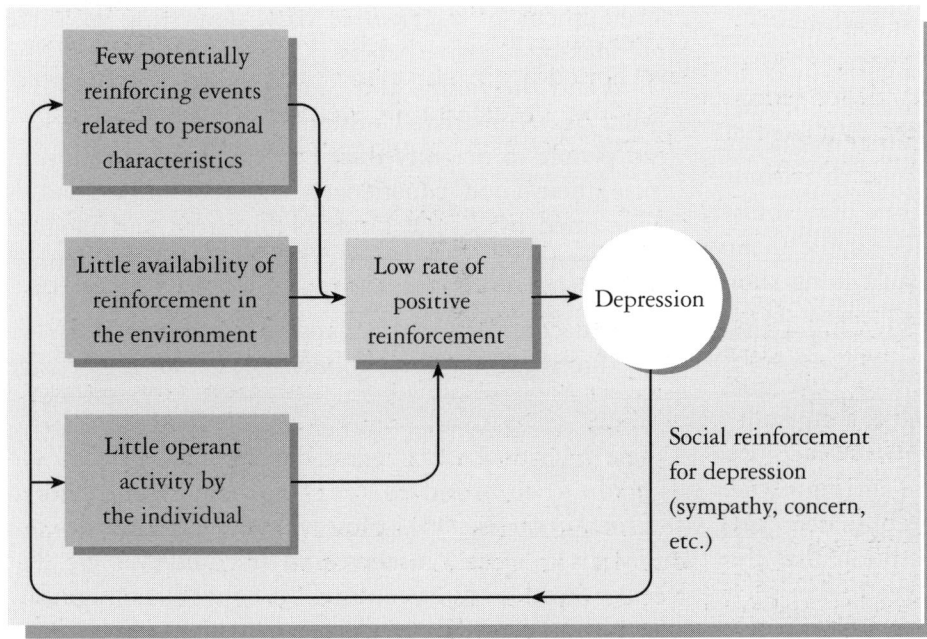

Figure 5.1   Lewinsohn's model of depression

pleasant experiences. However, whilst it is possible that depression *follows* a reduction in pleasant experiences, it is also possible that depression *precedes* a reduction in those experiences, and it is plausible to suggest that people who become depressed lower their participation in reinforcing events.

COGNITIVE–BEHAVIOURAL MODEL

Another explanation of depression represents a link between behavioural and *cognitive* perspectives and comes from research conducted by Seligman and his colleagues. Seligman & Maier (1967) conducted an experiment showing that dogs which were restrained so that they could not avoid electric shocks appeared to acquire a sense of passive resignation to the receipt of the shocks. Later, when the dogs were placed in a situation in which they *could* learn to escape a shock, they made no attempt to do so. Seligman termed this phenomenon *learned helplessness.*

Seligman and his colleagues argued that the behaviours exhibited by the dogs (such as lethargy, sluggishness, loss of appetite and so on) were similar to the behaviours exhibited by depressed humans. According to Seligman and his colleagues, depressed people (like dogs) learn from experience to develop an expectancy that their behaviours will be fruitless in bringing about a change in the environment. When people feel helpless to influence their encounters with pleasurable and unpleasurable stimuli, the consequence is depression.

The theory of learned helplessness was criticised because it failed to address the issue of why some depressed people tend to blame themselves for their depression, whilst others blame the external world, and the observation that depressed people tend to attribute their successes to luck rather than to their own ability. Abramson *et al.*'s (1978) revised version of the theory of learned helplessness went further than talking about a lack of control. The revised theory is based on the attributions or interpretations people make of their experiences. According to Abramson and his colleagues, people who attribute failure to *internal* ('It's my fault'), *stable* ('It's going to last forever') and *global* ('It's going to affect everything I do') causes and attribute their successes to luck are more likely to become depressed, because these factors lead to the perception that they are helpless to change things for the better. The researchers argue that this *attributional style* derives

from learning histories, especially in the family and at school.

Support for the learned helplessness theory of depression comes from research which indicates that questionnaires assessing how people interpret adversities in life predict (at least to a degree) their future susceptibility to depression. However, although cognitions of helplessness often do accompany depressive episodes, the pattern of cognition has been shown to change once the individual's depressive episode ends. According to Barnett & Gottlib (1988), people who were formerly depressed are actually no different from people who have never been depressed in terms of their tendency to view negative events with an attitude of helpless resignation. This finding could be interpreted as indicating that an attitude of helplessness is a symptom rather than a cause of depression.

A similar account to that advanced by Seligman has been proposed by Beck (1974), whose cognitive model of emotional disorders states that:

> 'an individual's emotional response to an event or experience is determined by the conscious meaning placed on it'.

Beck believes that depression is based in self-defeating *negative beliefs* and *negative cognitive sets* (or tendencies to think in certain ways) that develop as a result of experience. According to Beck, certain experiences in childhood and adolescence (such as the loss of a parent or criticism from teachers and other adults) leads to the development of a *cognitive triad* consisting of three interlocking negative beliefs. These concern the *self,* the *world* and the *future,* and cause people to have a distorted and constricted outlook on life. These beliefs lead people to magnify their bad experiences and minimise their good experiences. The cognitive triad is maintained by several kinds of distorted and illogical interpretations of real events that contribute to depression. We identified several kinds of illogical thinking that can contribute to feelings of depression when we introduced the cognitive model in Chapter 2 (see page 16).

There is evidence to suggest that depressed people do describe their world in the ways that Beck outlined (White *et al.*, 1985). However, correlations do not allow us to infer causality, and it could well be that feelings of depression and logical errors of thought are both caused by a third factor (which might be a biochemical imbalance: see below). Additionally, as Hammen (1985) has pointed out, the perception and recall of information in more negative terms might be the *result* of depression rather than the *cause* of it.

Recent research has looked at the role of *depressogenic schemata*, that is, cognitions that may precipitate depression, which remain latent until activated by *stress*. Haaga & Beck (1992) have specified several types of stressor that may activate dysfunctional beliefs in people. For example, *sociotropic* individuals may be stressed by negative interactions or rejections by others, whereas *autonomous* individuals may be stressed by a failure to reach personal goals. According to Teasdale's (1988) *differential activation hypothesis*, the increased accessibility of negative thoughts after an initial shift in mood may explain why some people suffer persistent rather than transient depression. Some of the attempts to examine Teasdale's and Haaga and Beck's proposals can be found in Scott (1994).

PSYCHODYNAMIC MODEL

Psychodynamic approaches to mood disorders were first addressed by Abraham (1911), who was once a student of Freud. However, it was Freud himself, in *Mourning and Melancholia* (1917), who attempted to apply psychodynamic principles. Freud noted that there was a similarity between the grieving that occurs when a loved one dies and the symptoms of depression. Freud saw depression as being excessive and irrational grief which occurs as a reaction to loss that evokes feelings associated with real or imagined loss of affection from the person on whom the individual was most dependent as a child.

Freud argued that both *actual losses* (such as the death of a loved one) and *symbolic losses* (such as the loss of a job or social prestige) lead us to re-experience parts of our childhood. Thus, depressed people become dependent and clinging or, in very extreme cases, regress to a childlike state. Freud believed that the greater the experience of loss in childhood, the greater was the regression that occurred during adulthood. The evidence for this account is, however, mixed. For example, whilst some studies do suggest that children who have lost a parent are particularly susceptible to depression later on (Roy, 1981), other studies have failed to find such a susceptibility (Lewinsohn & Hoberman, 1982).

Freud also argued that unresolved hostility towards one's parents, which has been repressed so that we are no longer consciously aware of it, was also important. When loss is experienced, anger is evoked and is turned *inward* on the self. The reason for this is that the outward expression of anger is unacceptable to the superego, and so is turned inwards. The self-directed hostility creates feelings of guilt, unworthiness and despair, which may be so intense as to motivate *suicide* (the ultimate form of inward-directed aggression). Freud further believed that grief was complicated by inevitable mixed feelings. As well as affection, Freud felt that mourners were likely to have had at least occasionally angry feelings towards the deceased. However, because such feelings are unacceptable, they too are redirected towards the self, leading to lowered self-esteem and feelings of guilt.

The above accounts explain the depression that occurs in response to some sort of environmental stress. Freud explains depression in the absence of any immediately identifiable stress as the *symbolic* loss of a loved one. A person might, for example, interpret a short-tempered response from a loved one as a sign that affection will no longer be returned.

Psychodynamic theorists see the occurrence of bipolar disorder as the result of the alternating dominance of personality by the superego (in the depressive phase of the disorder, which floods the individual with exaggerated ideas of wrong-doing and associated feelings of guilt and worthlessness) and the ego, which attempts to defend itself by rebounding and asserting supremacy, accounting for the elation and self-confidence that are part of the manic phase. As a response to the excessive display of ego, the superego dominates, resulting in feelings of guilt and again plunges the individual into depression.

At least four reasons suggest that the psychodynamic model is inadequate in explaining mood disorders in general, and depression in particular. First, there is no direct evidence that depressed people interpret the death of a loved one as desertion or rejection of themselves (Davison & Neale, 1990). Second, if anger is turned inward, we would not expect depressed people to direct excessive amounts of hostility towards people who are close to them. However, Weissman & Paykel (1974) reported evidence to suggest that this does occur. Third, as Crook & Eliot (1980) have observed, there is little evidence for a direct connection between early loss and the risk of depression in adult life.

Finally, since symbolic loss cannot be observed, this aspect of the theory cannot be experimentally assessed.

MEDICAL MODEL

Genetic influences

It has long been known that mood disorders tend to run in families. On the basis of this observation, it has been suggested that these disorders have a *genetic* basis. According to Weissman (1987), people with first-degree relatives (relatives with whom an individual shares 50% of his or her genes, i.e. parents and siblings) who have a mood disorder are ten times more likely to develop one than those people with unaffected first-degree relatives. Allen (1976) has reported a higher average concordance rate for bipolar disorder in identical twins (72%) than in non-identical twins (14%). These concordance rates for identical twins are the highest for *any* psychological disorder.

As far as major depression is concerned, Allen (1976) has reported an average concordance rate of 40% for identical twins and only 11% for non-identical twins. The fact that concordance rates for bipolar disorder and major depression differ suggests that, if genetic factors *are* involved, they are different for the two disorders. As we noted in Chapter 4, however, the data from families and twins is limited by the fact that families and twins usually share the same environment. However, as with schizophrenia, this problem has been at least partially overcome by adoption studies. For example, Wender *et al.* (1986) have shown that adopted children who later develop a mood disorder are much more likely to have a biological parent who has been diagnosed as having a mood disorder, becomes alcoholic or commits suicide, even though the adopted children are raised in very different environments.

Recent research has used DNA markers to try and identify the gene or genes that are involved in the mood disorders. This approach attempts to look at the inheritance of mood disorders within high-risk families and then locate a DNA segment that is inherited along with a predisposition to develop the disorder. One of the most publicised studies was reported by Egeland *et al.* (1987), who studied 81 people from four high-risk families, all of whom were members of the Old Order Amish community in Pennsylvania. 14 of the 81 were diagnosed as having a bipolar disorder, and all were shown to have specific genetic markers at the tip of chromosome 11. However, subsequent research has failed to replicate this finding in other populations in which bipolar disorder appears to be inherited. For example, a study by Hodgkinson *et al.* (1987) of three large Icelandic families and Detera-Wadleigh *et al.* (1987) of three North American families failed to find evidence of the chromosome 11 linkage. Whilst these data do not invalidate the data obtained by Egeland and her colleagues, other researchers (e.g. Kelsoe *et al.*, 1989) have failed to support the findings when the analysis was extended to other Amish relatives. Such a finding suggests at least two possibilites. For example, the gene for bipolar disorder may not actually be on chromosome 11, or several genes play a role, only one of which is on chromosome 11. This possibility is perhaps supported by the observation that a second gene located on the X chromosome has also been implicated in bipolar disorder (Baron *et al.*, 1987).

Research conducted by Ogilvie *et al.* (1996) has shown that cells use a gene called SERT to make a serotonin transporter protein which plays an important role in the transmission of information between neurons. In most people, part of this gene called the 'second intron' contains 10 or 12 repeating sections of DNA. However, in a significant number of people with depression, this part of the gene has only nine repeat sequences. Although it has yet to be established how this variation is involved in depression, the fact that serotonin is a neurotransmitter strongly implicated in depression (see below) and that the newer anti-depressant drugs such as Prozac (see Chapter 8) interact with the serotonin transporter protein, offers one of the strongest hints yet that there may be a genetic link with depression.

Biochemical influences

As we mentioned in Chapter 2, genes act by directing biochemical events. A number of researchers have looked at the *biochemical processes* that may play a causal role in affective disorders. Research has linked these disorders to chemical imbalances in the neurotransmitters *serotonin* and *norepinephrine*. An early theory advanced by Schildkraut (1965) was that too much norepinephrine at certain sites resulted in mania, whereas too little resulted in depression. Later research suggested that a similar role was played by serotonin.

Certainly, there is some evidence to support the causal role played by these neurotransmitters. For example, animals given drugs that diminish norepinephrine production become sluggish and inactive, which are two symptoms of depression (Wender & Klein, 1981). Similar effects occur when humans are given *reserpine*, which is used to treat high blood pressure. Additionally, drugs which are effective in reducing depression (see Chapter 8, page 85) increase brain levels of norepinephrine and serotonin. The drug *iproniazid* (which is used to treat tuberculosis) produces elation and euphoria in individuals and it increases norepinephrine and serotonin levels. Lithium carbonate (which is used to treat mania: see Chapter 8, page 86) decreases norepinephrine and serotonin levels.

Research also suggests that lower than normal levels of compounds that are produced when norepinephrine and serotonin are broken down by enzymes are found in the urine of depressed people (Teuting *et al.*, 1981), suggesting lower than normal activity of norepinephrine and serotonin-secreting neurones in the brain. Abnormally high levels of norepinephrine-derived compounds have been found in the urine of manic people (Kety, 1975), and the level of these compounds fluctuates in people with bipolar disorder (Bunney *et al.*, 1972).

However, Schildkraut's theory was dealt a serious blow by the finding that whilst norepinephrine *and* serotonin are lower in depression, lower levels of serotonin are also found in mania. Thus, it cannot be a simple case of an excess or deficiency of the neurotransmitters that is responsible for mania and depression respectively. An attempt to reconcile these observations has been proposed by Kety in his *permissive amine theory of mood disorder* (norepinephrine and serotonin are examples of *biogenic amines*, hence the theory's name). According to Kety, serotonin plays a role in limiting norepinephrine levels. When serotonin levels are normal, so are norepinephrine levels, and only normal highs and lows are experienced. However, when serotonin is deficient, it cannot play its limiting role and so norepinephrine levels fluctuate beyond normal high and low levels, leading to mania and depression.

However, whilst drugs that alleviate depression increase levels of norepinephrine and serotonin, they do so only in the period immediately after the drug has been taken. Within a few days, the neurotransmitter levels return to baseline. The problem for Kety's theory is that antidepressant effects do *not* occur during the period when transmitter levels are elevated. All anti-depressant drugs generally take a period of time before they alleviate depression (see Chapter 8, page 85). This would suggest that depression cannot be explained simply in terms of a change in neurotransmitter levels. What is more likely is that the drugs act to reduce depression by increasing the *sensitivity* of receiving neurones, thereby allowing them to utilise limited supplies of the neurotransmitters in a more effective way (Sulser, 1979).

The role of neurotransmitters in mood disorders is further complicated by the fact that antidepressant drugs are not always effective in the reduction of depression, that not everyone suffering from depression shows reduced levels of the neurotransmitters, and that not everyone displaying mania shows increased levels of norepinephrine. Whilst it seems likely that neurotransmitters *do* play a role in mood disorders, their exact role remains to be determined.

External factors and biochemical influences

Despite the reservations concerning both genetic and biochemical findings, there is general agreement that mood disorders probably do have an organic basis. If a gene is involved, its exact mode of transmission must be complex, given the variation in the severity and manner of the expression of mood disorders. It could be that serotonin acts as the regulator or it could be that serotonin and norepinephrine play different roles in different types of mood disorders. Also, we cannot rule out the possibility that neurotransmitter levels occur as a result of the mood disorder rather than acting as a cause of it. For example, environmental stimuli may cause depression which then leads to biochemical changes in the brain. Miller *et al.* (1977) showed that levels of norepinephrine are lower in dogs in whom learned helplessness has been induced. The dogs did not inherit such levels but acquired them as a result of their experiences. Whilst the evidence suggests that affective disorders are heritable and that biochemical factors are involved, the exact cause-and-effect relationships remain to be established.

Seasonal variation in the incidence of depression has been recognised since the time of the ancient Greeks. Two sub-types of what is known as *seasonal affective disorder* have been of particular interest. *Summer depression* is associated with loss of appetite, weight and sleep. *Winter depression*, by contrast, is associated with increased appetite, weight and sleep. Wurtman & Wurtman (1989) have argued that summer depression

Figure 5.2   Exposure to bright light has been shown to be effective for some individuals in the treatment of seasonal affective disorder (SAD). However, the processes underlying SAD and light therapy are still unclear

is associated with deficiences in serotonin levels, whilst Wehr & Rosenthal (1989) see the desynchronisation of the rhythm of *melatonin* (a hormone secreted by the *pineal gland* and which influences serotonin production) as the result of decreasing natural light exposure in winter. In the case of summer depression, a mechanism other than decreasing light exposure must play a role. Laboratory studies of non-human animals conducted by Rudolph *et al.* (1993) have shown that changes in magnetic field exposure, which alters the direction of the magnetic field, are correlated with decreased melatonin synthesis and decreased serotonin production. On the basis of Rudolph *et al.*'s. findings, Kay (1994) hypothesised that geomagnetic storms might partly account for the bimodal annual distribution of depression (that is, summer *and* winter depression). Kay reported a statistically significant 36% increase in male hospital admissions for depression in the second week following such storms and believes that the effects of geomagnetic storms on melatonin synthesis and serotonin production are the same in humans as in non-human animals.

In a related study, Bush (cited in Whittell, 1995) has investigated the very high suicide rate in the remote Alaskan hinterland, where suicide levels among the state's 15–24 year olds have risen to six times the US average. Bush argues that there is a link between the *aurora borealis* (or Northern lights), which is a source of changes in geomagnetism, and electrical activity in the brain. Bush believes that the solar flares of the borealis can be guarded against by wearing special dark glasses. However, other researchers are sceptical of her claims. Hallinan (cited in Whittell, 1995), for example, believes that the most serious health risk in watching the aurora borealis is a cricked neck!

Sex differences in depression

As we mentioned earlier (see page 52), there are differences between the sexes as far as depression is concerned. Cochrane (1995) has shown that when all relevant factors are controlled for, depression contributes most highly to the overall rate of treatment for mental disorders in women. According to Williams & Hargreaves (1995), women are 2–3 times more likely than men to become clinically depressed.

A number of factors have been advanced to account for the sex difference. These include hormonal fluctuations associated with the menstrual cycle, childbirth, the menopause and the taking of oral contraceptives. However, the evidence concerning these factors is weak. For example, although one in ten women who have just given birth are sufficiently depressed to need medical or psychological help, no specific causal hormonal abnormality has been identified, and it is just as plausible to suggest that social factors (such as the adjustment to a new role) are as important as any proposed physical factors (Callaghan & O'Carroll, 1993; Murray, 1995). Indeed, when women who have given birth are compared with non-pregnant women of the same age, the rate of depression is very similar (and, in fact, is slightly *lower* in the women who have just given birth: see Cooper *et al.*, 1988).

Cochrane (1995) has summarised a number of non-biological explanations of women's greater susceptibility to depression. For example, girls are very much more likely to be sexually abused than boys, and victims of abuse are at least twice as likely to experience clinical depression in adulthood as compared to non-abused individuals. Abuse alone, then, might account for the sex difference. An alternative account is based on the fact that the sex difference is greatest between the ages of 20 and 50, the years when marriage, child-bearing, motherhood and the *empty nest syndrome* will be experienced by a majority of women. Although women are increasingly becoming part of the labour force, Brown & Harris (1978) have noted that being a full-time mother and wife, having no employment outside of the home, and lacking an intimate and confiding relationship are increasingly being seen as risk factors for depression. The acceptance of a traditional female gender role may contribute to *learned helplessness* (see page 54), because the woman sees herself as having little control over her life.

Cochrane (1983) has argued that depression may be seen as a *coping strategy* that is available to women. Not only is it more acceptable for women to admit to psychological problems, but such problems may represent a means of changing an intolerable situation. As Callaghan & O'Carroll (1993) have observed:

'Unhappiness about their domestic, social, and political circumstances lies at the root of many women's concerns. This unhappiness must not be medicalised and regarded as a "female malady"'.

Conclusions

Like schizophrenia, depression is a serious mental disorder which has a number of distinct characteristics. A number of explanations have been advanced to explain the disorder. All of these have received some support from research studies, although we are still some way from a single accepted explanation for the disorder.

SUMMARY

- At one extreme of **mood/affective disorder** is **manic disorder/mania**, characterised by wild and unrealistic activity and a flight of ideas. At the other extreme is **depressive disorder**. Mania usually occurs in conjunction with depression (**bipolar disorder**, the term used also when mania occurs alone); **unipolar disorder** refers to episodes of depression alone. **Manic-depressive** refers to both the unipolar and bipolar forms of affective disorder.

- Depression is the most common psychological disorder; this can be a normal response to certain life events or just part of 'everyday life'. To be diagnosed as having **clinical depression**, a person must display persistent low mood for at least two weeks, plus at least five of the following: weight loss/gain over several weeks, **insomnia/hypersomnia**, serious loss of energy/tiredness, **agitated depression**, marked loss of interest in previously enjoyed activities, self-reproach or excessive/inappropriate guilt, reduced ability to think/concentrate, suicidal thoughts/plan for committing suicide/actual suicide attempt.

- Psychiatrists have traditionally distinguished between **endogenous** and **exogenous/reactive** depression; however, this is controversial and 'endogenous' no longer denotes the origins of the depression, but refers to a cluster of symptoms.

- The duration and frequency of periods of mania and depression involved in **bipolar disorder** vary from person to person, and they may be separated by long periods of normal functioning or follow each other very rapidly.

- While depression can occur at any age, bipolar disorder, which is much less common than depression, generally appears in the early 20s and is equally prevalent in men and women. It is disproportionately more common among creative people.

- **Behavioural** approaches to depression stress the role of **reinforcement**, such that loss of a loved one or one's job result in a reduction in positive reinforcement. The attention and concern shown by others may reinforce the depressed behaviour, but these may be withdrawn over time, exacerbating the depression and producing a vicious cycle.

- People lacking **social skills** are prime candidates for depression since they are unlikely to receive reinforcement from others. While depressed people report fewer pleasant experiences than non-depressed people, depression could **precede** a

- reduction in pleasant experiences as easily as following it.
- Seligman argues that **learned helplessness** in dogs (e.g. lethargy, sluggishness, loss of appetite) is similar to the behaviour of depressed people. Depression results from the expectancy, based on experience, that it is impossible to change one's environment. However, learned helplessness on its own cannot account for the **attributional style** of depressed people. According to Abramson *et al.*, people who attribute failure to **internal/stable/global** causes and success to luck are more likely to become depressed, although an attitude of helplessness might be a symptom rather than a cause of depression.
- According to Beck's **cognitive model**, depression is based in self-defeating **negative beliefs** and **negative cognitive sets.** Certain experiences in childhood and adolescence lead to the development of a **cognitive triad**, concerning the **self**, the **world** and the **future.** These beliefs lead people to exaggerate their bad experiences and to minimise their good experiences.
- Evidence in support of Beck's model is only correlational: biochemical factors may be the cause of both feelings of depression and illogical thought, and recall of information in a negative way might be the result of depression rather than a cause.
- **Depressogenic schemata** may be activated by rejections from others (in **sociotropic** individuals) or a failure to reach personal goals (in **autonomous** individuals). The **differential activation hypothesis** tries to explain why some people suffer persistent rather than transient depression.
- According to Freud's **psychodynamic** approach, grieving that follows the death of a loved one is similar to depression, which is an excessive/irrational grief in response to loss that evokes feelings associated with childhood dependency. Both **actual** and **symbolic losses** cause us to re-experience parts of our childhood, and depression may involve a regression to a childlike dependency. There is mixed evidence for the claim that the greater the loss in childhood, the greater the adult regression.
- The **anger** aroused by loss is turned **inward** on the self, which creates feelings of guilt, unworthiness and despair; in extreme cases, this can take the form of **suicidal** tendencies. These feelings are likely to be exaggerated by unacceptable anger towards the deceased which are also redirected towards the self.
- Psychodynamic theorists see bipolar disorders as the alternating dominance of personality by the **superego** (during the depressive phase) and the **ego** (manic phase). However, the evidence suggests that the psychodynamic model is inadequate in explaining both mood disorders in general and depression in particular.
- The observation that mood disorders run in families has led to the suggestion that they have a genetic basis, which is supported by the incidence of these disorders among first-degree relatives and concordance rates in identical compared with non-identical twins. However, any factors that are involved seem to be different for bipolar disorder and major depression.
- As with schizophrenia, adoption studies help to overcome the problem arising from the fact that families and twins usually share the same environment.
- Recent attempts have been made to identify the gene(s) involved in the mood disorders. Members of 'high-risk' families have been studied, as in the Old Order Amish community in Pennsylvania, in which chromosome 11 seemed to be implicated. However, other studies in other populations have failed to replicate these results. Other genes on other chromosomes may be involved.
- Recent research has shown that cells use a gene (SERT) to make a serotonin transporter protein which plays an important role in communication between neurons. A part of this gene (the 'second intron') usually contains 10–12 repeating sections of DNA, but many depressed people have only nine. Since serotonin is strongly implicated in depression and newer antidepressants (such as Prozac) interact with the serotonin transporter protein, there is good reason to believe that genetic factors are involved in depression.
- Genes may produce chemical imbalances in the neurotransmitters serotonin and norepinephrine, which seem to play a causal role in affective disorders. **Reserpine**, used to treat high blood pressure, produces sluggishness and inaction. Antidepressant drugs, as well as **iproniazid**, used to treat tuberculosis, producing elation/euphoria, increase levels of these two neurotransmitters in the brain; lithium carbonate, used to treat mania, decreases levels of these transmitters.
- Depressed people show lower than normal activity of norepinephrine and serotonin-secreting neurons in the brain, while manic people show the reverse pattern for norepinephrine. However, manic people also show lower levels of serotonin.

Kety's **permissive amine theory of mood disorder** attempts to reconcile these conflicting findings.

- However, the antidepressant effects of drugs do not occur when transmitter levels are raised, and antidepressants take time to exert their effect. This suggests that the drugs increase the **sensitivity** of receiving neurons, so allowing them to utilise limited supplies of the neurotransmitters more effectively.
- Antidepressant drugs do not always reduce depression, not all depressed people show reduced levels of the neurotransmitters, and not all manic people show increased levels of norepinephrine. All this suggests that the exact role of neurotransmitters in mood disorders is still unclear.
- While it is generally agreed that mood disorders probably have an organic basis and are heritable, it is possible that neurotransmitter levels are caused by the mood disorder, which may be brought about by environmental stimuli; the exact cause-and-effect relationship remains to be discovered.
- Two sub-types of **seasonal affective disorder** of special interest are **summer depression**, associated with deficiencies in serotonin levels, and **winter depression**, associated with desynchronisation of the rhythm of **melatonin** (produced by the **pineal gland**) resulting from decreased natural light.
- Based on studies of non-human animals, it has been proposed that geomagnetic storms might partly account for the occurrence of both summer and winter depression, i.e. these storms affect both melatonin synthesis and serotonin production.
- The higher incidence of depression in women has been attributed to a number of factors, including hormonal fluctuations associated with the menstrual cycle, childbirth, the menopause, and taking oral contraceptives. However, evidence for the influence of these factors is weak, and several non-biological explanations have been proposed, including the greater likelihood that women have been sexually abused as children and the stress associated with marriage, childbearing, motherhood and the 'empty nest syndrome'. Acceptance of the traditional female gender role may contribute to **learned helplessness.**
- Rather than being medicalised as a 'female malady', depression may represent a **coping strategy** for women, a socially acceptable means of changing an intolerable situation.

6

ANXIETY DISORDERS

Introduction and overview

All of us have experienced *anxiety* at some point in our lives. Indeed, researchers generally agree that mild or moderate anxiety is *biologically adaptive* in that it produces enhanced vigilance and a more realistic appraisal of a situation, which allows us to develop appropriate coping responses. In some people, however, the experience of anxiety may be so overwhelming that it interferes with normal everyday functioning.

Anxiety disorders is a category in DSM-IV that is subsumed by the category *Neurotic, stress-related and somatoform disorders* in ICD-10 (see Boxes 3.1 and 3.2 on pages 23–25). DSM recognises four types of anxiety disorder. These are *panic disorders and generalised anxiety disorder*, *phobic disorders* (which ICD-10 calls *phobic anxiety disorders*), *obsessive-compulsive disorder* and *post-traumatic stress disorder* (which ICD-10 includes under the heading *stress and adjustment disorders*). Our aim in this chapter is to describe the characteristics associated with each of the four disorders identified by DSM-IV and to examine the various explanations that have been advanced to explain their origins.

The characteristics of panic disorder and generalised anxiety disorder

Anxiety can be described as a general feeling of dread or apprehensiveness which is typically accompanied by a variety of physiological reactions. These include increased heart rate, rapid and shallow breathing, sweating, muscle tension and a dryness of the mouth. In both *panic disorder* (*PD*) and *generalised anxiety disorder* (*GAD*), the anxiety is 'free-floating', that is, it occurs in the absence of any obvious anxiety-provoking object or situation. Thus, a person feels anxious, but does not know why the anxiety is occurring.

The physiological reactions that occur with unpredictable and repeated attacks of anxiety and panic are similar to those that occur during a heart attack. As well as the reactions described above, a person may also experience chest pain and a tingling in the hands or feet, and it is not uncommon for people experiencing panic disorder to actually *believe* that they are having a heart attack. Other symptoms commonly reported are *derealisation* (the feeling that the world is not real) and *depersonalisation* (the loss of a sense of personal identity, which is manifested as a feeling of detachment from the body). Panic attacks can last for a few minutes to several hours. Although they usually occur during wakefulness, Dilsaver (1989) has reported evidence for their occurrence during sleep. Box 6.1 describes a typical case.

Box 6.1   A typical case of panic disorder

During the times when this 38-year-old man was experiencing intense anxiety, it often seemed as if he were having a heart seizure. He experienced chest pains and heart palpitations, numbness and shortness of breath, and he felt a strong need to breathe in air. He reported that in the midst of this, he developed a feeling of tightness over his eyes and he could only see objects directly in front of him. He further stated that he feared he would not be able to swallow.

The intensity of the anxiety was very frightening to him, and on two occasions his wife had rushed him to hospital because he was in a state of panic, sure that his heart was going to stop beating and he would die. His symptoms were relieved after he was given an injection of tranquiliser medication. He began to note the location of the doctor's offices and hospitals in whatever vicinity he happened to be, and he became extremely anxious if medical help were not close by.

(adapted from Leon, 1990)

Panic disorder may be so terrifying to people experiencing it that they can be driven to suicide. In many cases, panic disorder is accompanied by *agoraphobia*, that is, a fear of finding oneself in a situation from which escape might be difficult or help not available should a panic attack occur (see below). Because panic disorder occurs without any apparent cause, sufferers also experience *anticipatory anxiety*, a worry about when the next attack will occur and the avoidance of situations in which it has occurred.

GAD is characterised by persistent high levels of anxiety and worry about things, which is accompanied by the physical sensations we described for PD. However, although the physical symptoms associated with GAD are more persistent than in PD, they are less intense. The physical, cognitive and emotional problems caused by GAD lead those people experiencing the disorder to become tired, irritable, socially inept and to have difficulty functioning in an effective way.

EXPLANATIONS OF PD AND GAD

The *behavioural*, *cognitive*, *psychodynamic* and *medical* models emphasise conditioning, cognitions, internal conflicts and genes and biochemistry respectively as the causes of PD and GAD. As we mentioned earlier, some people develop anticipatory anxiety (see above) and actively avoid those situations in which they believe PD will occur. As Clark (1993) has noted, the cues associated with the situations in which anxiety is aroused can lead to it being experienced. This is *reinforced* by a reduction in the fear component of the disorder. However, the *origins* of all cases of PD are probably not capable of explanation in conditioning terms, and it seems likely that classical conditioning increases the severity of PD rather than causes it (Sue *et al.*, 1994).

It has been shown that certain cognitions can act as what Belfer & Glass (1992) term *internal triggers* for PD. Clark (1993) has argued that the core disturbance in panic is an abnormality in thinking. When external or internal stressors cause an increase in physiological activity, this activity is noticed but interpreted in *catastrophic* ways (such as 'I am having a heart attack'). This leads to yet more physiological activity, which only confirms the catastrophic thinking and so a *positive feedback loop* between cognitions and bodily activity is experienced. Although there is some evidence to support this perspective on PD, some people do not report being aware of particular thoughts during a panic attack. It is also not clear why catastrophic thoughts *should* be characteristic of the disorder.

The psychodynamic model sees GAD as the result of unacceptable unconscious conflicts that the ego has blocked. These impulses are powerful enough to produce constant tension and apprehension, but since they are unconscious, the person does not know what the source of anxiety is. Psychodynamic theorists argue that, to defend ourselves, we try to repress the impulses, but our defences are occasionally weakened and PD occurs. Alternatively, PD may represent unresolved *separation anxiety*. According to Klein & Rabkin (1981), PD may be experienced later in life when a threat of separation is either perceived or actually occurs.

The evidence suggests that there could be a *genetic* component in PD and GAD. Research conducted by Balon *et al.* (1989) indicates that around 40% of first-degree relatives of a person with PD have the disorder themselves, whilst Slater & Shields (1969) have reported a higher concordance rate in identical twins (49%) than in non-identical twins (4%). Although environmental factors cannot be ruled out, what might be inherited is a predisposition towards anxiety in the form of a highly reactive autonomic nervous system. This idea, originally proposed by Eysenck (1967), has some supporting evidence. Thus, some people with GAD demonstrate *autonomic lability*, that is, they are more easily aroused by environmental stimuli.

More recently, Papp and his colleagues (1993) have argued that PD is triggered by a dysfunction in receptors that monitor the amount of oxygen in the blood. By incorrectly informing the brain that oxygen levels are low, fear of suffocation and hyperventilation result. PD is accompanied by an elevated blood level of *lactic acid*, which is a by-product of muscular activity. In *biological challenge tests*, sodium lactate is given to people with PD and, in most of them, a panic attack occurs.

According to George & Ballenger (1992), this may be because the *locus coeruleus*, which is part of the brain associated with anxiety, is overly sensitive to anything that is *anxiogenic* (or anxiety-inducing). However, and as Sue *et al.* (1994) have noted, the results of biological challenge tests are influenced by *expectations*. People informed they will experience pleasant sensations report less anxiety than those informed they will experience unpleasant sensations. Even if biological factors do play a role, then, it is likely that they can be modified by cognitive factors.

The characteristics of phobic disorders

Being afraid of something that might objectively cause us harm is a normal and acceptable reaction. However, some people show a strong, persistent and *irrational* fear of, and desire to avoid, a particular object, activity or situation. Such behaviour, when it interferes with normal everyday functioning, defines a phobia. Encountering the phobic stimulus results in intense anxiety being experienced. Although phobics usually acknowledge that their anxiety is out of proportion to the actual danger posed by the phobic stimulus, this understanding does little to reduce the fear, and they are highly motivated to avoid it. Phobias towards many

different objects, activities and situations have been identified, some of which are shown in Box 6.2.

Box 6.2   Some varieties of phobias

Acrophobia (high places)
Ailurophobia (cats)
Algophobia (pain)
Anthropophobia (men)
Aquaphobia (water)
Arachnophobia (spiders)
Astraphobia (storms, thunder, lightning)
Belonophobia (needles)
Cancerophobia (cancer)
Claustrophobia (enclosed spaces)
Cynophobia (dogs)
Hematophobia (blood)
Monophobia (being alone)
Mysophobia (contamination or germs)
Nycotophobia (darkness)
Ochlophobia (crowds)
Ophidiophobia (snakes)
Pathophobia (disease)
Pyrophobia (fire)
Siderophobia (railways)
Taphophobia (being buried alive)
Thanatophobia (death)
Triskaidekaphobia (thirteen)
Xenophobia (strangers)
Zoophobia (animals or a specific animal)

DSM-IV identifies three categories of phobia. These are *agoraphobia*, *social phobia* and *specific phobias*. *Agoraphobia* is defined as a fear of open spaces but, as we mentioned earlier (see page 63), it typically involves the fear of being in situations from which escape may be difficult or help unavailable. In extreme cases, agoraphobics become 'prisoners' trapped in their own homes and dependent on others. Agoraphobia accounts for around 10–50% of all phobias, and the vast majority of agoraphobics are women. The phobia typically occurs in early adulthood.

Social phobia was identified as an entity in the UK in 1970, but was not included in DSM until 1980 (Menninger, 1995). It is an intense and excessive fear of being in a situation in which one is exposed to possible scrutiny by others. It is also characterised by the fear that, in a particular situation, one will act in a way which will be humiliating or embarrassing for the self or others. Three types of social phobia can be

Figure 6.1   Having to make a speech in front of any kind of audience is likely to induce some degree of anxiety in most people. As a social phobia, anxiety over public speaking is an intense and excessive fear of being exposed to scrutiny by other people; it is an example of performance social phobia

distinguished. *Performance* social phobia is characterised by excessive anxiety over activities like public speaking or being in a restaurant. In *limited interactional* social phobia, anxiety occurs only in specific situations, such as interacting with an authority figure. *Generalised* social phobia involves displaying anxiety in most social situations. Social phobia accounts for around 10% of all phobias and, like agoraphobia, the vast majority of social phobics are women. Social phobia typically arises in adolescence.

A *specific phobia* is an extreme fear of a specific object (such as spiders) or situation (such as being in an enclosed space). The phobias identified in Box 6.2 are all examples of specific phobias. Taken together, specific phobias are the most common phobic disorders, but they are also the *least disruptive* to a person. Phobias are the most common type of anxiety disorder and whilst there are differences between the sexes with respect to the likelihood of developing agoraphobia or social phobia, there are no differences between the sexes for most of the specific phobias. Specific phobias usually develop in childhood, but can occur at any time. The *nosophobias* (or 'illness and injury' phobias, such as cancerophobia and thanatophobia – see Box 6.2) tend to occur in middle age.

EXPLANATIONS OF PHOBIC DISORDERS

Supporters of the *psychodynamic* model see phobias as the *surface* expression of a much deeper conflict between the id, ego and superego which has its origins in childhood. In a very famous case study, Freud (1909) described a five-year-old boy, known as 'Little Hans', whose phobia of horses kept him from going out of the house. Freud believed that phobias were expressions of unacceptable wishes, fears and fantasies that are displaced (or shifted) from their original, internal source onto some external object or situation that can be easily avoided. In Hans' case, Freud saw the boy's fear of horses as an expression of anxieties related to his œdipal complex. Since Hans unconsciously feared and hated his father (whom Hans perceived to be a rival for his mother's affection), he displaced this fear onto horses, which he could avoid more easily than his father.

Although appealing to supporters of the psychodynamic model, Freud's explanation was challenged by supporters of the *behavioural* model. They noted that Hans' phobic response *only* occurred in the presence of a large horse pulling a heavily loaded cart at high speed and that this phobia had developed *after* Hans had witnessed a terrible accident involving a horse pulling a cart at high speed. As we noted in Chapter 2 (see page 15), the evidence (e.g. Watson & Rayner, 1920) indicates that phobias can be classically conditioned, and the behavioural model's account of Hans' phobia is at least as plausible as Freud's interpretation.

For some researchers (e.g. Wolpe, 1969), classical conditioning explains the development of *all* phobias. Certainly, the pairing of a neutral stimulus with a frightening experience is acknowledged by some phobics as marking the onset of their phobia. Moreover, the *resilient* nature of some phobias (that is, their *resistance to extinction*) can also be explained in conditioning terms. According to Mowrer's (1947) *two-process* or *two-factor theory*, phobias are acquired through classical conditioning (factor 1) and maintained through operant conditioning (factor 2), because the avoidance of the phobia and the associated reduction in anxiety is *negatively reinforcing* (although Rachman's (1984), *safety signal hypothesis* sees avoidance as being motivated by the *positive* feelings of safety).

However, the fact that some phobics are unable to recall any traumatic experience involving their phobia and that profound trauma does not inevitably lead to the development of a phobia is difficult for the behavioural model to explain. Studies also indicate that certain classes of stimuli (including snakes) can more

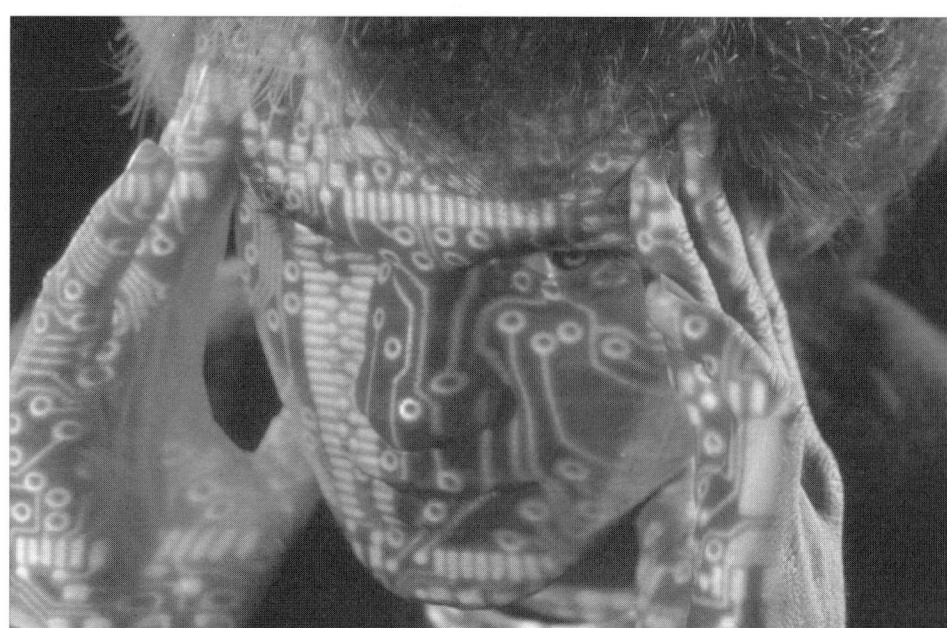

Figure 6.2   Technophobia is a feeling of fear or frustration experienced by people unfamiliar with modern digital and computer technology

easily be made a conditioned stimulus than others (including, for example, flowers). To explain this, Rosenhan & Seligman (1984) have argued for an interaction between organic and conditioning factors that biologically predisposes us to acquire phobias towards certain classes of stimuli. According to the concept of *preparedness* or *prepared conditioning*, we are genetically prepared to fear things that were sources of danger in our evolutionary past. Hugdahl & Öhman (1977) and Menzies (cited in Hunt, 1995) have shown that, in laboratory studies, people are more 'prepared' to acquire fear reactions to some stimuli (such as snakes) than to others. However, such studies do *not* show biological preparedness. Because we live in a society in which many people react negatively to certain animals, learning experiences rather than genetic factors might prepare us to fear these stimuli.

According to Rachman (1977), many phobias are acquired on the basis of information transmitted through *observation* and *instruction*. As Murray & Foote (1979) have noted, although preparedness for direct conditioning does not seem to be relevant, a preparedness for observational and instructional learning is possible. Slater & Shields' (1969) observation of a 41% concordance rate amongst identical twins and only a 4% rate amongst non-identical twins is suggestive of a genetic role in phobic disorders. However, in the absence of data relating to identical twins reared *apart*, the role played by genetic factors is unclear. In the case

of *neurological* factors in phobic disorders, it may well be that there is a relationship between a person's arousal level and the likelihood of a phobia developing, although the finding that high levels of physiological arousal are not associated with specific phobias casts doubt on the generality of such a proposal (Tallis, 1994).

The characteristics of obsessive-compulsive disorder

As its name suggests, in *obsessive-compulsive disorder* (OCD), the profound sense of anxiety is reflected in obsessions and compulsions. *Obsessions* are recurrent thoughts or images that do not feel voluntarily controlled and are experienced as senseless or repugnant. *Compulsions* are irresistable urges to engage in repetitive behaviours which are performed according to rituals or rules as a way of reducing or preventing the discomfort associated with some future undesirable event.

Of course, all of us have thoughts and behaviour patterns that are repeated, but such thoughts and behaviours would only be considered to represent a problem when they cause personal distress or interfere with our daily life. As Tallis (1994) has remarked, OCD has undergone a dramatic change in status over the last decade. Whilst it was once regarded as a rare example of the neuroses, it now occupies a central position in clinical psychology and contemporary psychiatry. In the United States at least, OCD is the fourth most common of all psychological problems. In Britain, an estimated one to one and a half million people suffer from OCD. The evidence suggests that females are slightly more likely to be diagnosed as experiencing OCD and that the disorder usually begins in young adulthood, although it can begin in childhood.

Frequently, the obsessive thoughts take the form of violent images, such as killing oneself or others. However, such thoughts can take other forms. According to Sanavio (1988), the four most common obsessional characteristics are *impaired control over mental processes* (such as repetitive thoughts of the death of a loved one), *concern of losing control over motor behaviours* (such as killing someone), *contamination* (being contaminated by, for example, germs) and *checking behaviours* (such as a concern over whether a door has been locked). Whatever form they take, such thoughts cannot be resisted and provide no joy to the sufferer.

Often, a compulsion arises from an obsession. For example, a person who persistently thinks about contamination by germs may develop complex rituals for avoiding contamination, and these may be repeated until the person is satisfied that cleanliness has been achieved (even if the hands become raw as a result of being washed over 500 times a day [Davison & Neale, 1990]). Shakespeare's character Lady Macbeth, who acquired a hand-washing compulsion after helping her husband murder the King of Scotland, is perhaps the most famous fictional sufferer of OCD (see Figure 6.3). The late billionaire Howard Hughes, who wore gloves all the time, walked on clean paper, bathed repeatedly and refused to see people for fear of being contaminated by them, is perhaps the most well-known non-fictional sufferer (although, as Illman & Taylor (1995) have noted, the footballer Paul Gascoigne's inability to leave his house unless all of his towels are perfectly straight, suggests a potential challenger to Hughes!). Compulsives recognise that their behaviours are senseless, yet if prevented from engaging in them, they experience intense anxiety which is reduced when the compulsive ritual is carried out (Hodgson & Rachman, 1972). A typical case of obsessive thoughts leading to compulsive actions is shown in Box 6.3.

Figure 6.3   Shakespeare's Lady Macbeth, who acquired a hand-washing compulsion after helping her husband murder the King of Scotland. This compulsion was an attempt to remove obsessive thoughts about her blood-stained hands ('out damned spot'). RSC production, 1988

> **Box 6.3   A case of obsessive thoughts leading to compulsive behaviour**
>
> Shirley K., a 23-year-old housewife, complained of frequent attacks of headaches and dizziness. During the preceding three months, she had been disturbed by recurring thoughts that she might harm her two-year-old son either by stabbing or choking him (the obsessive thought). She constantly had to go to his room, touch the boy and feel him breathe in order to reassure herself that he was still alive (the compulsive act), otherwise she became unbearably anxious. If she read a report in the daily paper of the murder of a child, she would become agitated, since this reinforced her fear that she, too, might act on her impulse.
>
> (taken from Goldstein & Palmer, 1975)

EXPLANATIONS OF OCD

Comings & Comings' (1987) finding that people with OCD often have first-degree relatives with some sort of anxiety disorder suggests that there might be a *genetic* basis to OCD. However, Shafran's (cited in Tallis, 1994) finding that, in over half of the families of an OCD sufferer, members become actively involved in the rituals, indicates the potential infuence of *learning* (which would lend support to the behavioural model). This might be particularly applicable to the development of OCD in childhood: children with a parent who engages in ritual behaviour may see such behaviour as the norm (see below).

There is some evidence to suggest that people with OCD show a different pattern of *brain activity* as compared with non-OCD controls. Several studies have shown that, in OCD, there is increased metabolic activity in the frontal lobe of the left hemisphere. For example, McGuire *et al.* (1994) have reported that, when drugs are given which reduce this activity, the symptoms of OCD decline. However, whether OCD is a consequence of increased activity, a cause of it or merely a correlate is unclear at present. The fact that OCD can be treated using drugs which increase the availability of the neurotransmitter *serotonin* has led some researchers to suggest that a deficiency of serotonin may be implicated in OCD.

According to the *psychodynamic model*, obsessions are *defence mechanisms* (see Box 2.2, page 13) that serve as ways of occupying the mind and displacing more threatening thoughts. Laughlin (1967), for example, sees the intrusion of obsessive thoughts as preventing the arousal of anxiety:

'by serving as a more tolerable substitute for a subjectively less welcome thought or impulse'.

Certainly, something like this might be practised by athletes who 'psych themselves up' before a competitive event and, from a psychodynamic perspective (and indeed from a cognitive perspective: see Chapter 2), we might suggest that this functions to exclude self-defeating doubts and thoughts. However, whilst a psychodynamic account may be intuitively appealing, it is hard to see what thoughts of killing someone (which, as we noted earlier, is one of the more common obsessional thoughts) are a more tolerable substitute for.

The *behavioural model* sees OCD as developing because it reduces anxiety. If a particular thought or behaviour reduces anxiety, then it should (because it is reinforcing) become more likely to be engaged in. This *anxiety-reduction hypothesis* is helpful in explaining the maintenance of OCD, but does not tell us why the disorder develops in the first place. However, the *superstition hypothesis* does. On the basis of his work with pigeons, Skinner (1948) argued that what we call 'superstition' develops as a result of a chance association between a behaviour and a reinforcer. In Skinner's experiments, pigeons were given food at regular intervals irrespective of their behaviour. After a while, the pigeons displayed idiosyncratic movements, most likely because these were the movements they happened to be making when the food was given.

O'Leary & Wilson (1975) believe that the superstition hypothesis can account for many compulsive rituals. Amongst professional soccer players, for example, many superstitious behaviours exist. These include always being last onto the pitch, putting the left sock on before the right and kicking the ball into the net three times before the match starts. Such behaviours may occur because they have, in the past, been associated with success. If such rituals are not permitted, anxiety is aroused (and, in the case of one professional soccer player, actually led to him being transferred to another club because of a dispute over who would wear the number 7 shirt). Whilst chance associations between behaviours and reinforcers might explain the persistence of some *behaviours*, the development of intrusive *thoughts* is, of course, much more difficult for the behavioural model to explain.

The characteristics of post-traumatic stress disorder

During the First World War, many soldiers experienced *shell shock*, a descriptive label coined by C. S. Meyers for a shock-like state which followed the traumatic experiences that occurred as a result of prolonged combat. Prior to Myers' description of it as a clinical condition, it had been taken as a symptom of cowardice in the face of the enemy and sometimes resulted in summary trial and execution. In World War II, the term *combat exhaustion* was used to describe a similar reaction which was characterised by feelings of terror, agitation or apathy and the inability to sleep.

Today, the term *post-traumatic stress disorder* (PTSD) is used to describe an anxiety disorder that occurs in response to an extreme psychological or physical experience. As well as war, such experiences include a physical threat to one's self or one's family, witnessing the death of other people, being part of a natural or man-made disaster or any other traumatic event which is outside the range of normal human experience. In Britain, several disasters associated with PTSD have been extensively researched. These include the Piper Alpha oil rig disaster, the bombing of the PanAm airliner that crashed at Lockerbie, and the death of over 90 soccer spectators at the Hillsborough football ground.

The dramatic capsize of the cross-channel ferry *The Herald of Free Enterprise* in Zeebrugge has also been the subject of much research. Studies of children, adolescents and their families who survived the *Herald of Free Enterprise* disaster have shown that even very young children can be emotionally upset by such a trauma. Yule (1993), for example, reports that child survivors of recent disasters show symptoms which are characteristic of PTSD, including distressing recollections of the event, avoidance of reminders and signs of increased physiological arousal manifested as sleep disturbances and poor concentration. Often, these children do not confide their distress to parents or teachers for fear of upsetting them. Thus, their school work is affected and they are often thrown off their educational career course. However, when asked sympathetically and straightforwardly, they usually share their reactions with psychologists and others. Other research has also confirmed the view that PTSD may be experienced by children. For example, Pynoos *et al.* (1993) found a strong correlation between children's proximity to the epicentre of the 1988 Armenian earthquake and the overall severity of the core components of PTSD, with girls reporting more persistent anxiety than boys.

PTSD may occur immediately following a traumatic experience or weeks, months and even years later. In the Vietnam war, for example, there were relatively few cases of shell shock or combat fatigue, most probably because of the relatively rapid turnover of soldiers in and out of the fighting zone. However, on their return home, Vietnam veterans found adjusting to civilian life much more difficult than the soldiers in the two World Wars.

As well as experiencing tiredness, apathy, depression,

social withdrawal and nightmares, veterans reported *flashbacks* as a consequence of either witnessing or participating in a traumatic event. When studied, they also showed *hyperalertness*, exaggerated startle reactions and reported feeling guilty that they had survived but others had not. Like at least some people experiencing PTSD, the veterans also reported using alcohol, drugs or violence to try and curb the disturbing symptoms (as have the survivors of *The Herald of Free Enterprise* disaster: Joseph *et al.*, 1993). At least some of the veterans cut themselves off from society to escape the sense of not being able to fit in as a result of what they had witnessed.

One civilian disaster that led to PTSD in those who survived it was the collision between two jumbo jets that killed 582 passengers on the island of Tenerife in 1977. A combination of environmental and human factors led to a Dutch jumbo jet colliding with an American airliner. Many passengers were killed instantly, but some survived. The experiences of one of the passengers are described in Box 6.4.

> ### Box 6.4 A case of post-traumatic stress disorder
>
> Martin's story is tragic. He lost his wife of 37 years and blames himself for her death, because he sat stunned and motionless for some 25 seconds after the Dutch jumbo jet hit. He saw nothing but fire and smoke in the aisles, but he roused himself and led his wife to a jagged hole above and behind his seat. Martin climbed out onto the wing and reached down and took hold of his wife's hand, but 'an explosion from within literally blew her out of my hands and pushed me back and down onto the wing'. He reached the runway, turned to go back after her, but the plane blew up seconds later.
>
> Five months later, Martin was depressed and bored, had 'wild dreams', a short temper and became easily confused and irritated. 'What I saw there will terrify me forever,' he says. He told the psychologist who interviewed him that he avoided television and movies, because he couldn't know when a frightening scene would appear.
>
> (adapted from Perlberg, 1979)

One interesting phenomenon that has recently been the subject of research interest is apparent PTSD amongst people in their 60s and 70s who seem to be disturbed by their experiences in World War II. As Bender (1995) has observed, this is hardly surprising if it is assumed that they have been bothered *continuously* since the war. However, this assumption appears to be false, as most survivors got on with their lives, raised families and so on. For some reason, the memories seem to be coming back to disturb them now that they have retired (see below).

EXPLANATIONS OF PTSD

Unlike other anxiety disorders, the *origins* of PTSD seem amenable to explanations on largely, if not exclusively, *environmental* grounds. Whilst people who have a phobia or suffer from obsessive-compulsive disorder tend not to reveal background factors that are common, all sufferers of PTSD share the experience of a profoundly traumatising event or events, even though these may be markedly different from one another with respect to other characteristics.

Kolb (1987) has argued that *classical conditioning* is at least involved in PTSD. Thus, PTSD sufferers often show reactions to stimuli which were present at the time of the trauma. Hunt (cited in Bender, 1995), for example, interviewed veterans of the Normandy landings in World War II around the time of the 50th anniversary events in 1994. Many reported still being troubled by their memories of the war in general, but in particular reported being adversely affected by specific memories which had been revived by the anniversary commemorations.

As with phobias, however, classical conditioning cannot be the only mechanism involved, since not everyone who is exposed to a traumatic event develops PTSD. In a review of the literature, Green (1994) has reported that PTSD develops in about 25% of those who experience potentially traumatic events, although the range is quite large. According to Green, it is about 12% for accidents and 80% for rape, with a *dose-effect* relationship between the severity of the stressor and the degree of consequent psychological distress. Presumably, individual differences (in terms of prior experiences, personal characteristics and so on) in the way in which people perceive events as well as the *recovery environment* (such as support groups) also play an influential role.

Paton (1992), for example, found that relief workers at Lockerbie reported that there were differences between what they expected to find and what they actually encountered, and that this was a source of stress. The same finding was reported by Dixon *et al.* (1993) in their study of PTSD amongst 'peripheral' victims of the *Herald of Free Enterprise* disaster. For relief workers, then, some way of increasing predictability (and hence

Figure 6.4 Despite being trained to deal with emergency situations, members of the emergency services cannot be prepared for major disasters, such as the Lockerbie, Hillsborough and Herald of Free Enterprise disasters. Police involved in the 1989 Hillsborough disaster were awarded (in 1996) substantial financial compensation for the 'mental injury' they suffered (post-traumatic stress disorder) and can be considered peripheral victims of the disaster

control) that would minimise the differences between what is expected and what is observed would be useful. Amongst the Normandy veterans, Hunt found that support systems, in the form of comradeship, were *still* important and were used by veterans as a means of coping with the traumatic memories (and often the physical consequences) of their war experiences.

The return of memories many years after a traumatic event, as reported by veterans of World War II, suggests that keeping busy with socially valued life roles (such as being a parent, spouse and worker) enables a person to *avoid* processing the traumatic memories. The unfortunate consequence of this, however, is that war memories do not get integrated into a person's views about the world. Bender (1995) suggests that to resolve the discrepancy, people must process the traumatic experience and integrate it into their views about the world. In conditioning terms, thinking about the traumatic event would lead to *extinction* of the responses associated with it.

Although it is likely that social/psychological factors cause the onset of PTSD, researchers are still interested in understanding the *biological processes* that are associated with the disorder. The observation of similarities between PTSD and withdrawal from opioid drugs, such as morphine, and the finding that stress-induced analgesia was reversed by *naloxone* (a substance that reverses the pharmacological action of morphine) in PTSD combat victims exposed to a combat movie, has led Van der Kolk *et al.* (1989) to suggest that *disturbed opioid function* occurs in PTSD. According to other research conducted by Krystal *et al.* (1989), the *locus coeruleus* acts as an 'alarm centre' and plays a pivotal role in the genesis of PTSD. In support of this, Davidson (1992) notes that drugs which are effective in treating PTSD also prevent the development of *learned helplessness* in animals exposed to inescapable shock (see Chapter 5, page 54) when these drugs are infused directly into the locus coeruleus.

Conclusions

In this chapter, we have examined the characteristics of the anxiety disorders and the explanations of them that have been advanced. Some explanations are more powerful than others, depending on which of the four anxiety disorders they are trying to account for. As with the disorders considered in Chapters 4 and 5, however, there is still much debate among researchers as to how these disorders can best be explained.

SUMMARY

- While mild/moderate anxiety can be seen as **biologically adaptive**, it can be so intense as to interfere with normal, everyday functioning.
- DSM-IV has a separate category for **anxiety disorders** which are included within ICD-10's **neurotic, stress-related and somatoform disorders**. DSM distinguishes **panic disorder (PD)** and **generalised anxiety disorder (GAD)**, **phobic disorders, obsessive compulsive disorder** and **post-traumatic stress disorder**.
- Both **PD** and **GAD** involve **free-floating anxiety**. Anxiety and panic attacks, which usually occur during wakefulness but can occur during sleep, are typically accompanied by various physiological reactions which are similar to those that occur during a heart attack, including increased heart rate, rapid/shallow breathing, sweating,

- muscle tension and dry mouth, chest pain and tingling in hands/feet.
- Other symptoms of PD include **derealisation** and **depersonalisation**. PD can drive people to suicide. It is often accompanied by **agoraphobia** and **anticipatory anxiety**.
- GAD is characterised by persistent high levels of anxiety and worry and involves the same physical symptoms as PD; in GAD these are more persistent but less intense. People with GAD are tired, irritable, socially inept and find it difficult to function effectively.
- The cues **associated** with the situations in which anxiety is aroused can produce anxiety, which is **reinforced** by a reduction in the fear component. However, although classical conditioning may increase the severity of PD, conditioning principles

are unable to explain its **origins**.

- Certain cognitions can act as **internal triggers** for PD, and the core disturbance may be an abnormality in thinking, such that physiological activity caused by stressors is interpreted in 'catastrophic' ways, setting up a **positive feedback loop** between cognitions and bodily activity. However, not everyone reports particular thoughts, and it is not obvious why catastrophic thoughts should be characteristic of the disorder.
- According to the psychodynamic model, GAD is the result of unacceptable unconscious conflicts that are repressed by the ego but which are powerful enough to cause constant tension/apprehension. Alternatively, PD may represent unresolved **separation anxiety**.
- Studies of first-degree relatives and concordance rates for identical and non-identical twins suggest that there could be a **genetic component** in PD and GAD. What might be inherited is a predisposition towards anxiety in the form of a highly reactive autonomic nervous system (**autonomic lability**), as originally proposed by Eysenck.
- PD may be triggered by a dysfunction in receptors that monitor the amount of oxygen in the blood, causing fear of suffocation and hyperventilation. Supporting evidence for this link comes from raised blood levels of **lactic acid** which accompany PD and the results of **biological challenge tests**, implicating the **locus coeruleus**. However, these results are likely to be influenced by cognitive factors, such as **expectations**.
- It is the **irrational** nature of the fear involved in a **phobia**, together with its interference with everyday functioning, particularly the avoidance of the feared stimulus, that makes it a disorder.
- **Agoraphobia** accounts for 10–50% of all phobias, affects mostly women and typically occurs in early adulthood. Three types of **social phobia** are **performance**, **limited interactional** and **generalised**; together they account for 10% of all phobias, also affect mainly women, and typically appear in adolescence.
- **Specific phobias** are the most common phobic disorders, but are also the least disruptive. They affect males and females equally and usually develop in childhood, although they can occur at any time; the **nosophobias** tend to occur in middle age.
- According to Freud, phobias are the **surface** expression of some underlying conflict between the id, ego and superego, originating in childhood. Unacceptable wishes/fears/fantasies are displaced onto some external object/situation, as

illustrated in Little Hans' phobia of horses, which could more easily be avoided than his father, the real source of his conflict.

- Behaviourist psychologists reject Freud's explanation, arguing instead that Hans' phobia had been classically conditioned; according to Wolpe, all phobias can be explained in this way. The **resilience/resistance to extinction** of some phobias can be explained in terms of Mowrer's **two-process/-factor theory**, referring to classical and operant conditioning (**negative reinforcement** of avoidance behaviour through anxiety reduction) respectively. According to the **safety signal hypothesis**, avoidance is motivated by **positive** feelings of safety.
- However, not all phobics remember a traumatic experience related to their phobia, and profound trauma does not always result in a phobia. In addition, some classes of stimuli can more easily become the object of a phobia than others, which has been explained in terms of **preparedness/prepared conditioning**. The results of studies claiming to demonstrate preparedness, however, can be explained in terms of non-genetic factors.
- Many phobias may be acquired through **observation** and **instruction**. It is possible that there is a preparedness not for direct conditioning but for observational/instructional learning.
- Despite the far higher concordance rate for phobias among identical compared with non-identical twins, in the absence of data for identical twins reared apart, the role of genetic factors remains unclear. High levels of physiological arousal are not associated with specific phobias, suggesting that it is unlikely that neurological factors are involved.
- While **obsessive-compulsive disorder (OCD)** was once thought to be a rare neurosis, it is now the fourth most common of all psychological problems in the USA, and in Britain there are up to one and a half million sufferers, with females being slightly more likely to be diagnosed than males. It usually first appears in young adulthood.
- The four most common obsessional characteristics are **impaired control over mental processes**, **concern about losing control over motor behaviour**, **contamination** and **checking behaviours**.
- Compulsions often arise from obsessions, as in the case of hand-washing rituals which represent attempts to avoid contamination. Examples of famous sufferers from such compulsions are Lady Macbeth and Howard Hughes. Compulsives

recognise that their behaviours are senseless, but they experience great anxiety if prevented from engaging in them.

- Although there might be a genetic basis to OCD, relatives of sufferers often become actively involved in their rituals, implying the potential role of learning; this may be especially relevant in the case of childhood sufferers.
- Several studies have shown that OCD sufferers display increased metabolic activity in the left frontal lobe compared with non-sufferers. But these findings are consistent with OCD being a cause of increased activity or a consequence of it; they may simply be correlated. A deficiency of **serotonin** has also been implicated.
- According to the psychodynamic model, obsessions are **defence mechanisms**, which prevent more threatening, self-defeating thoughts from entering consciousness. While this may be intuitively appealing, it is not always clear what certain obsessions are a more acceptable substitute for.
- While the **anxiety reduction hypothesis** is helpful in explaining the maintenance of OCD, it cannot account for its original development, unlike Skinner's **superstition hypothesis**. This can account for many compulsive rituals, such as those of professional footballers. However, while chance associations might explain the persistence of certain **behaviours**, the behavioural model has much more difficulty explaining the development of intrusive **thoughts**.
- In World War II, **combat exhaustion** replaced **shell shock**, used during World War I. Today, **post-traumatic stress disorder (PTSD)** is used to describe the response to an extreme psychological/physical experience, such as being part of a natural/man-made disaster, as in the Hillsborough football disaster and the *Herald of Free Enterprise* disaster.
- Even very young children can show symptoms of PTSD, including distressing recollections of the event, avoidance of reminders and signs of increased physiological arousal, as in sleep disturbances and poor concentration. They often fail to confide their distress, with the result that school work is affected.
- PTSD may occur immediately following the traumatic experience or many years later. Vietnam war veterans were much more likely to experience difficulties on their return to civilian life than while fighting. They reported **flashbacks**, **hyper-alertness** and **guilt**. As with other PTSD sufferers, veterans used alcohol, drugs or violence to try to stop the disturbing symptoms.
- Unlike other anxiety disorders, PTSD sufferers all share the experience of a profoundly traumatising event. **Classical conditioning** is involved to the extent that sufferers often show reactions to stimuli present at the time of the trauma. However, not everyone exposed to a traumatic event develops PTSD; this will depend on the nature and severity of the stressor, as well as individual differences and the **recovery environment**.
- The return of memories many years after a traumatic event (as reported by World War II veterans) suggests that socially valued life roles help the person to avoid processing these memories. But this prevents those memories becoming integrated into the person's world view, so that **extinction** of the associated responses cannot take place.
- Similarities between PTSD and opioid withdrawal, plus the finding that stress-induced analgesia was reversed by **naloxone** in PTSD combat victims exposed to a combat movie, have led to the proposal that **disturbed opioid function** occurs in PTSD.
- The **locus coeruleus** may act as an 'alarm centre', playing a crucial role in the genesis of PTSD. When infused directly into the locus coeruleus, drugs which are effective in treating PTSD also prevent the development of **learned helplessness** in animals exposed to inescapable shock.

7

EATING DISORDERS

Introduction and overview

As identified in DSM-IV, eating disorders are characterised by physically and/or psychologically harmful eating patterns. Two broad categories of disorder are recognised. These are *anorexia nervosa* and *bulimia nervosa*. In ICD-10, these disorders are characterised as 'behavioural syndromes associated with physiological disturbances and physical factors' (see Box 3.1, page 23). Although there are several types of eating disorder (see, for example, Parry-Jones & Parry-Jones, 1994), our aim in this chapter is to describe the characteristics associated with anorexia nervosa and bulimia nervosa and to examine the explanations of these disorders that have been advanced.

The characteristics of anorexia nervosa

Although the characteristics of what we now call anorexia nervosa have been known about for several hundred years, it is only recently that the disorder has attracted much interest. As Sue *et al.* (1994) have noted, this increased attention is the result of a greater public knowledge of the disorder and the recent increase in its incidence (although we should note that Fombonne (1995) has recently disputed claims about

such an increase which he attributes to changes in the diagnostic criteria concerning weight loss: see below).

Anorexia nervosa seems to occur primarily in females. Some studies suggest that female *anorectics* outnumber males by a factor of 20:1, whilst others suggest a figure of 10:1 (Fombonne, 1995). The disorder usually has its onset in adolescence between the ages of 12 and 18, the period between 14 and 16 being most common (Hsu, 1990). However, in some cases, the onset occurs later in adult life or before adolescence. Lask & Bryant-Waugh (1992), for example, have reported cases of the disorder in children as young as 8. Estimates of the incidence of anorexia nervosa vary, but a study conducted in America by Lewinsohn *et al.* (1993) suggests that 4 in 1,000 females may experience the disorder. In Britain, the figure is somewhat higher, with estimates ranging from 10 in 1,000 to 40 in 1,000 (Sahakian, 1987), with around 70,000 people recognised as anorectic (Brooke, 1996). Box 7.1 describes a typical case of anorexia nervosa:

> **Box 7.1   A typical case of anorexia nervosa**
>
> Frieda had always been a shy, sensitive girl who gave little cause for concern at home or in school. She was bright and did well academically, although she had few friends. In early adolescence, she had been somewhat overweight and had been teased by her family that she would never get a boyfriend unless she lost some

weight. She reacted to this teasing by withdrawing and becoming very touchy. Her parents had to be careful about what they said. If offended, Frieda would throw a tantrum and march off to her room – hardly the behaviour they expected from their bright and sensitive 15-year-old.

Frieda began dieting. Initially her family was pleased, but gradually her parents sensed that all was not well. Meal times became battle times. Frieda hardly ate at all. Under pressure, she would take her meals to her room and later, having said that she had eaten everything, her mother would find food hidden away untouched. When her mother caught her deliberately inducing vomiting after a meal, she insisted they go to the family doctor. He found that Frieda had stopped menstruating a few months earlier. Not fooled by the loose, floppy clothes that Frieda was wearing, he insisted on carrying out a full physical examination. Her emaciated body told him as much as he needed to know, and he arranged for Frieda's immediate hospitalisation.

(adapted from Rosenhan and Seligman, 1984)

As Box 7.1 illustrates, anorexia nervosa is characterised by a prolonged refusal to eat adequate amounts of food which results in deliberate weight loss. As the case of 'Frieda' shows, the loss of body weight is often accompanied by the cessation of menstruation (*amenorrhea*). For a diagnosis of anorexia nervosa to be considered, the individual must weigh less than 85% of his or her normal or expected weight for height, age and sex. As a result of the significant weight loss, anorectics take on an emaciated appearance. In one dramatic case, Bliss & Branch (1960) described a woman whose weight dropped from 180 to 60 pounds. Anorectics also show a decline in their general health, which is accompanied by many physical problems (Sharp & Freeman, 1993). These include low blood pressure and body temperature, constipation and dehydration. Hsu (1990) reports that in 5–15% of cases, anorexia nervosa is fatal.

Literally, anorexia nervosa means 'nervous loss of appetite'. However, anorectics are often both hungry and preoccupied with thoughts of food. For example, they may constantly read recipe books and may prepare elaborate meals for their friends. Anorectics themselves, however, will avoid most calorie-rich foods, such as meat, milk products, sweets and other desserts, and will often limit their consumption to little more than a lettuce leaf and carrot. Anorectics also demonstrate a reduced pleasure in eating. Although studies indicate that anorectics do not experience deficiencies in taste, Sunday & Halmi (1990) have shown that they have a *low hedonic responsiveness* to taste and an aversion to the oral sensation of fat.

Anorexia nervosa is also characterised by an intense fear of being overweight which does not diminish even when a large amount of weight has been lost. As a consequence of the fear of becoming overweight, anorectics take extreme measures to lose weight. In DSM-IV, two sub-types of anorexia nervosa are identified, both of which contribute to the refusal to maintain a body weight above the minimum normal weight for the person's height, age and sex. The *restricting type* of anorectic loses weight through constant fasting and engaging in excessive physical activity. The *binge eating/purging type* alternates between periods of fasting and 'binge eating' (see below) in which food that is normally avoided is consumed in large quantities. Following this, the feelings of guilt and shame that are experienced as a result of the 'binge' lead the anorectic to use laxatives or self-induced vomiting to expel ingested food from the system.

One other characteristic of anorexia nervosa is a *distorted body image* in which the individual does not recognise the thinness of the body. Even though their appearance may show protruding bones, many anorectics still see themselves as being fat and deny that they are 'wasting away'. As Bruch (1978) has observed, anorectics:

'vigorously defend their gruesome emaciation as not being too thin ... they identify with the skeleton-like appearance, actively maintain it and deny its abnormality'.

As Cooper (1995) has noted, the fact that many people who would be diagnosed as anorectic do not perceive themselves as having a problem, suggests that data relating to both the incidence and prevalence of the disorder should be treated with caution.

EXPLANATIONS OF ANOREXIA NERVOSA

In the early 1900s, Morris Simmonds, a German pathologist, described the case of a girl who was emaciated, had stopped menstruating and showed severe atrophy of the pituitary gland. At the time, and for the quarter of a century that followed, it was believed that pituitary gland damage was the cause of anorexia nervosa. However, as Colman (1987) has noted, this belief was incorrect and what Simmonds had identified was, in fact, a disorder that actually produces very different symptoms from anorexia nervosa. In what is now called *Simmonds' disease*, damage to the pituitary gland is associated with a loss of pubic and underarm hair. This does not happen in anorexia nervosa, and the emaciation Simmonds observed in his patient is unusual except in terminal cases. It is not surprising, therefore, that attempts to treat anorexia nervosa by means of pituitary extracts were unsuccessful.

Despite this, some researchers have suggested that anorexia nervosa does have a *biological basis* and, instead of the pituitary gland, have implicated the *hypothalamus* as the brain structure whose dysfunction may lead to the disorder. Certainly, there is strong evidence to indicate that the hypothalamus plays an important role in the regulation of eating (see, for example, McIlveen & Gross, 1996). In one study, Kaplan & Woodside (1987) showed that when the neurotransmitter *norepinephrine* acts on part of the hypothalamus, animals begin eating and show a marked preference for carbohydrates. The neurotransmitter *serotonin*, by contrast, seems to induce satiation and suppress the appetite, especially for carbohydrates. Any condition which increased the effects of serotonin would, then, decrease eating. However, as Hsu (1990) has observed, there is not yet sufficient evidence to indicate whether brain dysfunction and changes in neurotransmitter levels are a cause of anorexia nervosa, an effect of it or merely a correlate.

Research reported by Park *et al.* (1995) examined four females with severe restrictive anorexia nervosa who spontaneously volunteered histories of glandular fever-like illnesses immediately preceding the onset of their eating disorder. Park and his colleagues suggest that viral- or immune-induced alterations in central homeostasis, particularly involving *corticotrophin-releasing hormone*, could trigger and perpetuate a behavioural response leading to a particularly severe form of restrictive anorexia nervosa, a suggestion which is speculative but biologically plausible.

Some researchers have suggested that anorexia nervosa may have a *genetic basis*. Strober & Katz (1987), for example, have shown a tendency for anorexia nervosa to run in families, with the first- and second-degree relatives of anorectic individuals being significantly more likely to develop the disorder as compared to the first- and second-degree relatives of a control group of non-anorectics.

Other researchers have conducted twin studies to investigate the possible role of genetic factors in anorexia nervosa. Askevold & Heiberg (1979), for example, have reported a 50% concordance rate for identical twins brought up in the same environment, and they see this as strong evidence that genes play an important role. However, in the absence of concordance rates for fraternal and identical twins reared apart, Askevold and Heiberg's claim is difficult to evaluate. Other research, conducted by Holland *et al.* (1984), reported a concordance rate of 55% for identical twins brought up in the same environment and 7% for fraternal twins. Although this difference hints at a genetic role in anorexia nervosa, the concordance rate suggests, as Treasure & Holland (1991) have noted, that if genes do play a role, it is likely to be a small one.

As well as theories based on biological, biochemical and genetic factors, there are also theories of anorexia nervosa that are more social and psychological in their orientation. Supporters of the *psychodynamic model* propose that the disorder may represent an unconscious effort by a girl to remain pre-pubescent. It has been argued that, as a result of overdependence on the parents, some girls fear becoming sexually mature and independent. As we saw earlier on (see page 75), anorexia nervosa is associated with the cessation of menstruation, and psychodynamic theorists see this as enabling the anorectic to circumvent growing up and achieving adult responsibilities. Certainly, in order to achieve puberty, we must attain a particular level of body fat, and there is evidence to suggest that anorectics will eat, provided they do not gain weight.

An alternative psychodynamic account proposes that anorexia nervosa may allow a girl to avoid the issue of her sexuality. The weight loss that occurs in the disorder prevents the rounding of the breasts and hips, and the body takes on a 'boy-like' appearance. At least some psychodynamic theorists see this as a way of avoiding the issue of sexuality in general, and the prospect of pregnancy in particular.

In contrast to the view that anorexia nervosa is the result of overdependence on the parents, yet another psychodynamic account sees the disorder as an attempt

Although there may be some truth in psychodynamic accounts of anorexia nervosa, there are at least two observations that challenge such accounts. First, some of them seem to apply only to females. It is impossible to see how the avoidance of the prospect of pregnancy could apply to male anorectics. Second, all of the accounts have difficulty in explaining the occurrence of anorexia nervosa after adolescence has been passed.

Supporters of the *behavioural model* see anorexia nervosa as a *phobia* (see Chapter 6) concerning the possibility of gaining weight. Indeed, Crisp (1967) suggested that anorexia nervosa might be more appropriately called *weight phobia*. The phobia is assumed to be the result of the impact of social norms, values and roles. In one study, Garner *et al.* (1980) discovered that the winners of Miss America and the centrefolds in *Playboy* magazine have consistently been below the average female weight and have become significantly more so since 1959. Thus, the cultural idealisation of the slender female (as represented by so-called supermodels) may be one cause of the fear of being fat. As Polivy & Herman (1985) have remarked, the pressures have become so great that, in America at least, normal eating for women is characterised by dieting!

In at least some occupations, such as ballet dancing and modelling, there is considerable pressure on women to be thin and, according to Garfinkel & Garner (1982), the incidence of anorexia nervosa in these occupations is much higher than in the population in general (although, as Cooper (1995) has observed, not all ballet dancers, models and so on, who diet to be slim develop eating disorders). For Wooley & Wooley (1983):

> 'an increasingly stringent cultural standard of thinness for women has been accompanied by a steadily increasing incidence of serious eating disorders in women.'

Support for the claim that societal norms can be extremely influential in this respect comes from evidence about eating disorders in other cultures. Lee *et al.* (1992), for example, have shown that in at least some non-Western cultures (including China, Singapore and Malaysia), the incidence of anorexia nervosa is much lower than in Western societies. Additionally, reported cases of anorexia nervosa in black populations of either Western or non-Western cultures are significantly lower than those in white populations.

According to Sui-Wah (1989), three factors are

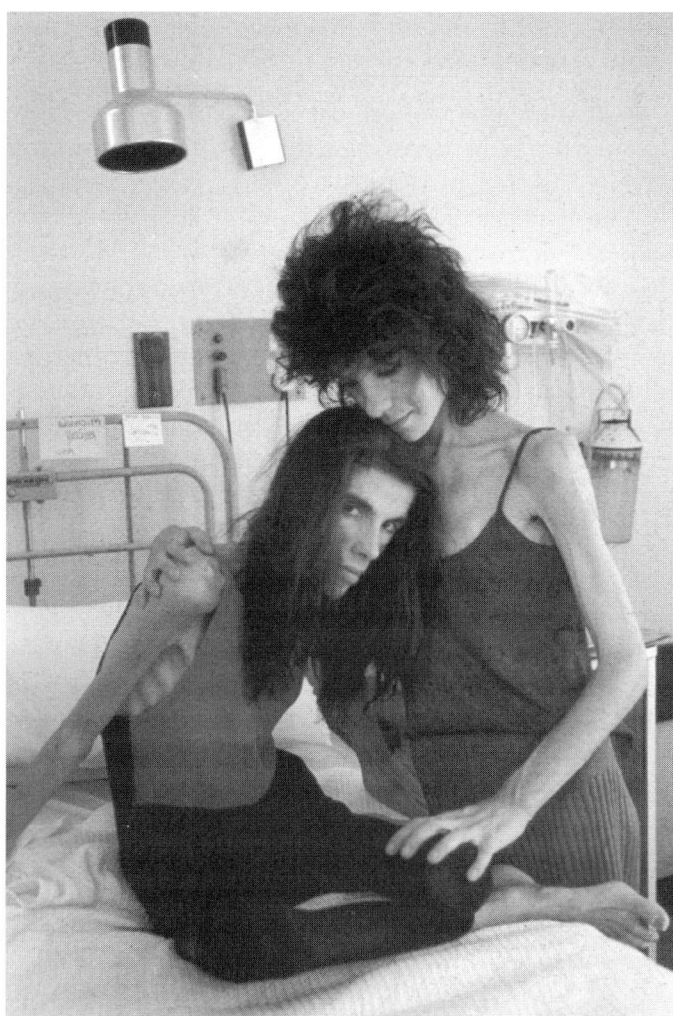

Figure 7.1 The much publicised English anorectic twins, Samantha and Michaela Kendall. Despite receiving treatment in the USA, Samantha eventually died. While their emaciated appearance is an obvious, external sign of anorexia nervosa, there are several theories of the cause of the disorder, including the genetic theory, based on the higher concordance rate found among monozygotic twins compared with dizygotic twins

by adolescents to *separate* themselves from their parents and establish an identity of their own. Psychodynamic theorists argue that the parents of anorectics tend to be domineering and that anorexia nervosa represents an attempt to exert individuality. Bemis (1978) notes that many female anorectics are 'good girls' who do well in school and are cooperative and well-behaved. Bemis argues that this leads them to feel that they have no choices and are being controlled by the desires and demands of others. One way of exerting individuality is to assume control over what is most concretely one's self – the body. Thinness and starvation, then, are signs of self-control and independence.

important in explaining the far fewer cases of anorexia nervosa in the Chinese. The first is the importance attached to food and eating in Chinese culture. A Chinese proverb says that 'of all the things in life, food is the most important'. Sui-Wah argues that, to the Chinese, food is 'a bit like God, paramount and ubiquitous'. Sui-Wah's second factor is that Chinese food is 'simply so delicious that one can hardly resist eating it' (a view that at least some of us would share!). The third factor is the Chinese custom of eating meals with the family. Everyone is expected to eat a certain amount, and it is difficult for individuals to go unnoticed if they depart from their usual quantity. As a result, there is always a social pressure for people to conform in order to avoid undue concern from other family members.

One puzzling observation that is difficult for theories to account for is the development of the disorder in those who are unable to see. As we noted earlier (see page 75), body image disturbance is one of the 'hallmarks' of anorexia nervosa. However, Yager *et al.* (1986) have described the case of a 28-year-old woman, blind from the age of 2, who had become anorectic at age 21. Touyz *et al.* (1988) reported a case of anorexia nervosa in a woman who had been blind from birth. Although neither research team was able to offer a satisfactory explanation for the development of the disorder, both agreed that blindness either from birth or from a very early age does not preclude the development of anorexia nervosa, and that people do not have to be actually able to see themselves to desire a slimmer physique.

The characteristics of bulimia nervosa

Literally, bulimia comes from the Greek *bous* meaning 'ox' and *limos* meaning 'hunger'. The disorder was first extensively investigated by Russell (1979), who saw it as 'an ominous variant' of anorexia nervosa. Instead of starving, bulimia nervosa is characterised by periodic

Figure 7.2   Kate Moss (left), well-known supermodel, and two models from *Yes!* magazine (right), demonstrating that physical beauty or ideal body shape/size can be defined in more than one way, within the same culture and at the same point in time

episodes of 'compulsive' or 'binge' eating, that is, the rapid and seemingly uncontrolled consumption of food, especially food which is rich in carbohydrates.

The binge is terminated either by abdominal pain or, in the case of the *purging type*, by the expulsion of food using diuretics, laxatives or self-induced vomiting. Some bulimics begin their binge by eating a coloured 'marker' food and, after they have finished, will continue purging until the marker has re-emerged (Colman, 1987). A typical binge might include the consumption of a large amount of ice cream, several packets of crisps, a pizza and several cans of fizzy drink. As well as their high calorific content, most foods consumed by bulimics have textures that aid rapid consumption. Thus, food tends to be 'wolfed down' rather than chewed properly. In the case of the *non-purging type*, strict dieting or vigorous exercise (rather than regular purging) occurs.

'Binge eating' itself is actually quite common. For example, Polivy & Herman (1985) discovered that many people admit to occasionally binge eating. In bulimia nervosa, however, the *frequency* of such behaviour is much higher, averaging at least two or three times a week and sometimes as often as 30 times a week. Box 7.2 describes a case which is typical of bulimia nervosa.

Box 7.2   A typical case of bulimia nervosa

Miss A. was a 22-year-old single clerk, who was referred by her doctor for treatment of 'psychiatric problems'. She had a three-year history of uncontrolled overeating. Although she was not originally obese, she disliked her 'square face' and developed a sensitive personality. After failing an examination and being unable to study in further education, she started to relieve her boredom and comfort herself by overeating. Her binges occurred four times per week and lasted one to three hours each. Triggers included feelings of emptiness and critical remarks from others. On average, she secretly consumed 800g of bread and biscuits. Such episodes were followed by abdominal bloating, guilt and dysphoria (inappropriate emotional feelings). There was nausea, but no vomiting. She took excessive laxatives (usually prune juice) to purge and 'calm' herself, restricted food intake and exercised excessively in the next 1–2 days. Her body weight fluctuated by up to 4 kg per week, but her menstrual cycle was normal.

Examination revealed a fully conscious girl who felt helpless over the 'attacks of overeating'. She desired a body weight of 45 kg and disparaged her waistline and square face, which made her 'look like a pig'. She found food dominated her life, and likened her problem to heroin addiction. There was a persistent request for laxatives.

(adapted from Lee *et al.*, 1992)

According to Cooper (1995), most bulimics are women, with fewer than 5% of cases presenting for treatment being men. The disorder usually begins in adolescence or early adulthood and generally appears later than is the case in anorexia nervosa. It also appears that bulimia nervosa is much more frequent than anorexia nervosa and may affect as much as 5% of the population. Like anorectics, bulimics have what ICD-10 calls 'an intrusive fear of fatness' and they are unduly concerned with their body weight and shape (and hence they take the drastic steps described above to control their weight). In a study conducted by Cutts & Barrios (1986), for example, bulimics were asked to imagine gaining weight. Physiological measures indicated an increased heart rate and muscle tension as compared with non-bulimic controls asked to perform the same task.

Whilst the discrepancy between actual body weight and desired body weight is generally no greater than among non-bulimics, Cooper (1995) reports that the discrepancy between *estimations* of body size and desired size is substantial. Although bulimics are mostly able to maintain a normal body weight, they tend to fluctuate between weight gain and weight loss. The binge-purge behaviour of the bulimic is typically accompanied by feelings of guilt. The purging of food produces feelings of relief and a commitment to a severely restrictive diet which ultimately fails (Sue *et al.*, 1994).

Clearly, bulimics recognise their eating behaviour to be abnormal and feel frustrated by it. However, they are unable to control the behaviour voluntarily. Because of the feelings of guilt, bingeing and purging are usually carried out in secret and, as a result of this, many bulimics go unrecognised even to close friends and family. Moreover, because there is not a constant loss of weight in bulimia nervosa, and because the bulimic's eating habits may appear normal in public, the estimate we gave for the number of cases must be treated with caution.

The purging does, however, produce some effects that might be noticeable to others. One of these is a 'puffy' facial appearance which is a consequence of swollen parotid glands caused by vomiting. Another is a deterioration in tooth enamel, which is caused by the stomach acid produced when vomiting occurs. A third effect is the development of calluses over the back of the hand which is caused by rubbing the hand against the upper teeth when the fingers are pushed into the throat in order to induce vomiting. There are many other physiological effects associated with bulimia nervosa. These include damage to the digestive tract, dehydration and nutritional imbalances. As well as these physiological effects, a number of psychological effects are associated with bulimia nervosa. These include anxiety, sleep disturbances and depression (see below).

Research also indicates that there are associations between *self-mutilative* behaviour and bulimia nervosa. Perhaps the oldest literary reference occurs in Ovid's *Metamorphoses*, in which Erysicthon, scorner of Gods and violator of the sacred groves of Ceres, was punished by being racked by famine and persecuted by a wild craving for food which nothing could satisfy. When 'his grievous malady' needed more food, 'the wretched man began to tear his limbs and rend them apart with his teeth and, by consuming his own body, fed himself' (Miller, 1983). Parry-Jones & Parry-Jones (1993) examined 25 bulimic cases reported from the late 17th to the late 19th centuries. They found four instances of self-mutilative behaviour and argue that such historical evidence offers some support for the suggested connection between eating disorders and self-mutilation.

An unusual form of self-mutilation was reported by Parkin & Eagles (1993) who studied three cases of *blood-letting* in association with bulimia nervosa. All three cases had some degree of medical training and began blood-letting after they had acquired sufficient expertise in the insertion of intravenous cannulae and the necessary implements. According to the researchers, each bulimic appeared to derive similar psychological benefit from the blood-letting and it appeared to serve much the same function as bingeing and vomiting in that it relieved feelings of anxiety, tension and anger.

EXPLANATIONS OF BULIMIA NERVOSA

As with anorexia nervosa, there are several theoretical approaches to understanding the causes of bulimia nervosa. As we mentioned earlier (see page 76), certain *neurotransmitters* have been implicated in the regulation of eating behaviour. As well as being a potential explanation for anorexia nervosa, it is possible that the neurotransmitters identified earlier are also implicated in bulimia nervosa. For example, abnormal neurotransmitter activity might account for the periodic carbohydrate bingeing that occurs in bulimia nervosa.

As well as neurotransmitters, *hormones* and *endorphins* have also been proposed as playing a mediating role in bulimia nervosa. Lydiard *et al.* (1993) reported that levels of *cholecystokinin octapeptide* (CCK-8), a neuroactive hormone implicated in the regulation of eating behaviour, were significantly lower in 11 drug-free female bulimics than 16 age-matched controls. Since there was no correlation between the mean frequency of binge eating or vomiting and scores on the *Eating Disorders Inventory*, the bulimics' unusual eating habits do not seem to be responsible for the decreased levels of CCK-8.

Other research has suggested that *plasma endorphins* are elevated in people with bulimia nervosa (and, interestingly, in those who self-mutilate: cf. Parkin & Eagles' (1993) study of blood-letting and bulimia nervosa described above). However, whether the elevated levels of plasma endorphins are a cause or a result of bulimia nervosa remains to be established. We should also note that the *genetic* evidence for bulimia nervosa is much weaker than that for anorexia nervosa. Kendler *et al.* (1991), for example, have reported a concordance rate of only 23% for identical twins and 9% for non-identical twins (see page 76).

One psychological approach to understanding bulimia nervosa has been termed the *disinhibition hypothesis* by Ruderman (1986). This hypothesis distinguishes between 'unrestrained' and 'restrained' eaters, the latter being people who constantly monitor their weight and are constantly going on diets. On some occasions, 'restrained' eaters may believe that they have overeaten, a belief which is sometimes accompanied by the thought that, since the diet has been broken, there is no reason why more should not be eaten. This *disinhibition* is held to lead to the consumption of more food, which is followed by purging in an attempt to reduce the weight that has been put on by the binge eating. As well as breaking a diet, other *disinhibiting factors* include alcohol. In Ruderman's view, the food intake pattern of highly weight-conscious people is characterised by an all-or-nothing rigidity which makes them susceptible to binge eating.

The fact that anorexia nervosa and bulimia nervosa share many characteristics has led some researchers to suggest that they can be explained in the same way. Other researchers (such as Garner, 1986) have argued that it is seriously misleading to consider the two disorders as being psychologically dissimilar. Echoing Garner, Bee (1992) has described them as 'variations on a basic theme' rather than distinctly different disorders. Garner has shown that, as well as sharing many psychological traits (such as perfectionism), anorectics and bulimics also share the same goal of maintaining a sub-optimal body weight. Moreover, a particular individual may often move *between* the two disorders in the quest for thinness.

What might be an interesting observation is the relationship between eating disorders and *sexual abuse*. According to Waller (1993), sexual abuse appears to be causally related to eating disorders, particularly those involving bulimic features. In a study of 100 women with eating disorders, Waller found that *borderline personality disorder* is a psychological disorder that explains at least a small part of the link between sexual abuse and bulimic behaviour, especially as regards the frequency of bingeing. The claimed link between sexual abuse and eating disorders has, however, been challenged (e.g. Cooper, 1995), and even if there is a link, other factors are surely involved. For example, it has often been reported that people with eating disorders have a personal history of affective disorder (particularly depression: see Chapter 5). In one study, Piran *et al.* (1985) found that among 18 patients with a lifetime history of major depression, the depressive symptoms preceded the emergence of the eating disorder by at least one year in eight cases, post-dated its onset in six, and occurred around the same time in the other four. It has also been shown that binge eating, mood and purging vary seasonally with bulimia nervosa. This might suggest that a vulnerability to depression (or seasonal affective disorder: see Chapter 5) may increase the predisposition to eating disorders, and an episode of depression might contribute to either the initation of its symptoms or its maintenance (Cooper, 1995).

Conclusions

Several theories of anorexia nervosa and bulimia nervosa have been advanced. Although some theories are more plausible than others and have more supporting evidence, there is as yet no theory whose explanatory power is superior over all others. Possibly, the two eating disorders we have described do not have single discrete causes, and there may be complex chains of events which interact to precipitate them.

SUMMARY

- In DSM-IV, **anorexia nervosa** and **bulimia nervosa** are two broad categories of physically and/or psychologically harmful eating patterns. They are also included within ICD-10.
- Although the characteristics of what we now call anorexia nervosa have been known about for centuries, it has only recently attracted much interest, due to greater public knowledge and increased incidence (although the latter claim has been disputed).
- Anorexia nervosa occurs predominantly in females and usually first appears in adolescence (especially between 14 and 16), although it can occur in childhood and later in adult life. In Britain, estimated incidence is higher than in the USA, ranging from 10–40 per 1,000 females.
- Anorexia nervosa is characterised by a **prolonged refusal to eat** adequate amounts of food, resulting in **deliberate weight loss**; this is often accompanied by **amenorrhea**. To be diagnosed **anorectic**, the individual must weigh less than 85% of his/her normal/expected weight for height/age/sex; this means that anorectics will look emaciated. They tend to have poor general health, and in 5–15% of cases, anorexia nervosa is fatal.
- Anorectics are often both hungry and preoccupied with thoughts of food, but they will avoid

most calorie-rich foods and show a reduced pleasure in eating in the form of a **low hedonic responsiveness** to taste and an aversion to the oral sensation of fat.

- Because of their intense fear of being overweight, which does not diminish even when a large amount of weight has been lost, anorectics take extreme measures to lose weight. The **restricting type** of anorectic engages in constant fasting/excessive physical activity, while the **binge eating/purging type** alternates between periods of fasting and 'binge eating'. The resulting guilt and shame lead to the use of laxatives or self-induced vomiting.

- Anorectics also have a **distorted body image**, so that they see themselves as being fat, even when they have a skeleton-like appearance for others.

- It was originally believed that anorexia nervosa was caused by damage to the pituitary gland. But this was based on a confusion between anorexia nervosa and **Simmonds' disease**. Not surprisingly, attempts to treat anorexia nervosa using pituitary extracts were unsuccessful.

- Damage to the **hypothalamus** has been proposed as an alternative cause of anorexia nervosa. There is strong evidence for the claim that the hypothalamus plays an important role in the regulation of eating. When **norepinephrine** stimulates the hypothalamus of animals, they start eating and show a marked preference for carbohydrates, while **serotonin** produces the opposite effect. However, it is still unclear as to whether brain dysfunction/changes in neurotransmitter levels are a cause of anorexia nervosa, are caused by it or are merely a correlate.

- Another suggestion is that viral- or immune-induced alterations in central homeostasis, particularly involving **corticotrophin-releasing hormone**, could trigger and maintain a behavioural response leading to an especially severe form of restrictive anorexia nervosa.

- There is some tendency for anorexia nervosa to run in families, and there is a 50% concordance rate for identical twins reared together. However, in the absence of concordance rates for fraternal and identical twins reared apart, it is difficult to assess the possible role of genetic factors. But this role is likely to be only small.

- According to the psychodynamic model, anorexia nervosa may represent an unconscious attempt by a girl to remain pre-pubescent. The cessation of menstruation enables the anorectic to avoid growing up and assuming adult responsibilities. Alternatively, being anorectic may allow a girl to avoid the issue of her sexuality; the weight loss results in a body with a 'boy-like' appearance.

- Again, it may represent an attempt by adolescents to **separate** themselves from their parents and establish their own identity. Consistent with this is the observation that the parents of anorectics tend to be domineering and that many female anorectics are 'good girls'. Assuming control of the most concrete aspect of one's self is a way of exerting choice and individuality.

- One problem with psychodynamic accounts is that many points apply only to females; another is that they focus on anorexia nervosa as an adolescent disorder and so cannot apply to onset after adolescence.

- According to the **behavioural** model, anorexia nervosa is a **phobia** of gaining weight (**weight phobia**), resulting from the impact of social norms, values and roles. The cultural idealisation of the 'slender female' may be one cause of the fear of being fat, such that dieting has become part of 'normal' eating, for American women at least.

- This is supported by the finding that the incidence of anorexia nervosa is much higher in occupations, such as ballet dancing and modelling, in which there is considerable pressure to be thin, compared with the general population. Also, in at least some non-Western cultures, the incidence of anorexia nervosa is much lower than in Western societies, as it is in black populations compared with white, regardless of culture.

- According to Sui-Wah, lower rates of anorexia nervosa among Chinese women can be explained in terms of the importance attached to food/eating in Chinese culture, the deliciousness of Chinese food and the Chinese custom of eating meals with the family.

- Being **blind** does not prevent the development of anorexia nervosa, which is difficult to explain, given the importance of distorted body image as a characteristic of the disorder.

- **Bulimia nervosa** is characterised by frequent episodes of compulsive/'binge' eating (commonly two to three times per week but sometimes as much as 30 times), which is ended either by abdominal pain or by the use of diuretics/laxatives/self-induced vomiting (**purging type**). Typically, the food is high in calories and is easily consumed. The **non-purging type** counteracts the food intake either by strict dieting or vigorous exercise.

- Over 95% of bulimics are women. The disorder usually begins in adolescence/early adulthood, generally later than anorexia nervosa, which is much less common than bulimia nervosa. Like anorectics, bulimics are fearful of fatness and unduly concerned with their body weight/shape.

- Bulimics display a substantial discrepancy between estimations of body weight and desired weight compared with non-bulimics. Although able to maintain a normal body weight, bulimics tend to fluctuate between weight gain and loss. This binge-purge pattern is associated with guilt feelings and so is usually carried out in secret, making detection even by close friends/relatives more difficult.
- Bulimics recognise the abnormal nature of their eating behaviour, but are unable to control it. Because there is no constant weight loss and eating in public may seem quite normal, estimates of the number of cases are likely to be **underestimates**.
- Frequent vomiting causes a 'puffy' facial appearance, a deterioration in tooth enamel and calluses over the back of the hand. Other effects include damage to the digestive tract, dehydration and nutritional imbalances.
- Bulimia nervosa is also associated with **self-mutilative** behaviour, an unusual form of which is **blood-letting**, which seems to serve the same basic function as bingeing and vomiting, i.e. relief from anxiety, tension and anger.
- One proposed explanation of bulimia nervosa is that norepinephrine and serotonin are involved, as they are thought to be in anorexia nervosa. **Hormones** and **endorphins** may also play a mediating role. For example, **cholecystokinin octapeptide (CCK-8)** levels were found to be significantly lower in drug-free bulimics than controls; however, there was no evidence that the bulimics' unusual eating habits were causing these decreased levels of CCK-8.
- **Plasma endorphins** are raised in bulimics, but it is unclear which is cause and which is effect. The genetic evidence for bulimia nervosa is much weaker than for anorexia nervosa.
- According to the **disinhibition hypothesis**, when 'restrained eaters' believe that they have overeaten, their eating may become 'disinhibited', which is then followed by purging in an effort to reduce the weight that has been put on by the binge eating. Highly weight-conscious people display an all-or-nothing rigidity, making them susceptible to binge eating.
- There is debate among researchers as to whether anorexia and bulimia nervosa are variations on a basic theme or distinct disorders. Not only do anorectics and bulimics share many psychological traits, they also share the goal of maintaining a sub-optimal body weight; the same individual may also alternate **between** the two disorders.
- Sexual abuse appears to be causally related to eating disorders, especially those involving bulimic features, with **borderline personality disorder** partly linking the two. However, being vulnerable to depression (or seasonal affective disorder) may increase the predisposition to eating disorders, and an episode of depression might contribute either to its initiation or its maintenance.

<h1 style="text-align:center">PART 3</h1>
<h1 style="text-align:center">Therapeutic approaches</h1>

8

THERAPIES BASED ON THE MEDICAL MODEL

Introduction and overview

As we saw in Chapter 2, the medical model views mental disorders, like physical disorders, as being caused largely if not exclusively by physical factors. As a result, therapeutic approaches favoured by the medical model are physical and are collectively known as *somatic therapy*. As David (1994) has observed, the early and middle parts of this century saw the introduction of a variety of extraordinary treatments for mental disorders, whose names conjure up disturbing images of what they involved. These include *carbon dioxide inhalation therapy, nitrogen shock therapy, narcosis therapy, insulin coma therapy* and *malaria therapy*.

Although a large number of somatic approaches to therapy have been abandoned, three continue to be used (and their names too may conjure up disturbing images). These are *chemotherapy, electroconvulsive therapy* and *psychosurgery*. Our aim in this chapter is to describe the procedures involved in these therapeutic approaches and consider some of the issues that surround their use.

Chemotherapy

The use of *drugs* to treat mental disorders has been by far the most influential of the somatic approaches we will consider in this chapter. Indeed, according to SANE (1993b), a quarter of all the medications pre-scribed in Britain through the National Health Service are *psychotherapeutic* drugs. Three main types of psychotherapeutic drug can be identified. These are the *neuroleptics*, the *antidepressant and antimanic drugs* and the *anxiolytics*.

THE NEUROLEPTICS

The neuroleptics were the forerunners of the 'drug revolution' in the treatment of mental disorders. They were introduced in the 1950s following the accidental discovery by French researchers that they calmed psychotic individuals. Since they lessened the need for *physical restraint* (such as straitjackets) of seriously disturbed individuals, they were seen as a great advance in treatment. Neuroleptics are also known as *major tranquillisers*, although this term is misleading because they generally tranquillise without impairing consciousness. The term *antipsychotics* is also used to describe them because they are mainly used to treat schizophrenia and severe disorders, such as mania and amphetamine abuse. Some examples of neuroleptics, their mode of action and side-effects associated with them are illustrated in Box 8.1.

> **Box 8.1   The neuroleptic drugs**
>
> **Examples**: The most widely used group are the *phenothiazines* and include *chlorpromazine* (marketed under the trade names *Thorazine* and *Largactil*). The *butyrophenone* group includes *haloperidol* (*Haldol*) and *droperidol* (*Droleptan*).

One of the more recent neuroleptics is *clozapine* (*Clozaril*), a member of the *dibezazepines* group, which was developed to avoid the side-effects (see below) of the phenothiazines.

Mode of action: Most neuroleptics block a particular type of *dopamine* receptor (called D2) in the brain with the result that dopamine cannot excite post-synaptic receptors (see Chapter 4, page 46). Neuroleptics also inhibit the functioning of the hypothalamus (which also contains dopamine secreting neurons). The hypothalamus plays a role in arousal, and neuroleptic drugs prevent arousal signals from reaching higher parts of the brain. Rather than blocking D2 receptors, clozapine blocks the recently discovered D4 receptors.

Side-effects: Of the many that have been reported, the more extreme include blurred vision, *neuroleptic malignant syndrome* (which produces delirium, coma and death) and *extrapyramidal symptoms*. These consist of *akathisia* (restlessness), *dystonia* (abnormal body movements, one of which is known as the 'Thorazine shuffle'), and *tardive dyskinesia*. Tardive (late onset) dyskinesia (movement disorder) is an irreversible condition which resembles Parkinson's disease. Some of these side-effects can be controlled by the use of other drugs such as *procyclidine* (*Kemadrin*).

Attempts to limit the side-effects of neuroleptics include *targeted strategies* or *drug holidays*, in which the drugs are discontinued during periods of remission and reinstituted when early signs of relapse occur. *Agranulocytosis* (a decrease in the number of infection-fighting white blood cells) is a side-effect of clozapine and some other neuroleptics, which occurs in about 2% of users, and is potentially fatal. Blood tests must be given on a regular basis. When the cell count drops too low, the drug's use must be *permanently* discontinued. Newer neuroleptics such as *risperidone* (marketed under the trade name *Risperdal*), may avoid many of the side-effects described above (NSF, 1994). *Olanzapine*, which has a similar action to clozapine but without the haematological complications, has recently been approved by the Food and Drug Administration in America. It is expected to become available in Britain in early 1997 (Wick, 1996).

Neuroleptics are effective in reducing the *positive* symptoms of schizophrenia (see Chapter 4, page 46), which allows other forms of therapy to be used when the symptoms are in remission. However, some people fail to respond to the drugs, especially those displaying the *negative* symptoms of schizophrenia, such as apathy and withdrawal (see Chapter 4, page 46). The drugs do not *cure*, but reduce the prominent symptoms of schizophrenia. Relapse occurs after several weeks if the drugs are stopped. Additionally, neuroleptics are of little value in treating social incapacity and other difficulties in adjusting to life outside the therapeutic setting. As a result, relapse is common.

THE ANTIDEPRESSANT AND ANTIMANIC DRUGS

Antidepressants are classified as *stimulants* and were introduced in the 1950s. As well as being used to treat depression, the drugs have also been used in the treatment of anxiety, agoraphobia, obsessive-compulsive disorder and eating disorders. Box 8.2 shows some examples of antidepressants, their mode of action and some of the side-effects associated with them.

Box 8.2   The antidepressants

Examples: *The monoamine oxidase inhibitor* (*MAOI*) group includes *phenelzine* (marketed under the trade name *Nardil*). The *tricyclic* group includes *imipramine* (*Tofranil*). The *tetracyclic* group includes *fluoxetine* (*Prozac*). Because of their mode of action (see below), the tetracyclics are also known as *Selective Serotonin Reuptake Inhibitors* (*SSRIs*).

Mode of action: MAOIs are so called because they inhibit (or block) the uptake of the enzyme that deactivates *norepinephrine* and *serotonin*. Thus, they are believed to act directly on these neurotransmitters (see Chapter 5, page 57). The tricyclic group prevents the reuptake of norepinephrine and serotonin by the cells that released them, making these neurotransmitters more likely to reach receptor sites. The tetracyclics block the action of an enzyme that removes serotonin from the synapses between neurons (hence serotonin levels are elevated).

Side-effects: MAOIs require special dietary requirements to be adhered to. Amine-rich food (such as some cheeses, pickled herrings and yeast extracts) must be avoided. Failure to avoid amine-rich foods results in the accumulation of amines, which leads to cerebral haemorrhage. Both MAOIs and the tricyclics are associated with cardiac arrhythmias and heart block, dry mouth, blurred vision and urinary retention. Recent findings with the tetracyclics suggest that drugs like Prozac are also not free from serious side-effects.

As Box 8.2 illustrates, there are several types of anti-depressant drug, none of which exerts immediate effects. For example, the *tricyclics* can take up to four weeks before a noticeable change in behaviour is observed (and with individuals who are so depressed that they are contemplating suicide, this is clearly a drawback). When mood improves, psychological therapies can be used to try and get at the root of the depression. MAOIs are generally less effective than tricyclics. Because of dietary requirements and the fact that they have more side-effects than tricyclics, MAOIs are the least preferred antidepressant drug.

1987 saw the introduction of *Prozac*, an SSRI anti-depressant (see Box 8.2) which has been termed the 'happy pill' and its users 'the happy, shiny people'. Because Prozac was believed to have fewer side-effects than the tricyclics, it was widely prescribed as a treatment for depression. However, one month's supply of an SSRI costs £20, whereas the same supply of a tricyclic costs only £1. The claim that Prozac can increase happiness and create a 'more interesting personality' has produced astonishing sales. More than 15 million people worldwide take the drug, including 500,000 in Britain.

Although antidepressants are effective when used in the short term with severe depression, they are not useful when taken on a long-term basis. Indeed, they do not alleviate depression in all people, and controlled studies (e.g. NIMH, 1987) suggest their effectiveness is no greater than psychotherapy (see Chapter 9) and cognitive therapy (see Chapter 11). As Box 8.2 illustrates, one side-effect of antidepressants (especially the tricyclics) is *urinary retention*. Controversially, this side-effect has been used to treat *nocturnal enuresis* (bedwetting) in children, even when other simple measures have not been tried.

Lithium carbonate was first approved for use as an anti-manic drug in 1970, but was actually first used in the mid-nineteenth century for what Garrod (1859) called *gouty mania*. The drug is used to treat bipolar disorder and unipolar depression (see Chapter 5) as well as mania. Lithium salts (such as *lithium carbonate* and *lithium citrate*) flatten out cycles of manic behaviour. Once the manic phase in bipolar disorder has been eliminated, the depressed phase does not return. The salts of lithium appear to be 'miracle drugs', in that within two weeks of taking them, 70–80% of manic individuals show an improvement in mood. Box 8.3 shows some examples of antimanic drugs, along with their mode of action and the side-effects associated with them.

Box 8.3   The antimanic drugs

Examples: The inorganic salts lithium carbonate and lithium citrate are marketed under a variety of trade names including *Camoclit* and *Liskanum* (both lithium carbonate) and *Litarex* and *Piradel* (both lithium citrate).

Mode of action: By increasing the re-uptake of *norepinephrine* and *serotonin*, it is believed that lithium carbonate exerts its effects by decreasing the availability of these neurotransmitters at various synaptic sites.

Side-effects: These include depressed reactions, hand tremors, dry mouth, weight gain, impaired memory and kidney poisoning. If lithium becomes too concentrated in the bloodstream, side effects include nausea, diarrhoea and, at very high levels, coma and death. As a result, users' blood is regularly checked.

THE ANXIOLYTIC DRUGS

These are classified as *depressants* and are also known as *antianxiety drugs* or *minor tranquillisers*. Anxiety was first treated with synthetic *barbiturates* (such as *phenobarbitol*). However, because of the side-effects produced by these drugs and because of the introduction of other anxiolytic drugs, their use gradually declined. Anxiolytics are used to reduce anxiety and tension in people whose disturbances are not severe enough to warrant hospitalisation. The drugs are effective in reducing the symptoms of generalised anxiety disorders (see Chapter 6), especially when used in the short term and in combination with psychological therapies. They are also used to combat withdrawal symptoms associated with opiate and alcohol addiction. However, anxiolytics are of little use in treating the anxiety that occurs in sudden, spontaneous panic attacks. Some examples of anxiolytic drugs, their mode of action and some of the side-effects associated with their use are illustrated in Box 8.4.

Box 8.4   The anxiolytic drugs

Examples: The *propanediol* group includes *meprobamate* (marketed under the trade name *Miltown*). The *benzodiazepine* group includes *chlordiazepoxide* (*Librium*) and *diazepam* (*Valium*).

Mode of action: The general effect of anxiolytic drugs is to depress central nervous system activity, which produces a decrease in the activity of the sympathetic branch of the autonomic nervous system. This produces decreased heart and respiration rate and reduces feelings of nervousness and tension. Since benzodiazepine receptor sites exist in the brain, that group possibly exert their effect by mimicking or blocking a naturally occurring substance.

Side-effects: These include drowsiness, lethargy, tolerance, dependence, withdrawal (manifested as tremors and convulsions) and toxicity. *Rebound anxiety*, that is, anxiety which is even more intense than that originally experienced, can occur when their use is stopped. Rebound anxiety may be physiological *or* psychological in origin. Newer anxiolytics (such as *Busparin* and *Zopiclone*) seem to be as effective as established anxiolytics, although worrying side-effects have also been reported with them.

The use of the term *minor tranquillisers* suggests that anxiolytic drugs are 'safe'. However, one of the dangers of these drugs is that overdose can lead to death, especially when taken with alcohol. As Box 8.4 shows, anxiolytics also produce addiction. Although it is generally agreed that the use of anxiolytics should be limited to people whose anxiety is clearly handicapping their work, leisure and family relationships, they are all too commonly prescribed. Indeed, one of the anxiolytics, *Valium*, is the most prescribed of all drugs. An astonishing 8,000 tons of *benzodiazepines* were consumed in the United States alone in 1977! As with other drugs,

their use with children (to relieve acute anxiety and related insomnia caused by fear) is controversial.

Electroconvulsive therapy

In 1933, Sakel (cited in Fink, 1984) found that inducing a hypoglycaemic coma by means of insulin seemed to be effective in the treatment of certain psychoses. A little later, von Meduna observed that schizophrenia and epilepsy appeared to be *biologically incompatible*, that is, schizophrenia rarely occurred in epilepsy and vice versa. Drawing on his observation that those psychotic individuals prone to epilepsy showed less severe symptoms following an epileptic fit, von Meduna advocated inducing major epileptiform fits in psychotics in order to 'drive out' and hence 'cure' their schizophrenia.

Von Meduna used a cerebral stimulant called *Cardiazol* in order to induce the epileptic fit. However, this method was unsatisfactory, not least for the fact that the stimulant gave rise to feelings of impending death during the conscious phase of its action! Various alternatives to Cardiazol were tried until, after visiting an abattoir and seeing animals rendered unconscious by means of electric shocks, Cerletti and Bini (reported in Bini, 1938) advocated passing an electric current across the temples in order to induce an epileptic fit. Although there have been refinements to the procedures originally used by Cerletti and Bini, today *electroconvulsive therapy* (ECT) is administered in essentially the same way (see Figure 8.1 overleaf). A summary of the procedures involved in the administration of ECT is shown in Box 8.5.

Box 8.5   The procedures used in electroconvulsive therapy

Following a full physical examination, which is necessary because heart conditions, chest diseases and peptic ulcers can be accentuated by ECT, the person is required to fast for three to four hours prior to treatment and empty the bladder immediately before treatment is given. Whilst the person is being psychologically prepared for treatment, dentures, rings and other metallic objects are removed and a loose-fitting gown worn.

45–60 minutes before treatment, an *atropine sulphate* injection is given. This drug prevents the

---

heart's normal rhythm from being disturbed and inhibits the secretion of mucus and saliva. An anxiolytic drug such as *Valium* may also be given if a person is particularly apprehensive. With the person lying supine, head supported by a pillow, a short-acting anaesthetic followed by a muscle relaxant is given, the latter ensuring that a reduced convulsion will occur. Oxygen is given before and after treatment, and a mouth gag is applied to prevent the tongue or lips being bitten.

In *bilateral* ECT, saline-soaked lint-covered electrodes are then attached to each temple. In *unilateral* ECT, two electrodes are attached to the temple and mastoid region of the non-dominant cerebral hemisphere. With the chin held still, a current of around 200 milliamps, flowing at 110 volts, is passed from one electrode to another for a brief period (around 0.5–4 seconds). Because of the use of muscle relaxants, the only observable sign of the fit is a slight twitching of the eyelids, facial muscles, and toes. When the convulsion is

complete and the jaw relaxed, an airway is inserted into the mouth and oxygen given until breathing resumes unaided. The person is turned into the left lateral position, head on the side, and is carefully observed until the effects of the muscle relaxant and anaesthetic have worn off and recovery is complete.

(adapted from McIlveen *et al.*, 1994)

Typically, a number of ECT treatments occurring over several weeks will be administered, the total number being gauged by the individual's response (Freeman, 1995). Although ECT was originally used to treat schizophrenia, its usefulness with that disorder has been

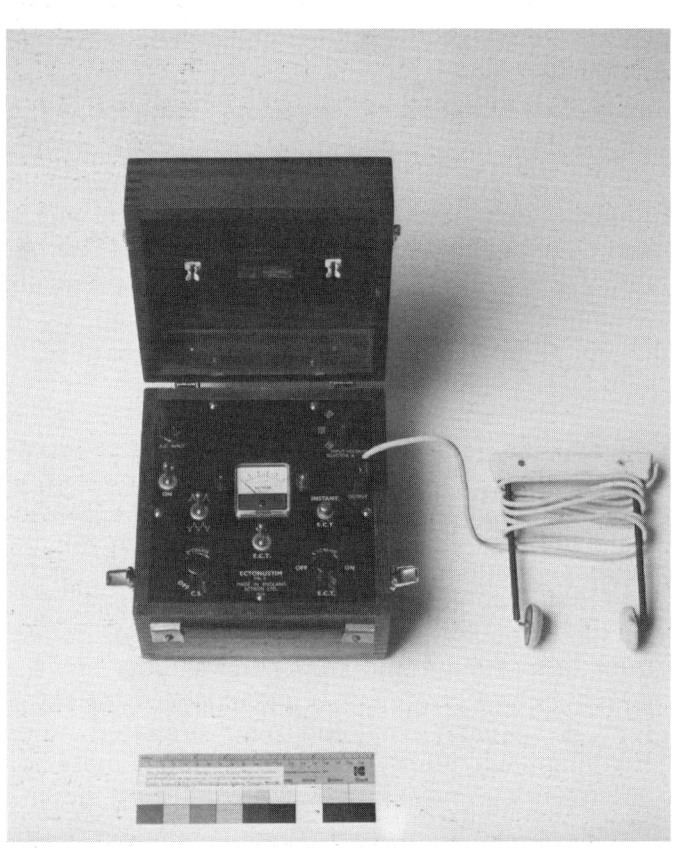

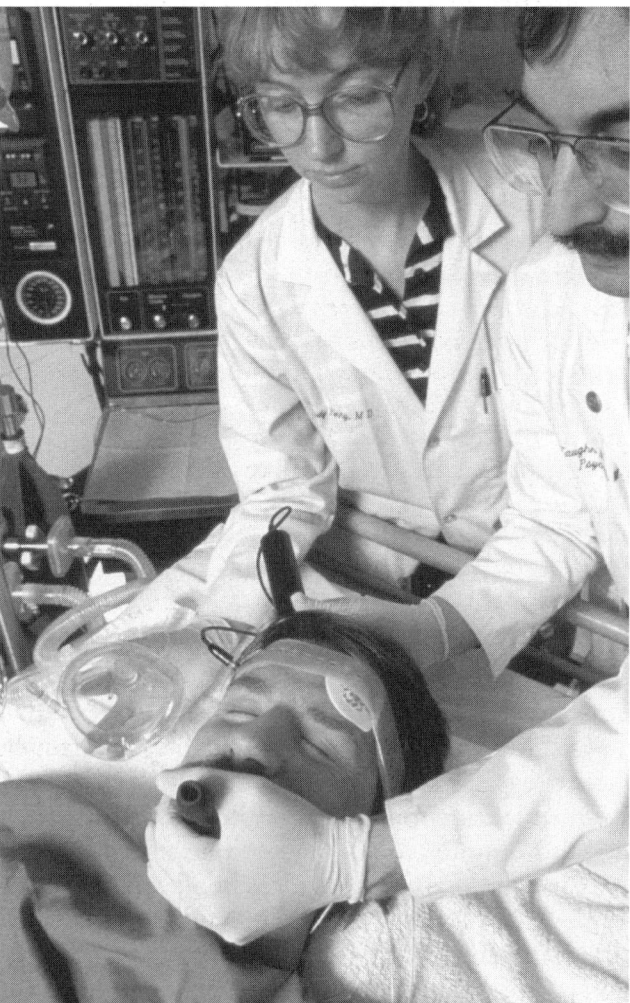

Figure 8.1 **The electroconvulsive therapy (ECT) equipment shown on the left dates from 1950, since when the procedure has become very much safer and more sophisticated. The right-hand photo shows the procedure as it is carried out today. Despite the technical improvements, ECT is a highly controversial treatment**

seriously questioned, and today it finds its primary use in the treatment of severe depression, bipolar disorder and certain obsessive-compulsive disorders. According to Wesseley (1993), ECT is 'highly effective' in the treatment of severe depression and particularly useful with those who harbour suicidal feelings because its effects are immediate (unlike the antidepressant drugs, which take time to produce a noticeable improvement in mood: see page 86).

Whilst ECT's effectiveness in the treatment of certain disorders is beyond dispute, the use of the therapy has been questioned on the grounds that it is not known why its beneficial effects occur. According to one theory, the therapy's effectiveness can be explained in terms of the *anterograde* and *retrograde amnesia* that occur as a side-effect. However, *unilateral ECT* (see Box 8.5), which minimises the disruption of memory, is also effective in reducing depression. As a result, a 'memory loss' theory of the effectiveness of ECT is unlikely to be true.

Another theory suggests that, given the nature of ECT and the negative publicity the therapy has received, a person will deny his or her symptoms in order to avoid the 'punishment' the therapy is perceived as being, and this extinguishes the abnormal behaviour. The proposal that ECT acts as a 'punishment' has been tested by applying *sub-convulsive shocks*, that is, shocks which do not produce a convulsion. However, sub-convulsive shocks do not seem to bring about any change in behaviour and, since they are equally as unpleasant as convulsive shocks, a 'punishment' theory account of ECT is also unlikely to be true.

Perhaps the most plausible account of why ECT produces behaviour change is that which suggests that the therapy produces a variety of *biochemical changes* in the brain, which are greater than those produced by other somatic approaches (such as antidepressant drugs). However, there are many physiological changes which occur when ECT is administered, and it is difficult to establish which of these are important. Since ECT appears to be most effective in the treatment of depression and since, as we saw in Chapter 5, both norepinephrine and serotonin have been strongly implicated in that disorder, it is most likely that these neurotransmitters are affected.

ECT has also been criticised on ethical grounds. Indeed, in Berkeley, California, in 1982, the therapy was outlawed by voter referendum and the administration of ECT was punishable by a fine of up to $500 and six months in jail. As we noted earlier, ECT has a negative public image which derives from horrific descriptions of the treatment in books and films. Some opponents of ECT (e.g. Heather, 1976) have described the therapy as being 'about as scientific as kicking a television set because it is not working'. Certainly, the primitive methods once used were associated with bruises and bone fractures (as a consequence of the restraint used by nursing staff during the convulsion) and with pain when an individual failed to lose consciousness during the treatment. However, the use of muscle relaxants minimises the possibility of fractures, and the use of anaesthesia rules out the possibility of the individual being conscious during treatment (see Box 8.5).

Yet whilst ECT is now considered to be a 'low-risk' therapeutic procedure, Breggin (1979) has argued that there is evidence that brain damage can occur following its administration (at least in animals sacrificed immediately after receiving ECT). Breggin has also pointed out that, whilst ECT is typically seen as a treatment of 'last resort', which should be preceded by a careful assessment of the costs and benefits for a particular individual, such assessments are not always routine. Although this may be true in the United States, under Section 58 of the Mental Health Act (1983), ECT's use in Britain requires an individual's consent or a second medical opinion before it can be administered.

Psychosurgery

Psychosurgery is a term which refers to surgical procedures that are performed on the brain in order to treat mental disorders. The term is properly used when the intention is to *purposely* alter a person's psychological functioning. Thus, whilst removing a brain tumour, for example, might affect a person's behaviour, it would not be considered a psychosurgical procedure.

Psychosurgical techniques, albeit primitive ones, have been carried out for a long time (see Chapter 2 and *trephining*). In medieval times, psychosurgery involved 'cutting the stone of folly' from the brains of those considered to be 'mad'. Modern psychosurgical techniques can be traced to the Second International Neurological Conference held in London in 1935, when Carlyle

Jacobsen and his colleagues reported the effects of removing the pre-frontal areas (that is, the forwardmost portion) of the pre-frontal lobes in chimpanzees. The researchers reported that the procedure abolished the violent outbursts that some of the chimpanzees had been prone to.

In the audience at the conference was Antonio de Egas Moniz, a Portugese neuropsychiatrist. Moniz was sufficiently impressed by the findings of Jacobsen and his colleagues to persuade a colleague, Almeida Lima, to carry out surgical procedures on the frontal lobes of schizophrenics and other disturbed individuals in an attempt to reduce their aggressive behaviour. The procedure involved severing the neural connections between the pre-frontal lobes and the hypothalamus and thalamus, the rationale being that thought (mediated by the cortex) would be disconnected from emotion (mediated by lower brain centres).

The *leucotomy* or *pre-frontal lobotomy* seemed to be successful in reducing the aggressive behaviour shown by unmanageable patients. The original 'apple corer' technique involved drilling a hole through the skull covering on each side of the head and then inserting a blunt instrument which was rotated in a vertical arc. This procedure followed the unsuccessful technique of injecting alcohol to destroy areas of the frontal lobe brain tissue, which produced incredibly poor results. Moniz and his colleagues originally used the 'apple corer' technique on schizophrenics and people who

were compulsive and anxiety-ridden. After a year of using the procedure, a 70% 'cure' rate was claimed by Moniz and Lima. The 'apple corer technique' and a later 'refinement' of it devised by Walter Freeman (see below) are shown in Figure 8.2.

Also at the 1935 conference in London was Walter Freeman, a neurologist who was not trained as a surgeon. With his associate James Watts, Freeman developed and popularised the psychosurgical technique that became known as the 'standard' pre-frontal lobotomy. In the absence of alternative therapeutic techniques and with the seemingly high success rate claimed by Moniz and others, the pre-frontal lobotomy became extremely popular. Estimates vary as to the number of operations performed in the United States following Freeman and Watts' pioneering work. Kalinowsky (1975) puts the figure at around 40,000. A more conservative estimate (Valenstein, 1980) puts it at around 25,000. The 'showman' in the Freeman and Watts 'double act' was Freeman. Tucker (1994) has described Freeman as 'a large man, with a large beard and an impressive speaker who habitually wore a stetson at conferences'. Although Freeman was not surgically trained, he developed his own psychosurgical technique called the *transorbital lobotomy* which is shown in Figure 8.2.

Psychosurgery was largely abandoned in the late 1950s following the introduction of the psychotherapeutic drugs, and for a variety of other reasons which are summarised in Box 8.6.

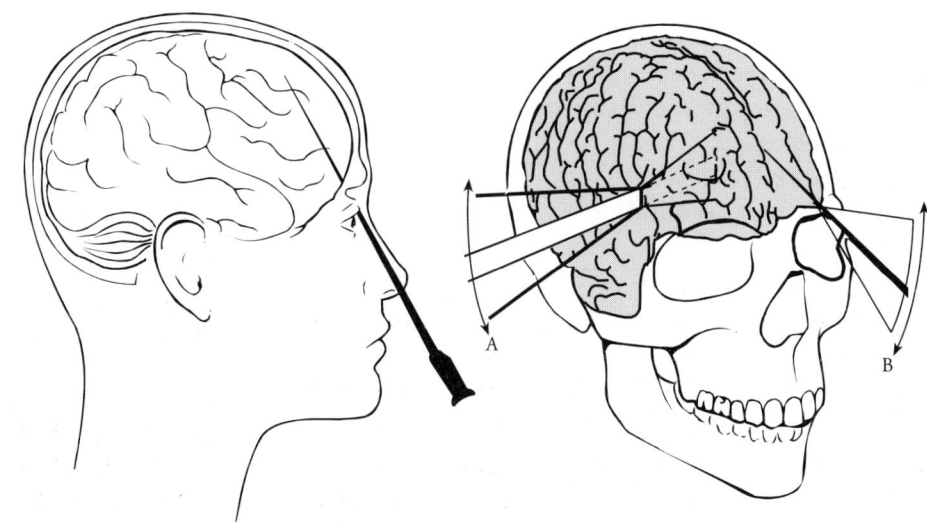

Figure 8.2   The picture on the left shows a transorbital lobotomy, as devised by Freeman who, together with Watts, developed and popularised the 'standard' pre-frontal lobotomy. The 'apple corer' technique (shown on the right) is the procedure originally used by Moniz and colleagues on schizophrenics and people suffering from compulsive and anxiety disorders. Both of these techniques represent a refinement of the Moniz technique

Box 8.6 Some reasons for the abandonment of psychosurgery

Lack of scientific basis: The theoretical rationale for the operation devised by Moniz was vague and misguided, with researchers not *entirely* clear as to why beneficial effects should occur. Indeed, David (1994) has questioned whether even now our knowledge of the frontal lobes (or what he calls 'frontal lobology') is anything more than 'psychiatry's new pseudoscience'. Also, according to Valenstein (1990), Moniz's reports of success were exaggerated. Although awarded the Nobel prize for medicine in 1949 'for his discovery of the therapeutic value of leucotomy in the treatment of some psychoses', it is ironic that Moniz was shot and paralysed by a patient on whom he had performed a lobotomy!

Consistency and irreversibility: There is a lack of consistency in the outcomes produced by psychosurgery. Behaviour change is produced in some individuals but not others, though who will be affected and how is difficult to predict. Psychosurgical procedures cannot be reversed.

Side-effects: Some of the severe and permanent side-effects associated with psychosurgery are (in no particular order):

- apathy
- impaired judgement
- reduced creativity
- epileptic-type seizures
- severe blunting of emotions
- intellectual impairments
- hyperactivity
- distractability
- impaired learning ability
- overeating
- partial paralysis
- memory loss
- personal slovenliness
- childlike behaviour
- indifference to others
- death

Lack of evaluation: One surgeon noted that the *cingulotomy* (see below) produces 'little or no changes in intellectual and discriminative ability' using the ability to knit after the operation as the criterion for change (Winter, 1972).

Consent: Psychosurgical techniques were routinely used with people who could not give their consent to the operation. However, section 58 of the revised Mental Health Act in Britain did introduce stringent provisions regarding information to those referred for psychosurgery and their consent to treatment (Rappaport, 1992).

Given the reasons identified in Box 8.6, it is perhaps surprising to learn that, although controversial, psychosurgery is still performed today. However, it is seen very much as treatment of last resort which is used only when other treatment methods have failed to produce a response. It is also occasionally used for pain control in the terminally ill. According to Snaith (1994), over 20 operations a year are conducted in Britain.

Modern lobotomies involve cutting two tiny holes in the forehead to allow radioactive rods to be inserted in the frontal lobe in order to destroy tissue. Other psychosurgical techniques involve the destruction of small amounts of tissue in precisely located areas of the brain. For example, the *tractotomy* interrupts the neural pathways between the limbic system and hypothalamus (which are believed to play a role in emotion) in the hope of alleviating depression. According to Verkaik (1995), psychosurgical techniques reduce the risk of suicide in severe depression from 15% to 1%. The *cingulotomy* cuts the cingulum bundle (a small bundle of nerve fibres connecting the pre-frontal cortex with parts of the limbic system). This is used to treat obsessive-compulsive disorder, and evidently does so effectively (Hay *et al.*, 1993). In fortunately very rare cases, our knowledge about the effects of psychosurgery has been advanced by unintended cases of it, as illustrated in Box 8.7.

Box 8.7 A case of unintended psychosurgery

Mr A., a 19-year-old man, was found with blood running down his face, the result of shooting himself through the mouth with a .22 calibre rifle. Mr A. had been diagnosed as suffering from obsessive-compulsive disorder (OCD) at the age of 15 when his minor checking and hand-washing rituals began to interfere with his everyday life. Various treatment methods failed to produce any beneficial effects and he eventually left treatment, although he returned after two failed suicide attempts. In addition to his earlier OCD symptoms, he had to repeat ideas in order to gain perfection, and had to recall 50 different chants.

Treatment with drugs had no effects, and Mr A.'s mother eventually threatened him with commital to a mental institution. When Mr A. complained to her about how wretched he felt, she replied 'Go and shoot yourself'. Five minutes later he did exactly that. Three weeks after surgery, Mr A. began to show an improvement, in that whilst his obsessions were still present, their frequency and intensity were much reduced.

Two years after being discharged, his mood was consistently calm and cheerful, and his obsessions were minimal. It is unlikely that the observed changes were coincidental to the self-inflicted psychosurgery. The early onset of Mr A.'s disorder, its progressively worsening course, the dramatic and almost immediate effects of the unintended psychosurgery, and the sustained improvement over two years virtually rule out *spontaneous remission* (see Chapter 13, page 138).

(adapted from Solyom *et al.*, 1987)

Even more controversial than electroconvulsive therapy, psychosugery continues to have a negative image amongst both professionals and the public. However, according to Valenstein (1973):

'There are certainly no grounds for either the position that all psychosurgery necessarily reduces all people to a 'vegetable status' or that it has a high probability of producing miraculous cures. The truth, even if somewhat wishy-washy, lies in between these extreme positions'.

Conclusions

Somatic therapies, which derive from the medical model of abnormality, have a long history of use in the treatment of abnormal behaviour. In this chapter, we have described and evaluated three somatic approaches to therapy. Although controversial, somatic therapies continue to be used today in the treatment of mental disorders.

SUMMARY

- Therapeutic approaches favoured by the medical model are physical (**somatic therapy**). Although many extraordinary treatments introduced in the early and middle 20th century (such as 'nitrogen shock therapy' and 'insulin coma therapy') have been abandoned, **chemotherapy, electroconvulsive therapy** and **psychosurgery** continue to be used.
- **Chemotherapy** has been the most influential of the somatic approaches; one estimate is that a quarter of all medications prescribed in Britain through the National Health Service are **psychotherapeutic drugs**. The three main types are **neuroleptics, antidepressants** and **antimanic drugs**, and **anxiolytics.**
- The **neuroleptics** were introduced in the 1950s and were seen as a great advance in treatment since they reduced the need for **physical restraint**. They are also known as **major tranquillisers**, although they generally tranquillise without impairing consciousness, and **antipsy-**

- **chotic** drugs, since they are mainly used to treat schizophrenia, mania and amphetamine abuse.
- The most widely used neuroleptics are the **phenothiazines**, which include **chlorpromazine (Thorazine/Largactil)**. The **butyrophenones** include **haloperidol (Haldol)** and **droperidol (Droleptan)**. The **dibezazepines**, developed to avoid the side-effects of the phenothiazines, include **clozapine (Clozaril)**.
- Most neuroleptics block the D2 **dopamine** receptor in the brain, preventing dopamine from exciting post-synaptic receptors. They also inhibit the functioning of the hypothalamus, preventing arousal signals from reaching higher brain centres. Clozapine blocks the D4 receptors.
- The more extreme **side-effects** of the neuroleptics include blurred vision, **neuroleptic malignant syndrome**, and **extrapyramidal symptoms (akathisia, dystonia** and **tardive dyskinesia)**. Some of these can be controlled by the use of **procyclidine (Kemadrin)**.

- Other attempts to limit the side-effects include **targeted strategies/drug holidays**. Regular blood tests must be given in order to detect **agranulocytosis**. Newer neuroleptics, such as **risperidone (Risperdal)** and **Olanzapine** (recently approved in the USA and likely to be available in the UK early in 1997), may avoid many of these side-effects.
- Neuroleptics reduce the **positive** symptoms of schizophrenia, allowing other forms of treatment to be used, but not the **negative** symptoms or social incapacity/difficulties in adjusting to life outside hospital. The drugs do not **cure** and relapse occurs if they are stopped.
- **Antidepressants (stimulants)** were introduced in the 1950s and are used to treat anxiety, agoraphobia, obsessive-compulsive disorder, and eating disorders, as well as depression. The **monoamine oxidase inhibitor (MAOI)** group includes **phenelzine (Nardil)**. The **tricyclic** group includes **imipramine (Tofranil)**. The **tetracyclic** group (**selective serotonin reuptake inhibitors/ SSRIs**) includes **fluoxetine (Prozac)**.
- **MAOIs** inhibit the uptake of the enzyme that deactivates **norepinephrine** and **serotonin**. The **tricyclics** prevent the reuptake of these neurotransmitters, making it more likely that they will reach receptor sites. The **tetracyclics** block the action of an enzyme that removes serotonin from the synapses between neurons, thus raising serotonin levels.
- **MAOIs** require a diet free of amine-rich food, which would cause a cerebral haemorrage. Both MAOIs and the **tricyclics** are associated with cardiac arrhythmias and heart block, as well as other side-effects. The **tetracyclics** are also not free from serious side-effects.
- All the antidepressant drugs take time to exert their effects, which can be a problem if someone is contemplating suicide. MAOIs are generally less effective than tricyclics and are the least preferred antidepressant drug. **Prozac**, introduced in 1987, was thought to have fewer side-effects than the tricyclics and, despite being so much more expensive, has sold astonishingly well worldwide.
- Antidepressants are not useful when used on a long-term basis and may be no more effective than psychotherapy or cognitive therapy. Controversially, **urinary retention** has been used to treat **nocturnal enuresis** in children.
- **Lithium carbonate** (e.g. **Camoclit/Liskanum**), first used as an antimanic drug in 1970, is used with both bipolar disorder and unipolar depression as well as mania. Like other lithium salts, such as **lithium citrate** (e.g. **Litarex/Piradel**), lithium carbonate flattens out cycles of manic behaviour. It is extremely effective and works very quickly; in bipolar disorder, elimination of the manic phase prevents return of the depressed phase.
- Lithium salts increase the re-uptake of **norepinephrine** and **serotonin**. Side-effects include depressed reactions, hand tremors, dry mouth, weight gain, impaired memory and kidney poisoning. Blood is regularly checked for concentrations of lithium, which if too high can cause coma and death.
- The **anxiolytic drugs (depressants)** are also known as **antianxiety drugs/minor tranquillisers**. They replaced synthetic **barbiturates** (such as **phenobarbitol**) as treatment for anxiety in people who do not require hospitalisation. They are effective in reducing generalised anxiety disorders (especially when used short-term and in conjunction with psychological therapies), but not sudden panic attacks. They are also used to combat withdrawal symptoms associated with opiate and alcohol addiction.
- The **propanediol** group includes **meprobamate (Miltown)**. The **benzodiazepines** include **chlordiazepoxide (Librium)** and **diazepam (Valium)**. Anxiolytic drugs depress central nervous system activity, producing a decrease in the activity of the sympathetic branch of the autonomic nervous system. The benzodiazepines may mimic or block naturally occurring benzodiazepine in the brain.
- Side-effects include drowsiness, lethargy, tolerance, dependence, withdrawal and toxicity; they can kill, especially if combined with alcohol, suggesting that 'minor tranquillisers' is a misleading term. **Rebound anxiety** can occur when their use is stopped. Newer anxiolytics, such as **Busparin** and **Zopiclone**, produce their own worrying side-effects. **Valium** is the most prescribed of all drugs, and the use of anxiolytics generally with children is controversial.
- Following the discovery that inducing a hypoglycaemia coma could be used to treat certain psychoses, it was observed that schizophrenia and epilepsy rarely occur together and that psychotic individuals prone to epilepsy showed less severe symptoms following a fit. This led to von Meduna's proposal that schizophrenia could be cured by inducing major epileptic fits.
- Following the use of **Cardiazol** to induce the fit, Cerletti and Bini advocated passing an electric current across the temples instead. **Electroconvulsive therapy (ECT)** is still administered in essentially the same way. After a full

physical examination and fasting for three to four hours prior to treatment, an **atropine sulphate** injection is given, followed by an anxiolytic drug (e.g. **Valium**) if required. Then a short-acting anaesthetic is given, plus a muscle relaxant; oxygen is given before and after treatment and a mouth gag applied.

- In **bilateral ECT** electrodes are applied to each temple, while in **unilateral ECT,** two electrodes are attached to the temple/mastoid region of the non-dominant hemispere. A current of 200 milliamaps, at 110 volts, is passed from one electrode to another for about 0.5–4 seconds. A slight twitching of the eyelids, facial muscles and toes are the only visible signs of the fit.

- Typically, several treatments will be administered over a number of weeks. Having originally been used to treat schizophrenia, ECT is used today mainly to treat severe depression, bipolar disorder and certain obsessive-compulsive disorders. Its effects are immediate and substantial, but it is not known how it works.

- One theory sees its effectiveness lying in the **anterograde** and **retrograde amnesia** side-effect. But **unilateral** ECT is also effective, despite minimising memory disruption. An alternative theory claims that ECT acts as a 'punishment', but **sub-convulsive** shocks, while just as unpleasant ('punishing') as convulsive shocks, are ineffective.

- The most plausible account is the suggestion that ECT causes various **biochemical changes** more extensively than other somatic approaches. However, it is difficult to establish which of the many physiological changes produced by ECT are important, although norepinephrine and serotonin are the most likely neurotransmitters to be affected.

- ECT has been criticised on ethical grounds and was once outlawed in California. Despite its 'low-risk' status since the use of muscle relaxants and anaesthesia, it is claimed that brain damage can occur and that assessment of the suitability of ECT for individual patients is not routine, at least in the USA. Under the Mental Health Act, the patient must give consent or a second medical opinion must be sought.

- **Psychosurgery** refers to the **deliberate** attempt to alter a person's psychological functioning through the use of surgical procedures involving the brain. Modern techniques can be traced to 1935 and the abolition of violent outbursts in certain chimpanzees by removal of the pre-frontal areas of their pre-frontal lobes.

- This inspired Moniz and Lima to use surgical procedures with aggressive schizophrenics and other disturbed patients in which the neural connections between the pre-frontal lobes and the hypothalamus and thalamus were cut (**leucotomy/pre-frontal lobotomy**), thereby disconnecting thought from emotion. After using the 'apple corer' technique for a year, Moniz and Lima claimed a 70% 'cure' rate.

- Freeman and Watts developed the 'standard', widely used, pre-frontal lobotomy. Freeman also developed his own technique called the **transorbital** lobotomy.

- Psychosurgery was largely abandoned in the 1950s following the introduction of the psychotherapeutic drugs. The reasons for psychosurgery's beneficial effects are unclear and Moniz's success rates were exaggerated. There is a lack of consistency in the outcomes produced by psychosurgery, and the effects are irreversible. Many of the side-effects, cognitive, emotional and social, are serious and permanent. The Mental Health Act includes stringent provisions regarding patient consent to treatment.

- Despite its controversial nature, psychosurgery is still performed today, although only as a last resort. It is occasionally used for pain control in the terminally ill.

- Modern lobotomies involve insertion of radioactive rods into tiny holes in the forehead which destroy tissue in the frontal lobe tissue, or the destruction of small amounts of tissue in precise locations in the brain, as in the **tractotomy** (used to treat severe depression) and the **cingulotomy** (used to treat obsessive-compulsive disorder). Despite its apparent effectiveness, psychosurgery in general continues to have a negative image amongst both professionals and the public.

9

THERAPIES BASED ON THE PSYCHODYNAMIC MODEL

Introduction and overview

In Chapter 2, we noted that the psychodynamic model sees psychological disorders as stemming from the impulses of the id and/or the overdemanding superego. If the ego is too weak to cope with such conflicts, it defends itself by repressing them into the unconscious. However, the conflicts do not go away, but find expression through the behaviour of the person (and this is the disorder that is experienced).

For Freud and his followers, it is not enough to change a person's present behaviours. To bring about a permanent cure, the problems that are giving rise to the behaviours must also be changed. Because Freud believed that psychological problems had their origins in events that occurred earlier on in life, he did not see present problems as the *psychoanalyst's* domain on the grounds that people will already have received sympathy and advice from family and friends. If such support was going to help, argued Freud, it would have done so already and there would be no need for a psychoanalyst to be consulted.

According to Eisenberg (1995), there was a time 'when psychoanalysis was the only game in town'. However, whilst there are more than 400 psychotherapies (Holmes, 1996), the popularity of therapeutic approaches based on the psychodynamic model has declined over the years. For example, Smith (1982) reported that between 1961 and 1982, the proportion of therapists identifying themselves as psychoanalysts dropped from 41% to 14%. Nonetheless, therapies based on the psychodynamic model are, according to Laurance (1993), 'one of Britain's most recession-proof industries', and more than 100,000 people are currently receiving some form of therapy based on the psychodynamic model. Our aim in this chapter is to examine the processes involved in Freudian *psychoanalysis* and to briefly consider some of the therapeutic variations on it that have been devised.

Psychoanalysis

The purpose of *psychoanalysis* is to uncover the unconscious conflicts that are responsible for an individual's mental disorder. In Freud's words, psychoanalysis aims to 'drain the psychic abscess' and 'make the unconscious conscious'. The first step in psychoanalysis is thus to bring the conflicts into consciousness. Ultimately, this helps the individual (who is referred to as the *analysand*, that is, the person undergoing psychoanalysis) to gain *insight* or conscious awareness of the repressed conflict. The rationale is that once a person understands the reason for a behaviour, his or her ego can deal more effectively with it and resolve the conflict.

TECHNIQUES USED IN PSYCHOANALYSIS

Hypnosis

Ordinarily, the ego's defence mechanisms suppress conscious thoughts. As a result, the bringing of the unconscious into consciousness is not straightforward. Freud and his followers devised several methods to achieve this. Originally, Freud used *hypnosis*. The state produced by hypnosis seemed to allow his analysands to break through to things of which they were otherwise unaware. However, Freud abandoned hypnosis because afterwards some of his analysands denied the accuracy of what they had revealed during hypnosis, and others found the revelations to be premature and painful.

Dream interpretation

Another method involved the interpretation of the analysand's *dreams*. Freud believed that the content of dreams is determined by unconscious processes as well as by the 'residue' of the day. The unconscious impulses are expressed in dreams as a form of *wish fulfilment*. Freud believed dreams to be 'the royal road to the unconscious' and a rich source of information about hidden aspects of personality. For Freud, things that happened during the day evoked repressed childhood memories and desires. However, because some desires are too disturbing for an individual to face, even when asleep, these are expressed in symbolic form.

Freud used the term *manifest content* to describe the content of the dream as reported by the dreamer and *latent content* to refer to the dream's presumed hidden or symbolic content. The latent is transformed into the manifest by means of three distorting processes. *Displacement* refers to the role of symbols in dreams. In a dream, something (such as a king) appears in the manifest dream as a substitute for something else (perhaps the dreamer's father). *Condensation* is the process by which two or more images combine (or can be combined) to form a composite image which is invested with meaning and energy from both. For example, a king may represent the father, authority figures in general and/or wealthy and powerful people. *Concrete representation* refers to the expression of an abstract idea in a highly concrete way. The concrete image of a king, for example, could represent the abstract idea of authority, power and/or wealth.

Interpreting faulty actions and physiological cues

Other methods used by psychoanalysts include the *interpretation of faulty actions* (or *parapraxes*) and the *interpretation of physiological cues*. Freud saw what others have called *Freudian slips* as a route to the unconscious, because the errors and mistakes we make in everyday life represent unconscious thoughts finding their way into consciousness. Freud believed that repressed material could find expression through behaviour which is beyond conscious control, such as erroneous actions, forgetfulness and slips of the tongue and pen. The interpretation of physiological cues is used in conjunction with other methods. Blushing or pallor and changes in the timbre of a person's voice can all give a useful indication of the unconscious significance of ideas touched on in therapy.

Free association

The most widely used technique in psychoanalysis is *free association*. In this, the analysand lies on a comfortable couch so that the analyst cannot be seen (in order to prevent the analyst from distracting the analysand and interfering with concentration). The analysand is encouraged to say whatever comes to mind, no matter how trivial or frivolous it might seem. Freud called this the *basic rule of psychoanalysis*. He believed that, ordinarily, the ego acts as a *censor*, preventing threatening unconscious impulses from becoming conscious. By free-associating, the censor could be 'by-passed'.

Although free association is the most widely used technique, it takes several sessions before analysands 'open up'. Box 9.1 shows how analysands are typically introduced to the requirements of free association.

> **Box 9.1   Introducing an analysand to free association**
>
> In ordinary conversation, you usually try to keep a connecting thread running through your remarks, excluding any intrusive ideas or side issues so as not to wander too far from the point, and rightly so. But in this case, you must talk differently. As you talk, various thoughts will occur to you which you like to ignore because of certain criticisms and objections. You will be tempted to think, 'that is irrelevant or unimportant or nonsensical,' and to avoid saying it. Do not give in to such criticism. Report such thoughts in spite of your wish not to do so. Later, the reason for this injunction,

the only one you have to follow, will become clear. Report whatever goes through your mind. Pretend that you are a traveller, describing to someone beside you the changing views which you see outside the train window.

(taken from Ford & Urban, 1963)

During analysis, the analyst remains *'anonymous'* in that he or she expresses no emotion and does not evaluate the attitudes expressed by the analysand and does not reveal information about him or herself. The analyst needs to learn a great deal about the analysand, but the reverse is not true. This form of interaction ensures that the analysand does not form a close personal rela-

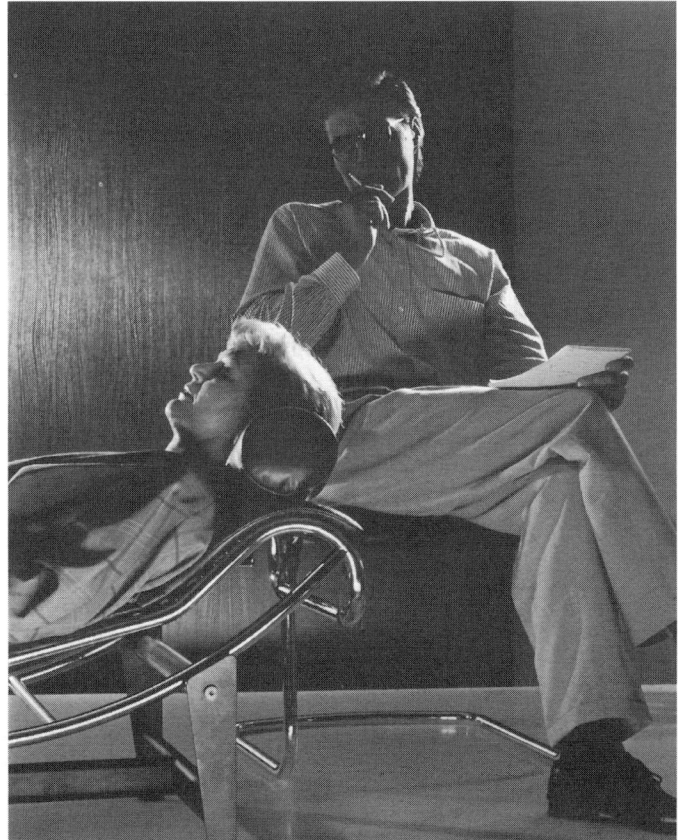

Figure 9.1 During psychoanalysis, the analysand usually reclines on a couch, while the analyst sits behind to avoid distracting the analysand. Although the analyst traditionally plays a passive role, occasionally he or she will offer an interpretation to help the analysand reach an insight

tionship with the analyst but views him or her purely as an 'anonymous and ambiguous stimulus'. Whilst the analysand free-associates, the analyst acts as a sort of *sounding board*, often repeating and clarifying what the analysand has said. Thus, the analysand tells a story and the analyst helps in its interpretation in terms of repressed conflicts and feelings.

The main form of communication between the analyst and analysand is in the form of the analyst's *interpretive comments*. In some cases, the analyst may need to draw attention to the analysand's *resistances*. Freud believed that what analysands do *not* say is as important as what they do say. During free association, analysands may express an unwillingness to discuss freely some aspects of their lives. For example, they may disrupt the session, change the subject whenever a particular topic comes up, joke about something as though it was unimportant, arrive late for a session or perhaps miss the session altogether. Freud's own description of resistance is shown in Box 9.2.

> **Box 9.2   Freud's description of resistance**
>
> The analysand endeavours in every sort of way to extricate himself from (the rule of free association). At one moment he declares that nothing occurs to him, at the next that so many things are crowding in on him that he cannot get hold of anything. Presently we observe with pained astonishment that he has given way first to one and then to another critical objection; he betrays this to us by the long pauses that he introduces into his remarks. He then admits that there is something he really cannot say – he would be ashamed to; and he allows this reason to prevail against his promise. Or he says that something has occurred to him, but it concerns another person and not himself and is therefore exempt from being reported. Or, what has now occurred to him is really too unimportant, too silly and senseless; I cannot possibly have meant him to enter into thoughts like that. So it goes on in innumerable variations.
>
> (Freud, 1894)

Freud saw resistance as natural because it is painful to bring unconscious conflicts into conscious awareness. It is also an indication that the analyst is getting close to the source of the problem and that the unconscious is struggling to avoid 'giving up its secrets'. Although resistance hinders therapy, it provides useful information for both analysand and analyst in the form of clues about the nature of the repressed conflict.

As therapy progresses, analysts may *privately deduce* the nature of what is behind the analysand's statements and may attempt to generate further associations. For example, the analysand may apologise for saying something he or she believes to be trivial. At this point the analyst may tell the analysand that what appears trivial may in fact relate to something important. By appropriately timing this interpretation, significant new associations may result. It is important to note that the analyst does not suggest what it is that is important in what the analysand has said. The goal is to help the analysand discover this him or herself.

As the therapy continues, the analyst may try to explain the analysand's behaviour in a way which is new to him or her. For example, analysands may be informed that their anger does not come from where they think it comes from, but rather that the reason for their anger is that the analyst reminds them of someone. Another approach is called *confrontation*. In this, the analyst tells the analysand exactly what is being revealed in the free associations. In *reconstruction*, the analyst provides hypothetical historical statements of hitherto buried fragments of the analysand's past. For example, the analysand may be told that the anger being expressed is a repetition of feelings experienced as a child and that the analyst stands for the objects of the anger.

Transference

Once interpretation is complete and the unconscious conflict has been brought into consciousness, the analyst and the analysand repeat and 'live out' the conflict. The associated feelings which have been repressed for so long then become available for 'manipulation' by the analyst. Freud called this process *transference* or *transference neurosis*. In this, the original source of the conflict is displaced on to the analyst who now becomes the object of the analysand's emotional responses. Depending on the nature of the conflict, the feelings may be positive and loving or negative and hostile. By exploring the transference relationship, psychoanalysis assumes that unconscious conflicts can be brought out into the open, understood and resolved. Thomas (1990) has this to say about transference:

'Over the years, it has become increasingly clear to practising analysts that the process of transference ... is one of the most important tools they have. It has become so central to theory and practice that many, though not all, analysts believe that making interpretations about transference is what distinguishes psychoanalysis from other forms of psychotherapy. When attention is focused on the transference and what is happening in the here and now, the historical reconstruction of childhood events and the search for the childhood origins of conflicts may take second place.'

Freud discovered that transference operated in both directions. For example, he found he could transfer his own feelings onto his own analysands. A male analysand, for example, could be viewed as a 'rebellious son'. Freud called the placing of clients into his own life *countertransference*. In order to avoid displacing their own repressed childhood feelings and wishes onto their patients, analysts must themselves undergo a *training analysis*. This permits them to understand their own conflicts and motivations so that they become *opaque* concerning their own behaviour and feelings in order to avoid countertransference with their analysands. Whether the avoidance of countertransference is absolutely necessary is, however, debatable. As Thomas (1990) has observed:

'In Freud's time, countertransference feelings were considered to be a failing on the part of the analyst. These feelings were to be controlled absolutely. Now, countertransference is considered an unavoidable outcome of the analytic process, irrespective of how well prepared the analyst is by analytic training and its years of required personal analysis ... most modern analysts are trained to observe their own countertransference feelings and to *use* these to increase their understanding of the analysand's transference and defences.'

The feelings associated with transference are the same for men and women. They include attachment to the analyst, overestimation of the analyst's qualities and jealousy against those connected with the analyst. In some cases, the process of transference takes on an exaggerated form which is known as *acting out* (or *abreaction* or *catharsis*), in which the analysand engages in the impulses that have been stirred up by the therapy. However, the analyst must convince the analysand that 'acting out' the conflict through transference does not constitute a true resolution of the problem. By itself, then, transference does not bring about the required change.

Quite clearly, transference is crucial because without it the analyst's interpretations would never even be considered by the analysand. Freud believed that psychoanalysis was ineffective with disorders like schizophrenia and depression because people with these disorders could not produce transference. Whilst Freud believed that the origins of schizophrenia and depression could be explained in psychodynamic terms, for some reason they reduce the capacity for transference, and since people experiencing those disorders are completely indifferent to the analyst, the analyst cannot influence them.

Achieving insight and working through

Once an analysand consciously understands the roots of the unconscious conflict, *insight* has been achieved, and the analysand must be helped to deal with the conflict in a mature and rational way. Whilst insight sometimes comes from the recovery of the memory of a repressed experience, the notion of psychoanalytic 'cures' resulting from the sudden recall of a single traumatic incident cannot be true, since psychodynamic therapists feel that troubles seldom stem from a single source. For Freud, analysands gained insight through a gradual increase in self-knowledge (a process of *re-education*). This gradual increase in self-knowledge, often involving repetitive consideration of all aspects of the conflict so as to allow the individual to face reality and deal with it effectively rather than deny and distort it, is called *working through*. Box 9.3 illustrates psychoanalytic interpretation.

Box 9.3   Psychoanalytic interpretation

The analysand is a middle-aged business man whose marriage has been marked by repeated strife and quarrels. His sexual potency has become tenuous. At times, he has suffered from premature ejaculation. At the beginning of one session, he began to complain about having to return to therapy after a long holiday weekend. He said, 'I'm not so sure I'm glad to be back in treatment, even though I didn't enjoy my visit to my parents. I feel I just have to be free.' He then continued with a description of his home visit, which he said had been depressing. His mother was bossy, aggressive, manipulative, as always. He feels sorry

for his father . . . 'She has a sharp tongue and a cruel mouth. Each time I see my father, he seems to be getting smaller; pretty soon he will disappear and there will be nothing left of him. She does that to people. I always feel that she is hovering over me, ready to swoop down on me. She has intimidated me, just like my wife. I was furious this morning. When I came to get my car, I found that someone had parked in such a way that it was hemmed in . . . I feel restrained by the city . . . I hate the feeling of being stuck in an office from nine until five.'

At this point, the analyst called to the analysand's attention the fact that throughout the material, in many different ways, the analysand was describing how he feared confinement, that he had a sense of being trapped. The analysand continued, 'You know I have the same feeling about starting an affair with Mrs X. She wants me to and I guess I want to also. Getting involved is easy. It's getting uninvolved that concerns me . . .'

In this material, the analysand associates being trapped in a confined space with being trapped in the analysis and with being trapped in an affair with a woman. At this point, the analyst is able to tell the analysand that his fear of being trapped in an enclosed space is the conscious derivative of an unconscious fantasy in which he imagines that if he enters the woman's body with his penis, it will get stuck; he will not be able to extricate it; he may lose it. The analyst goes on to say that one important goal of therapy would consist of making the analysand aware of childhood sexual strivings towards his mother, of a wish to have relations with her, and of a concomitant fear growing out of the threatening nature of her personality, and that, like a hawk, she would swoop down upon him and devour him. These interpretations would give him insight into the causes of his impotence and his stormy relations with women, particularly his wife.

(taken from Arlow, 1984)

In order to break down the complex ego defences which have been developed to cope with the conflict, and to bring about a lasting change in personality, the analysand and analyst need to work through every implication of the problem with complete understanding on the analysand's part. This is necessary to prevent the conflict from being repressed into the unconscious again. As a result the individual is strengthened and therefore becomes capable of handling different aspects of the conflict without having to resort to *defence mechanisms* (see Chapter 2, page 13). The ultimate goal of psychoanalysis, then, is a deep-seated modification of personality so as to allow people to deal with problems on a realistic basis.

Classical psychoanalysis is both intense, time-consuming and expensive (£25 to £35 per 50-minute session), involving perhaps three to six sessions per week over the course of several years. Moreover, during its course, an analysand may be vulnerable and helpless for long periods. This occurs when the analysand's old defences and resistances are broken down, but the ego is still not strong enough to cope adequately with the conflict. Although some psychoanalysts still rigidly adhere to Freud's protracted techniques, Holmes (1996) has argued that there has been a shift in the theoretical basis of psychoanalysis and that 'the Aunt Sally of classical Freudianism is simply not relevant to present-day psychoanalysis'. For Garfield & Bergin (1994):

'The cornerstones of early Freudian metapsychology were repression, the unconscious, and infantile sexuality. Contemporary psychoanalysis views all three in a different light'.

Analysts who are more flexible in fitting the therapeutic sessions to a person's needs are known as *psychoanalytically oriented psychotherapists* and we will briefly examine below some of the approaches that are used.

Psychoanalytically oriented psychotherapies

There are a number of psychoanalytically oriented psychotherapies, most of which involve briefer treatment and use face-to-face interaction rather than having the analysand lying on the couch facing away from the analyst (these are sometimes called *focal psychotherapies*). Although they also place emphasis on restructuring the entire personality, more attention is paid to the analysand's current life and relationships rather than early childhood conflicts. Freudian principles are still followed (the aim of therapy is still to gain insight and free expression is emphasised), but these therapies make it possible to treat those who cannot afford protracted

therapy or whose time is limited by other commitments (Cohn, 1994).

Perhaps the most influential of those who have revised Freudian therapeutic approaches are the *ego psychologists* or *ego analysts*. Rather than emphasising the role of the id, these therapists focus on the ego and the way in which it acts as the *executive* of personality (see Chapter 2). As well as being shaped by inner conflicts, contemporary analysts believe that personality may be shaped by the external environment and emphasise this in their therapeutic approaches. Box 9.4 briefly describes some of the influential contemporary analysts and their approaches.

Box 9.4   Contemporary therapeutic approaches derived from psychoanalysis

Ego analysts are sometimes referred to as the *second generation* of psychoanalysts. They believe that Freud over-emphasised the influence of sexual and aggressive impulses and underestimated the ego's importance. Erik Erikson, for example, spoke to clients directly about their values and concerns and encouraged them to consciously fashion particular behaviours and characteristics. For Erikson, the cognitive processes of the ego are constructive, creative and productive. This view is somewhat different to Freud's therapeutic approach of establishing conditions in which patients could 'shore up' the ego's position.

Unlike Freud, who saw analysands as perpetual victims of their past who could not completely overcome their childhood conflicts, Karen Horney saw them as capable of overcoming abuse and deprivation through self-understanding and productive adult relationships. Freud's emphasis on unconscious forces and conflicts was disputed by Anna Freud (Freud's daughter). She believed a better approach was to concentrate on the ways in which the ego perceives the world.

Melanie Klein and Margaret Mahler have stressed the child's separation from the mother and interpersonal relationships as being important in psychological growth. *Object-relations theorists* believe that some people have difficulty in telling where the influences of significant others end and their 'real selves' begin. Mahler's approach to therapy is to help people separate their own ideas and feelings from those of others so they can develop as true individuals.

As we noted earlier, one of the major distinctions between classical psychoanalysis and psychoanalytically oriented psychotherapies is in terms of the *time* that is spent in therapy. According to Roth & Fonagy (1996), there is a high 'relapse rate' in brief therapies of all types when those who have undergone treatment are followed up for long periods of time. The ultimate goal of therapy must be good outcome sustained at follow-up, but as Holmes (1996) has remarked:

'Modern health services seem always to be in a hurry; time is money; but the cost of major cardiac surgery is still far greater than, say, the 100–200 hours of psychotherapy that are needed to make a significant impact on borderline personality disorder. An emphasis on sufficient *time* is a central psychoanalytic dimension that should be preserved at all costs'.

Psychodynamic approaches to group therapy

According to Roberts (1995), the power of the group process for change and healing has been discovered, forgotten and rediscovered on numerous occasions in Britain. One of the earliest uses of *group psychotherapy* was at the Northfield Military Hospital in an attempt to treat neurotic and psychotic soldiers (see, for example, Bion, 1961). Since the pioneering work at Northfield, a variety of group approaches to psychodynamically-oriented therapy has been devised (reviewed by Brown & Zinkin, 1994). Two psychodynamic approaches to group therapy are *psychodrama* and *transactional analysis*.

PSYCHODRAMA

The originator of *psychodrama* was J. L. Moreno, a Viennese psychiatrist who believed that most human problems arise from the need to maintain social roles which may conflict with each other and a person's essential self. For Moreno, the conflict that this produces is the source of a person's anxiety. In the therapy, participants and other group members act out their emotional conflicts. The individual dramatising his or her conflicts is the *protagonist* and the protagonist chooses other members of the group to represent the key figures in the conflict. These *auxiliary egos* are briefed by being given a full description of the role they will play.

Once the protagonist has 'set the scene' by describing it in words and with the aid of very simple props, the interpersonal events are recreated by role play. For example, a male who is terrified of women may be literally 'put on stage' with a female group member who will play his mother. The two are then required to act out a childhood scene with, if necessary, other members of the group assuming the role of the father, brothers, sisters and so on. The aim is not for dramatic excellence but, in the example we have used, to reveal the sources of the individual's fear of women (Kipper, 1992).

This basic pattern can be varied in a number of ways. In *role reversal*, the 'actors' switch roles, whilst in *doubling*, the therapist or group leader also acts out the protagonist's role and suggests feelings, motives and so on that might be operating within the protagonist, but which he or she has not yet identified. *Mirroring* involves group members minimising or exaggerating the protagonist's behaviour in order to provide feedback.

Irrespective of the variation, the goal of psychodrama is to reveal to the protagonist why he or she is behaving in a particular way. For Moreno (1946), psychodrama is useful because (a) it helps to prevent destructive and irrational acting out in everyday life, (b) it enables feelings which cannot be adequately described or explained to be expressed more fully, and (c) it encourages individuals to reveal the deepest roots of their problems.

TRANSACTIONAL ANALYSIS

This approach to group therapy was originated by Berne (1964). According to Berne, personality is comprised of three *ego states*, and our behaviour at any given time is determined by one of the three states. The *parent* state is that part of personality which stands for the cautions and prohibitions upheld by society and which we learned from our own parents. The *child* state is the opposite, and is demanding, dependent and impulsive, seeking gratification of all its wishes *now*. The *adult* state is the mature, rational aspect of personality, which is flexible and adapts to new situations as they arise. It is important to note that Berne did not mean to imply that these three states equate with the id (child), ego (adult) and superego (parent), since the id, ego and superego are, to varying degrees, unconscious.

For Berne, we are capable of being fully conscious of the child and parent ego states.

Like Freud, Berne believed that psychological disorders occur when one of the ego states comes to dominate the personality. Berne felt that many interactions between people are *complementary*, that is, aspects of their personalities are matched. For example, the interaction between the adult states of two people produces a rational and mature interaction, as when one person says, 'These data don't make any sense' and the other replies, 'I agree. Let's run them through the computer again'. When the aspects of personality operating do not match, the interactions are *crossed*, and this is when problems arise (Baron, 1989). For example, a passenger in a car operating in the child state, might say, 'Come on, let's see if we can get 100 mph out of this car'. The driver, operating in the adult state, might reply, 'No way. If the police are about, we'll be in big trouble'.

In his book *Games People Play*, Berne (1964) argued that *crossed interactions* often take the form of 'games', that is, interactions which leave both people feeling upset or angry and prevent spontaneous and appropriate behaviour. In one of these, which Berne (1976) called *uproar*, one person baits another. The other responds in kind and the exchange escalates until one person storms off in anger. Transactional analysis concentrates on people's tendencies to manipulate others in destructive and non-productive ways. However, unlike psychoanalysis, transactional analysis focuses on the *present* rather than the past. Through role play, the ego states are identified as they are used in various personal transactions.

This *structural analysis* enables people to understand their behaviour and change it in a way which will give them greater control over their life. Although this is usually initially conducted on an individual basis, the person later participates in group *transactions* (or transactional analysis 'proper'). This involves experimenting by enacting more appropriate ego states and observing the effects of these on the self and others. By analysing such games, basic conflicts may come to the surface, and these can then be discussed openly, the aim being to show that whilst people's coping patterns may feel natural, they are actually destructive and there are better ways of relating to others.

Therapies based on the psychodynamic model: some issues

At least some people who have undergone psychoanalysis claim that it has helped them achieve insight into their problems and has provided long-term relief from the repressed feelings that were interfering with healthy functioning. However, although both Freud's theories and his therapeutic approach have been influential, they have also been the subject of much criticism, and there have been numerous explanations of 'why Freud was wrong' (e.g. Webster, 1995) and several calls to 'bury Freud' (e.g. Tallis, 1996). Perhaps the major problem with Freud's work is that it is difficult to study scientifically, since concepts like transference, insight, unconscious conflicts and repression are either vague or difficult to measure.

Evaluating the effectiveness of any therapeutic approach is, as we shall see in Chapter 13, extremely difficult. With psychoanalysis, however, the problems are particularly acute. Much of the evidence in favour of psychoanalysis derives from carefully selected case studies which may be biased. In cases where psychoanalysis fails to produce significant changes, analysts can blame the analysand. As Carlson (1988) has noted, if an analysand accepts an insight into a behaviour but does not change that behaviour, the insight is said to be merely *intellectual*.

This 'escape clause' makes the argument for the importance of insight completely circular and therefore illogical: if the analysand improves, the improvement is due to insight, but if the analysand's behaviour remains unchanged, then real insight did not occur. Carlson likens this to the logic of wearing a charm in the belief that it will cure an illness. If the illness is cured, then the charm works. If the illness is not cured, then the individual does not believe sufficiently in its power. We should also note that psychoanalysis is a *closed system*. A critic who raises questions about the validity of psychoanalysis is described as suffering from *resistance*, since the critic cannot recognise the 'obvious' value of the therapy.

Conclusions

In this chapter, we have examined therapies which are based on the psychodynamic model of abnormality. Although less popular than they once were, such therapies are still used today. However, there are a number of important issues surrounding their use, and at least some professionals believe them to be of little help in the treatment of mental disorders.

SUMMARY

- According to the psychodynamic model, if the ego is too weak to cope with conflicts with the id or superego, it defends itself by repressing them into the unconscious. But these conflicts express themselves through behaviour, i.e. the disorder. To achieve a permanent cure, it is not enough to change the present behaviours; the underlying problems must also be changed.

- According to Freud, if sympathy and advice from family and friends were going to help, there would be no need to consult a psychotherapist; the **psychoanalyst's** domain is not present problems but events that have occurred earlier in life.

- Although therapeutic approaches based on the psychodynamic model are still used, their popularity has declined over the past few decades.

- The purpose of **psychoanalysis** is to uncover the unconscious conflicts responsible for an individual's (**analysand's**) mental disorder and make them conscious, i.e. to provide the analysand with **insight** into the repressed conflicts in order to enable the ego to deal more effectively with them and to resolve them.

- Originally, Freud used **hypnosis** to break down the analysand's defences, but this was abandoned because some of his analysands denied the accuracy of their revelations or found them to be premature and painful.

- According to Freud's theory of **dream interpretation**, the **manifest content** of dreams is determined by unconscious processes as well as the 'residues' of the day, which evoke repressed childhood memories/desires (the **latent content**), some of which are too disturbing for an individual to face even while asleep; consequently, they are expressed symbolically as a form of 'wish fulfilment'.

- The latent content is transformed into the manifest content through **displacement, condensation** and **concrete representation**.

- Psychoanalysts also interpret faulty actions (**parapraxes** or **Freudian slips**), such as forgetfulness and slips of the tongue/pen, and **physiological cues**, such as blushing and changes in the voice. These represent ways in which repressed material finds its way into consciousness.

- **Free association** is the most widely used technique in psychoanalysis. The **basic rule** of psychoanalysis is that the analysand is encouraged to say whatever comes to mind, no matter how trivial/silly it might seem. By free-associating, the ego's normal role as **censor** of threatening unconscious impulses can be by-passed. Several sessions are needed before analysands 'open up'.

- The analyst remains **anonymous** and ambiguous, ensuring that the analysand does not form a close personal relationship with the analyst, who acts as a **sounding board**. The main form of communication are the analyst's **interpretive comments**, which will sometimes involve drawing attention to the analysand's **resistances**; these can range from changing the subject to arriving late for a session or missing the session altogether.

- Resistance is natural since it is painful to bring unconscious conflicts into conscious awareness; it also indicates that the analyst is getting close to the unconscious source of the problem and provides useful information as to the nature of the repressed conflict.

- As therapy progresses, the analyst may **privately deduce** the nature of what is behind the analysand's statements and may try to elicit further associations, thereby helping the analysand to discover for him/herself the importance of what underlies these statements. Other techniques include **confrontation** and **reconstruction**.

- Once the unconscious conflict has been brought into consciousness, the associated feelings become available for 'manipulation' by the analyst through the process of **transference/transference neurosis**. The feelings which are displaced onto the analyst may be positive/loving or negative/hostile. This represents another means of exploring and resolving unconscious conflicts.

- According to Thomas, many analysts believe that making interpretations about transference is what distinguishes psychoanalysis from other forms of psychotherapy. Freud also identified **counter-transference** which could and should be prevented by analysts undergoing a **training analysis**. However, while Freud saw counter-transference as a failing, most modern analysts take a much more positive view of its value for the analysand.
- Transference may sometimes take the form of **acting out/abreaction/catharsis**. As important as transference is, it does not on its own produce the required change; Freud believed that people with schizophrenia and depression will not benefit from psychoanalysis, because they are indifferent towards the analyst and so are unable to produce transference.
- While **insight** sometimes comes from the recovery of the memory of a repressed experience, this does not constitute a psychoanalytic 'cure', since psychodynamic theorists believe that problems rarely stem from a single source. For Freud, insight is achieved through a gradual process of 're-education' and increase in self-knowledge, involving **working through**.
- The ultimate goal of psychoanalysis is a deep-seated modification of personality so as to allow people to deal with problems in a realistic way and without having to resort to **defence mechanisms**.
- Classical psychoanalysis is not only expensive, but people will be vulnerable and helpless for long periods during the course of therapy, which can last several years, as their old defences are broken down and while their ego is not yet strong enough to cope with the conflict.
- Many contemporary psychoanalysts no longer see Freud's theory regarding the role of repression, the unconscious and infantile sexuality as central to psychoanalysis. This more flexible approach involves fitting therapy to a person's needs and is known as **psychoanalytically oriented psychotherapy**.
- Most psychoanalytically oriented psychotherapies (or **focal psychotherapies**) involve briefer treatment and use face-to-face interaction rather than the analysand lying on the couch with the analyst out of sight. Although Freudian principles are still followed, more attention is paid to the analysand's current life and relationships.

- Perhaps the most influential revisions of Freudian approaches have been made by the **ego psychologists/ego analysts** (the 'second generation' of psychoanalysts), who focus on the ego rather than the id. Personality is seen as being shaped as much by the external environment as by inner conflicts.
- **Erikson** spoke directly to clients about their values and concerns and encouraged them to consciously develop particular behaviours and characteristics; the ego is constructive and creative. For **Horney**, analysands are capable of overcoming childhood abuse/deprivation through self-understanding and productive adult relationships. **Anna Freud** criticised her father's emphasis on unconscious forces/conflicts. **Klein** and **Mahler** represent the **object-relations school of thought**, for whom therapy is aimed at helping people to separate their own ideas/feelings from those of others.
- Based on long-term follow-up, there is evidence of a high 'relapse rate' in all types of brief therapies. Such therapies may represent a false economy, since the cost of psychotherapy is still low compared with medical treatments such as major cardiac surgery.
- Several psychodynamic approaches to **group psychotherapy** have been devised. In Moreno's **psychodrama**, the individual acting out his/her emotional conflicts (the **protagonist**) chooses other group members to represent the key figures in the conflict (**anxiliary egos**). Following some preparation, the interpersonal events are recreated by role play, which may involve **role reversal**, **doubling**, and **mirroring**. Psychodrama helps to prevent destructive acting out in everyday life, to allow the full expression of feelings which cannot be adequately described/explained, and encourages individuals to reveal the deepest roots of their problems.
- Berne's **transactional analysis** is based on the view of personality as comprising three conscious **ego states**, namely the **parent**, **child** and **adult**. Psychological disorders arise when one ego state comes to dominate the personality.
- Many interactions between people are **complementary**, but when they are **crossed**, problems arise. Crossed interactions often take the form of 'games' (e.g. **uproar**). Transactional analysis concentrates on people's tendencies to manipulate others in destructive ways in the **present**. Role play is used to identify the ego states. Although this **structural analysis** is usually first conducted individually, the person later participates in group **transactions** (transactional analysis 'proper'), in

which games are analysed, aimed at showing that 'natural' coping patterns are actually destructive and that there are better ways of relating to others.

- Although Freud's theories and approach to therapy have been influential, they have also received much criticism, especially in relation to their unscientific nature. Trying to assess the effectiveness of psychoanalysis is particularly difficult and much of the supporting evidence comes from case studies which may be biased.
- Psychoanalysts also have 'escape clauses' if therapy fails to produce significant changes, and psychoanalysis is a **closed system** which enables criticisms to be explained away by using the very concepts that are being criticised.

10

THERAPIES BASED ON THE BEHAVIOURAL MODEL

Introduction and overview

As we saw in the previous chapter, the attempt by psychodynamic therapies to produce insight into the cause of a maladaptive behaviour *sometimes* results in a behaviour ceasing and being replaced by an adaptive behaviour. However, we also noted that insight often does *not* result in behavioural change. Also, the majority of psychodynamically-oriented therapies insist on using conflicts dating from *childhood* as a way of explaining present behaviours. For supporters of the behavioural model, it is much better to focus on the behaviour giving rise to a problem rather than the historical reasons for its development.

Therapies based on the behavioural model therefore attempt to change behaviour by whatever means are most effective. The term *behaviour therapy* has been used to describe any therapeutic approach deriving from the behavioural model. However, this does not allow us to determine whether the principles of classical or operant conditoning are being used as the treatment method. Walker (1984) has suggested that the term *behaviour therapy* be confined to those therapies which are based on *classical conditioning*. Those techniques based on *operant conditioning* are more appropriately described as *behaviour modification techniques*. Our aim in this chapter is to consider the application of thera-

pies based on the behavioural model to the treatment of mental disorders.

Therapies based on classical conditioning: behaviour therapy

As we saw in Chapter 2 (see page 15), Watson and Rayner (1920) showed that by repeatedly pairing a neutral stimulus with an unpleasant one, a fear response to the neutral stimulus could be classically conditioned. If maladaptive behaviours can be learned they can presumably be unlearned, since the same principles that govern the learning of adaptive behaviours apply to maladaptive ones. Therapies based on classical conditioning concentrate on stimuli that elicit new responses which are contrary to the old, maladaptive ones. In this section, we will consider three of these therapeutic approaches, which are designed to treat phobic behaviour. These are *implosion therapy*, *flooding* and *systematic desensitisation*. We will then consider two therapies which are designed to treat other disorders but which exert their effect by *creating* a phobia.

IMPLOSION THERAPY AND FLOODING

Implosion therapy and flooding both work on the principle that if the stimulus that evokes a fear response is repeatedly presented without the unpleasant experience that accompanies it, its power to elicit the fear response will be lost.

Implosion therapy

In implosion therapy, the therapist repeatedly exposes the person to vivid mental images of the feared stimulus in the safety of the therapeutic setting. This is achieved by the therapist getting the person to imagine the most terrifying form of contact with the feared object. The therapist uses *stimulus augmentation*, that is, vivid verbal descriptions of the feared stimulus, to supplement the person's imagery. After repeated trials, the stimulus eventually loses its anxiety-producing power and the anxiety extinguishes (or *implodes*) because no harm comes to the individual in the safe setting of the therapist's room.

Flooding

In flooding, the individual is forced to *confront* the object or situation that gives rise to the fear response. For example, a person who has a fear of heights might be taken to a tall building and physically prevented from leaving. By preventing avoidance of or escape from the feared object or situation, the fear response is eventually extinguished. In a dramatic illustration of the effectiveness of flooding, Wolpe (1973) describes a case in which an adolescent girl with a fear of cars was forced into the back of a car. The girl was then driven around continuously for four hours. Initially, her fear reached hysterical heights. Eventually, it receded and by the end of the journey had disappeared completely.

In a review of the literature, Emmelkamp and Wessels (1975) concluded that both implosion therapy and flooding are effective with certain types of phobia. However, for some people, both implosion therapy and flooding lead to increased anxiety, and the procedure is too traumatic. As a result, both therapies are used with considerable caution. One new approach which partially overcomes this problem is described in Box 10.1.

Box 10.1   Using virtual reality to treat phobias

Recently, a team of psychologists from Atlanta, Georgia, has created computer-generated virtual environments that have been tested on people suffering from a variety of phobias. The hardware consists of a head-mounted display and a sensor that tracks the movements of the head and right hand so that the user can interact with objects in the virtual environment. The equipment is integrated with a square platform surrounded by a railing. This aids exposure by giving the user something to hold on to and an edge to feel (see Figure 10.1 overleaf).

Software creates a number of virtual environments to confront different phobias. The ones for acrophobia (or fear of heights) include:

- three footbridges hovering 7, 50 and 80 metres above water
- four outdoor balconies with railings at various heights in a building ranging up to 20 floors high
- a glass elevator simulating the one at Atlanta's Marriott Hotel which rises 49 floors.

According to Barbara Rothbaum, leader of the research team, people using virtual reality 'had the same sensations and anxiety as they did *in vivo*. They were sweating, weak at the knees and had butterflies in the stomach. When the elevator went up and down, they really felt it. We are trying to help people confront what they are scared of.'

Rothbaum sees virtual reality as holding the key to the treatment of phobia because it is easier to arrange and less traumatic than real exposure to phobia-causing situations. Compared with a control group of acrophobics, Rothbaum and her team have reported a 100% improvement in 12 participants after two months of 'treatment'.

(based on Dobson, 1996)

SYSTEMATIC DESENSITISATION

As we have seen, both implosion therapy and flooding use extinction to alter behaviour. However, neither of them trains people to substitute the maladaptive behaviour (such as fear) with an adaptive and *desirable* response. In an early study, Jones (1924) showed that fear responses could be eliminated if children were given candy and other incentives in the presence of the feared object. Jones' method involved *gradually* introducing the feared object, bringing it closer and closer to the children whilst at the same time giving them candy, until they elicited no anxiety to its presence. For many

Figure 10.1 Head-mounted display, similar to that used by Barbara Rothbaum in the treatment of people with phobias. The computer program generates a number of virtual environments appropriate to different phobias. While inducing bodily responses identical to those that are experienced *in vivo*, virtual reality is easier to set up and is less traumatic (see Box 10.1)

Box 10.2	An anxiety hierarchy generated by a person with thanatophobia (where 1 = no anxiety and 100 = extreme anxiety)
Ratings	*Items*
5	Seeing an ambulance
10	Seeing a hospital
20	Being inside a hospital
25	Reading an obituary notice of an old person
30–40	Passing a funeral home
40–55	Seeing a funeral
55–65	Driving past a cemetery
70	Reading the obituary of a young person who died of a heart attack
80	Seeing a burial assemblage from a distance
90	Being at a funeral
100	Seeing a dead man in a coffin

(based on Wolpe & Wolpe, 1981)

years, Jones' work went unrecognised. In the 1950s, however, Wolpe (1958) popularised and refined it under the name *systematic desensitisation.*

The therapy requires that an individual initially constructs an *anxiety hierarchy,* that is, a series of scenes or events that are rated from lowest to highest in terms of the amount of anxiety they elicit. For example, on a scale of one (little anxiety) to ten (extreme anxiety), a person with a phobia of spiders might rate seeing a picture of a spider as 1 but rate being in a room with a spider as 10. Box 10.2 shows an anxiety hierarchy constructed by a person with thanatophobia (that is, a fear of death).

Once the hierarchy has been constructed, *relaxation training* is given. This will be the adaptive substitute response and is the one that most therapists use. The training aims to achieve complete relaxation, the essential task being to respond quickly to suggestions to feel relaxed and peaceful. After relaxation training, the person is asked to imagine as vividly as possible the scene at the bottom of the hierarchy that was constructed. Simultaneously, the person is told to remain calm and relaxed.

Wolpe was very much influenced by the concept of *reciprocal inhibition* which, as applied to phobias, maintains that it is impossible to experience two incompatible emotional states (such as anxiety and relaxation) at the same time. If the individual finds that anxiety is *increasing,* the image is terminated, and the therapist attempts to regain the sense of relaxation. When thinking about the scene at the bottom of the hierarchy no longer elicits anxiety, the next scene in the hierarchy is presented. *Systematically,* the hierarchy is worked through until the individual can imagine any of the scenes without experiencing discomfort. When this happens, the person is *desensitised.* Once the hierarchy has been worked through, the person is required to confront the anxiety-producing stimulus in the real world.

One of the problems with systematic desensitisation is its dependence on a person's ability to conjure up vivid images of encounters with a phobic object or situation. One way of overcoming this is to use photographs or slides displaying the feared object or situation. Another approach involves live or *in vivo* encounters. For example, a person who is afraid of spiders may be desensitised by gradually approaching spiders (this is, of course, the method used by Jones that we described at the beginning of this section!). According to Wilson & O'Leary (1978), *in vivo* desensitisation is almost always more effective and longer lasting than other desensitisation techniques.

The evidence suggests that systematic desensitisation, implosion therapy and flooding are all effective in dealing with specific fears and anxieties. As compared with one another, Marks (1987) has reported that flooding is more effective than systematic desensitisation, whilst Gelder *et al.* (1989) have shown that implosion therapy and systematic desensitisation do not differ in their effectiveness. In another study, Emmelkamp & Wessels (1975) have presented evidence indicating that flooding is more effective than implosion therapy.

The fact that flooding appears to be the superior of the three therapies suggests that *in vivo* exposure to the source of anxiety is crucial. The fact that implosion therapy and systematic desensitisation do not seem to differ in their effectiveness perhaps indicates that systematically working through a hierarchy is not necessary. Indeed, research has shown that presenting the hierarchy in reverse order (from most to least frightening), randomly or in the standard way (from least to most frightening), does not influence systematic desensitisation's effectiveness (Marks, 1987).

AVERSION THERAPY

The therapies we have just considered are all appropriate for people who want to remove an unpleasant feeling such as fear, which may occur in specific situations. Aversion therapy, by contrast, is used with people who want to *extinguish* the *pleasant* feelings that are associated with socially undesirable behaviours, such as excessive drinking or smoking. Unlike systematic desensitisation, which tries to substitute a pleasurable response for an aversive one, aversion therapy reverses this process and pairs an unpleasant event with a desired but socially undesirable behaviour. If this unpleasant event and desired behaviour are repeatedly paired, the desired behaviour will eventually come to elicit negative responses.

Perhaps the most well-known application of aversion therapy has been in the treatment of alcohol abuse. In one method, the problem drinker is given a drug that will induce nausea and vomiting, but *only* when combined with alcohol. When a drink is taken, the alcohol interacts with the drug to produce nausea and sickness. It does not take many pairings before alcohol begins to elicit an aversive fear (of becoming nauseous) response. In another method, the problem drinker is given a warm saline solution containing a drug which does induce nausea and vomiting without alcohol. Immediately before vomiting begins, an alcoholic beverage is given, and the person is required to smell, taste and swill it around the mouth before swallowing it. The aversive fear response may generalise to other alcohol-related stimuli, such as pictures of bottles containing alcohol. However, to avoid *generalisation* to all drinks, the individual may be required to take a soft drink in between the aversive conditioning trials.

Aversion therapy has been used with some success in the treatment of alcohol abuse and other behaviours (most notably cigarette smoking, overeating and children's self-injurious behaviour). The therapy has also found its way into popular culture. In Anthony Burgess's novel *A Clockwork Orange*, the anti-social 'hero', Alex, gains great enjoyment from rape and violent behaviour. When caught, he is given the choice between prison and therapy and elects to take the latter. He is then given a nausea-inducing drug and required to watch films of violence and rape. After his release, he feels nauseous whenever he contemplates violence and rape. However, because the therapy took place with the music of Beethoven playing, Alex acquires an aversion towards Beethoven as well!

One of most controversial (and non-fictional) applications of aversion therapy has been with sexual 'aberrations' such as homosexuality (e.g. Adams *et al.*, 1981). Male homosexuals, for example, are shown slides of nude males which are followed by painful but safe electric shocks. The conditioned response to the slides is intended to generalise to homosexual fantasies and activities beyond the therapeutic setting. In later sessions, the individual may be shown slides of nude women and an electric shock terminated when a sexual response occurs.

Figure 10.2   Photo of Alex (Malcolm McDowell) from Stanley Kubrick's very controversial film *Clockwork Orange* **(Warner Films). In the film, Alex, having been convicted of several violent crimes, opts to receive aversion therapy in preference to prison. Although he is successfully conditioned to feel nauseous whenever he contemplates violence or rape, he also acquires (inadvertently) an aversion towards Beethoven, previously his favourite composer**

Whatever it is used for, aversion therapy is not pleasant and is not an appropriate therapy to use unless an individual has *consented* to it (as might be the case with an individual whose continuation of an undesired behaviour, such as drinking, is more aversive than the treatment itself) or if all other approaches to treatment have failed. As we have noted, there is some evidence to suggest that the therapy is effective. However, those undergoing therapy often find ways to continue with their problem behaviour. As one alcoholic, the former footballer George Best, has written:

> 'When I was supposed to be swallowing those tablets that make you allergic to alcohol, I was sometimes hiding them behind my teeth and getting rid of them later. And even when I had the (emetic) implants, I was saying to myself: "when the effects of these pellets wears off, I'll have a good drink."'

Quite clearly, people have the cognitive abilities to discriminate between the situation in which aversive conditions occur and situations in the real world. In some cases, then, cognitive factors will 'swamp' the conditioning process, and this is one of the reasons why aversion therapy is not always effective.

We should note that aversion therapy does not involve classical conditioning alone and actually combines classical and operant conditioning. Once the classically conditioned fear has been established, the person is inclined to avoid future contact with the problem stimulus (which is an *operant* response) in order to alleviate fear of it (which is *negatively reinforcing*). We should also note that critics see aversion therapy as being inappropriate unless the individual learns an *adaptive* response. For this reason, most behaviour therapists try to *shape* (see page 112) new and adaptive behaviours at the same time as extinguishing existing and maladaptive ones.

COVERT SENSITISATION

Silverstein (1972) has argued that aversion therapy is unethical and has the potential for misuse and abuse. As a response to this criticism, some therapists use covert sensitisation as an alternative and 'milder' form of aversion therapy. The therapy is a mixture of aversion therapy and systematic desensitisation. Essentially, people are trained to punish themselves through using their *imaginations* (hence the term *covert*). *Sensitisation* is achieved by associating the undesirable behaviour with an exceedingly disagreeable consequence.

A heavy drinker, for example, might be asked to imagine being violently sick all over him- or herself on entering a bar, and feeling better only after leaving the bar and breathing fresh air. The individual is also instructed to rehearse an alternative 'relief' scene in which the decision not to drink, say, is accompanied by pleasurable sensations. According to some researchers (e.g. Cautela, 1967), covert sensitisation can be helpful in controlling overeating and cigarette smoking as well as excessive drinking.

Therapies based on operant conditioning: behaviour modification techniques

Behaviours that are under voluntary control are strongly influenced by their consequences. As we noted in Chapter 2 (see page 15), actions which yield positive outcomes tend to be repeated, whereas those which yield negative outcomes tend to be suppressed. Therapies based on classical conditioning usually involve *emotional responses* (such as anxiety), although *observable behaviours* (such as gradually approaching an object that elicits anxiety) are also influenced. Therapies based on operant conditioning are aimed *directly* at observable behaviours.

Several forms of therapy based on operant conditioning exist, all of which involve three main steps. The first is to identify the undesirable or maladaptive behaviour. Once this has been achieved, the next step is to identify the reinforcers that maintain such behaviour. The final step is to restructure the environment so that the maladaptive behaviour is no longer reinforced. One way to eliminate undesirable behaviours is to *remove* the reinforcers that maintain an undesirable behaviour, the idea being that removal of reinforcers will *extinguish* the behaviour they reinforce. Another way is to use aversive stimuli to *punish* voluntary maladaptive behaviours. As well as eliminating undesirable behaviours, operant conditioning can be used to increase desirable behaviours. This can be achieved by providing *positive reinforcement* when a behaviour is performed and making the reinforcement *contingent* on the behaviour being manifested voluntarily.

THERAPIES BASED ON EXTINCTION

As we noted above, people tend to engage in behaviours that are reinforced and tend to stop engaging in them if they are not reinforced. Supporters of the behavioural model believe that people learn to behave in abnormal ways when they are unintentionally reinforced by others for doing so (see Chapter 4, page 41). For example, a child who receives parental attention when he or she shouts is likely to engage in this behaviour in the future because attention acts as a reinforcer. If abnormal behaviours can be *acquired* through operant conditioning, they can be *eliminated* through it. In the case of a child who is disruptive, parents might be instructed to ignore the behaviour so that it is extinguished from the child's behavioural repertoire.

If this technique is to be effective, however, the therapist must be able to identify and eliminate the reinforcer that is maintaining the adaptive behaviour. As Crooks & Stein (1991) have observed, this is not always easy. Box 10.3 describes such a case.

> ### Box 10.3   Behaviour modification using extinction
>
> A 20-year-old woman reluctantly sought help for a problem described by her parents as 'compulsive face-picking'. Whenever the woman found some little blemish or pimple, she would pick and scratch at it until it became a bleeding sore. As a result, her face was unsightly. Everyone was distressed except the individual herself, who seemed remarkably unconcerned. The woman's family and her fiancé had tried several tactics to stop the face-picking, including appealing to her vanity, pleading and making threats.
>
> The therapist felt that the face-picking was being maintained by the attention her family and fiancé were giving it. As long as she continued picking at her face, the pattern of inadvertent reinforcement was maintained, and she would remain at the centre of attention. Once the therapist had identified the behaviours that were reinforcing the face-picking, the parents and fiancé were instructed not to engage in these and to ignore the face-picking entirely, and were told that it would probably get worse before it improved. After a temporary increase in face-picking had occurred, it was quickly extinguished when attention was no longer given. To prevent the behaviour from reappearing, the parents and fiancé were encouraged to provide plenty of loving attention and to support the woman contingent upon a variety of healthy, adaptive behaviours.
>
> (based on Crooks & Stein, 1991)

THERAPIES BASED ON PUNISHMENT

In aversion therapy (see page 109), an aversive stimulus, such as an electric shock, is used to classically condition a negative response to a desired but undesirable stimulus. Aversive stimuli can also be used to punish voluntary maladaptive behaviours. Cowart & Whaley (1971) studied an emotionally disturbed young child who persistently engaged in self-mutilating behaviour to such an extent that he had to be restrained in his crib in a hospital for the mentally retarded. Electrodes were attached to the child's leg, and the child was placed in the room with a padded floor (the self-mutilation involved violently banging the head against the floor). When the child began to engage in the self-mutilating behaviour, an electric shock was given. Initially, the child was startled by the shock, but continued his self-mutilation, at which point another shock was given. There were very few repetitions before self-mutilation stopped, and the boy could be safely let out of his crib.

It is generally agreed that therapies using punishment are not as effective as those employing positive reinforcement (see below) in bringing about behaviour change. At least one reason for not using punishment is the tendency for people to *overgeneralise* behaviour. Thus, those behaviours which are *related* to the behaviour that has been punished are also not engaged in. Moreover, punishment tends to produce only a temporary suppression of undesirable behaviour and unless another reinforcement-inducing behaviour pattern is substituted for the punished behaviour, it will resurface.

There are also ethical issues surrounding the use of punishment (particularly with very young children). In the Cowart and Whaley study, however, the infant was engaging in a behaviour which was clearly very harmful, and with these sorts of behaviour, punishment is in fact extremely effective. Presumably, the physical well-being that occurred from not self-mutilating was sufficiently reinforcing to maintain the new behaviour pattern.

THERAPIES BASED ON POSITIVE REINFORCEMENT

In an early demonstration that positive reinforcement can produce changes in the behaviour of disturbed individuals, Isaacs *et al.* (1960) described the case of a 40-year-old male schizophrenic who had not spoken to anyone for 19 years. Quite accidentally, one of the therapists discovered that the man loved chewing gum, and decided to use this as a way of getting him to speak.

Initially, the therapist held up a piece of gum. When the patient looked at the gum, it was given to him. The patient began to pay attention to the therapist and would look at the gum as soon as the therapist removed it from his pocket. Later, the therapist held up the gum and waited until the patient moved his lips. When this occurred, the gum was immediately given to the patient. However, the therapist then began to give the gum *only* when the patient made a sound. At the point when the patient reliably made a sound when the gum was shown, the therapist held the gum and instructed the patient to 'say gum'. After 19 years of silence, the patient said the word. After six weeks of this therapy, the patient spontaneously said 'Gum, please', and shortly afterwards began talking to the therapist. This approach is known as *behaviour shaping* and has been used with several types of disturbed individual, most notably the chronically disturbed and mentally retarded, who are extremely difficult to communicate with. The successful use of positive reinforcement in the treatment of anorexia nervosa (see Chapter 7) is shown in Box 10.4.

> **Box 10.4   Using positive reinforcement to treat anorexia nervosa**
>
> A young anorectic woman was in danger of dying because she had drastically curtailed her eating behaviour and weighed only 47lbs. In the first stage of therapy, the therapist established an appropriate reinforcer that could be made contingent upon eating. The reinforcer chosen was social, and whenever the anorectic swallowed a bite of food, she was rewarded by the therapist talking to her and paying her attention. If she refused to eat, the therapist left the room and she remained alone until the next meal was served (and note that this is not punishment, but rather is 'time out' from positive reinforcement).
>
> After a while, her eating behaviour gradually increased, and the therapist introduced other rewards contingent upon her continuing to eat and gain weight. These included having other people join her at meal times or being allowed to have her hair done. Eventually, the woman gained sufficient weight to be discharged from the hospital. Because people are likely to regress

if returned to a non-supportive institutional setting, the woman's parents were instructed in ways to continue reinforcing her for appropriate eating behaviours. At follow-up nearly three years later, the woman was still maintaining an adequate weight.

(based on Bachrach *et al.*, 1965)

In a study published in 1962, Ayllon and Haughton reported that staff at one hospital found it particularly difficult to get withdrawn schizophrenic individuals to eat regularly. Ayllon and Haughton noticed that the staff were actually exacerbating the problem by coaxing the patients into the dining room and, in some cases, even feeding them. The researchers reasoned that the increased attention was reinforcing the uncooperativeness of the patients and decided that the rules that operated in the hospital should be changed. For example, if patients did not arrive at the dining hall within 30 minutes of being called, they were locked out. Additionally, staff were no longer permitted to interact with patients at meal times. Because their uncooperative behaviour was no longer being reinforced, the patients quickly changed their eating habits. Then the patients were made to pay one penny in order to enter the dining hall. The pennies could be earned by showing socially appropriate *target behaviours*, and these also began to increase in frequency.

Ayllon and Haughton's approach was refined by Ayllon & Azrin (1968) in the form of a *token economy system*. In this, disturbed individuals are given tokens in exchange for behaving in desirable ways. The therapist first of all identifies what patients like. This may include watching television, smoking cigarettes, and so on. When a productive activity (such as making a bed or socialising with other patients) occurs, patients are given tokens that can be exchanged for 'privileges'. The tokens therefore become conditioned reinforcers for desirable and appropriate behaviours.

Research conducted by Ayllon and Azrin showed that the tokens were effective in eliciting and maintaining desired behaviours. The amount of time spent performing desired behaviours was high when the reinforcement contingencies were imposed and lowest when they were not. Ayllon and Azrin also discovered that the use of token economies had an effect on patient

and staff morale, in that the patients were less apathetic and less irresponsible, whilst the staff became more enthusiastic about their patients and the therapeutic techniques. One illustration of the effectiveness of the token economy system is shown in Figure 10.3.

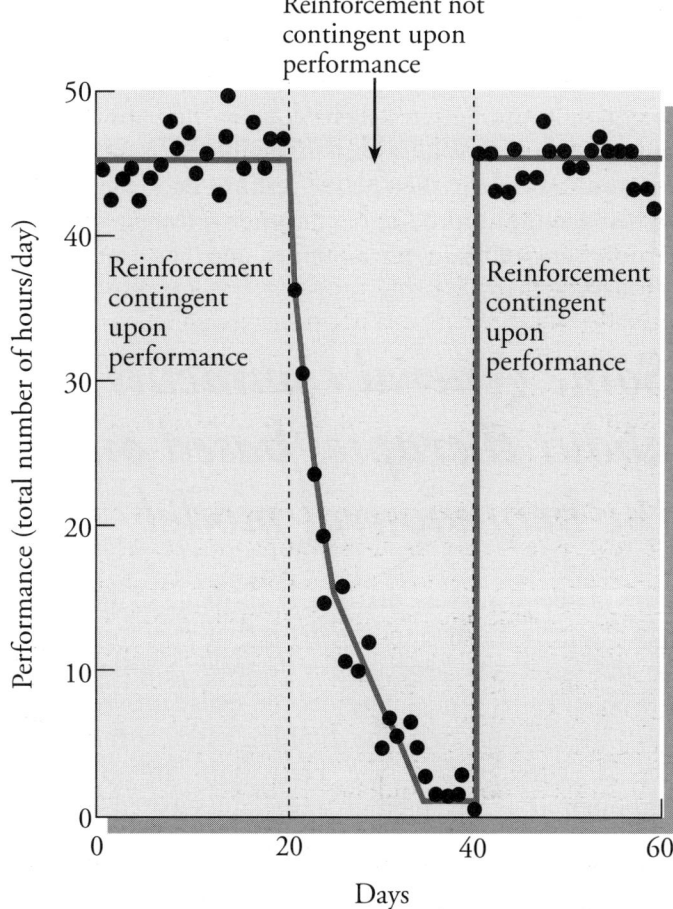

Figure 10.3   The effects of a token economy on the performance of hospitalised patients

As well as being used with the chronically disturbed, token economies have also been used in programmes designed to modify the behaviour of children with *conduct disorders*. In one study, Schneider & Byrne (1987) awarded tokens to children who engaged in helpful behaviours and removed the tokens for inappropriate behaviours, such as arguing or not paying attention. However, despite their effectiveness in producing behavioural change with a variety of disorders, issues have been raised about token economies.

Eventually tokens will have to be replaced by other social reinforcers, both within and outside the therapeutic setting. The individual is gradually 'weaned off' the tokens in the therapeutic setting and can be transferred to a 'half-way house' or some other community live-in arrangement where more social reinforcers can be used. Unfortunately, this is not always successful and there tends to be a high re-hospitalisation rate for discharged individuals.

Baddeley (1990) has argued that token economies can lead to 'token learning', by which he means that people might only indulge in a behaviour if they are directly rewarded for it. Whilst this might be effective within the confines of the therapeutic setting, Baddeley sees it as being quite unproductive in other settings, where it is necessary to learn on a subtler and less immediate reward system.

Some general comments about therapies based on the behavioural model

One of the criticisms that has been made of therapies based on the behavioural model is that they focus only on the observable aspects of a disorder. Supporters of the behavioural model consider the maladaptive behaviours they change to be the disorder, and that the disorder is 'cured' when the behaviours are changed. Although it is accepted that therapies based on the behavioural model can alter behaviour, critics argue that such therapies fail to identify a disorder's *underlying* causes. Critics argue that one consequence of failing to address a disorder's underlying causes is *symptom substitution*, in which removing one symptom of a disorder simply results in another, and perhaps more serious one, occurring in some other form.

As we noted earlier when we described the procedures involved in aversion therapy (see page 109), behaviours learnt under one set of conditions may not generalise to other conditions. Clearly, supporters of the behavioural model see behaviours as being controlled by the environment, so it is perhaps hardly surprising that behaviours altered in one context do not endure in a very different context. Indeed, Rimm (1976) sees this as the major limitation of behaviour therapy. To avoid this problem, therapists attempt to extend the generality of changed behaviours by working (as far as possible) in environments which are representative of real life. They also encourage people to avoid environments that elicit maladaptive behaviours, to return for follow-up treatment and teach them how to modify their behaviour on a continuing basis.

The most serious criticism of behaviour therapy and modification is ethical. Techniques involving punishment, in particular, have been criticised for exercising authoritarian control and for dehumanising and 'brainwashing' people. Another criticism is that behaviour therapists manipulate people and deprive them of freedom. As we have seen, it is the therapist, rather than the person, who controls the reinforcer, and therapists do not encourage people to seek insight concerning their disorder.

However, supporters of the behavioural model defend themselves by arguing that they do not treat disorders without consent and that, in a sense, we are all 'naïve behaviour therapists'. For example, when we praise people or tell them off for a particular behaviour, we are using behaviour modification techniques: all therapists are doing is using such approaches in a systematic and consistent way. Therapists who use behavioural methods are not attempting to control behaviour, but helping people to control their *own* behaviour.

Conclusions

There are a number of therapies based on the behavioural model. Some of these use classical conditioning techniques, whilst others use the techniques involved in operant conditioning. The various behaviour therapies and behaviour modification techniques have been applied to a number of mental disorders. Although supporters of the behavioural model see the therapies as being highly effective, opponents of the model believe that important criticisms which can be made of them limit their application.

SUMMARY

- In contrast with psychoanalysts, supporters of the behavioural model believe that we should focus on the behaviour that constitutes a problem rather than on the historical reasons for its development. Therapies based on the behavioural model try to change behaviour by whatever means are most effective.
- **Behaviour therapy** refers to those therapies based on **classical conditioning**, while those techniques based on **operant conditioning** are termed **behaviour modification**.
- If maladaptive behaviours can be acquired through classical conditioning, they can presumably be unlearned by the same principles. **Implosion therapy**, **flooding** and **systematic desensitisation** are all aimed at producing new responses to stimuli that are contrary to the old, maladaptive responses.
- **Implosion therapy** and **flooding** both work on the principle that if the fear-evoking stimulus is repeatedly presented without the fear response, the former will lose its power to elicit the fear response. In implosion therapy, the person is told to imagine the most terrifying form of contact of the feared object/situation, supplemented by **stimulus augmentation**, in the safety of the therapeutic setting. The stimulus eventually stops producing anxiety (**implodes**).
- In **flooding**, the individual **confronts** the feared object/situation; by being prevented from avoiding/escaping, the fear response eventually extinguishes. Both implosion therapy and flooding are effective with certain types of phobia, but they can lead to increased anxiety and are sometimes too traumatic. A recent approach which partially overcomes this problem is the use of **computer-generated virtual environments**; this is easier to arrange and less traumatic than real exposure and has produced encouraging results so far.
- Neither implosion therapy nor flooding trains people to substitute the maladaptive behaviour with an adaptive/**desirable** response. An early study by Jones involved **gradually** moving the feared object closer and closer to a child while giving it candy until no anxiety was elicited. In the 1950s, Wolpe popularised and refined this technique, calling it **systematic desensitisation**.
- The person initially constructs an **anxiety hierarchy**, after which **relaxation training** is given. Relaxation represents the adaptive substitute response used by most therapists. Systematic desensitisation is based on the principle of **reciprocal inhibition**. The person is then asked to imagine as vividly as possible the scene at the bottom of the hierarchy and to remain calm and relaxed.
- If the person experiences **greater** anxiety, the image is terminated and a relaxed state is regained. Once thinking about the scene at the bottom of the hierarchy no longer elicits anxiety, the next scene is presented and in this way the whole hierarchy is worked through **systematically**. When imagining any of the scenes can be done without experiencing any discomfort, the person is **desensitised**. Finally, the person has to confront the anxiety-producing stimulus in the real world.
- A problem with systematic desensitisation is its dependence on people's ability to vividly imagine the phobic object/situation. An alternative is *in vivo* exposure, which is invariably more effective and more permanent than other desensitisation techniques.
- While all these methods of treating phobias are effective, flooding appears to be more effective than systematic desensitisation, implosion therapy and systematic desensitisation seem to be equally effective (suggesting that systematically working through a hierarchy is not necessary), and flooding seems to be more effective than implosion therapy. The superiority of flooding suggests that *in vivo* exposure is the crucial factor.
- **Aversion therapy** is used with people who want to **extinguish** the **pleasant** feelings associated with socially undesirable behaviours (e.g. excessive drinking/smoking). This is achieved by repeatedly pairing an unpleasant event with a desired behaviour, until the desired behaviour eventually elicits negative responses.
- In one version, the problem drinker is given a drug that induces nausea/vomiting **only** when combined with alcohol. Only a few pairings are required for alcohol alone to elicit an aversive response. An alternative method involves drinking a warm saline solution containing a drug which induces nausea/vomiting without alcohol. Immediately before vomiting begins, an alcoholic drink is given, to be swilled around the mouth before swallowing. In order to prevent generalisation of the aversive response to all drinks, a soft drink

may be given between aversive conditioning trials.

- Apart from alcohol abuse, aversion therapy has been used with some success in the treatment of smoking, overeating and children's self-injurious behaviour. It has been popularised through Anthony Burgess' novel *A Clockwork Orange*.

- One of the most controversial applications of aversion therapy has been with (male) homosexuals, who are shown slides of male nudes, which are followed by electric shocks. The conditioned fear response to the slides is meant to generalise to homosexual fantasies/activities outside the therapeutic setting. Later in treatment, a sexual response to slides of nude women will terminate an electric shock.

- Aversion therapy is not pleasant and should not be used without **consent** or only as a last resort. It will not be effective if cognitive factors 'swamp' the conditioning process, such as discriminating between the conditioning situation and real-world situations.

- Aversion therapy involves both classical conditioning (by which the original aversive response is acquired) and operant conditioning (avoidance of the problem stimulus/situation which is negatively reinforced by reduction of fear). Most behaviour therapists try to **shape new/adaptive behaviours** at the same time as extinguishing existing/maladaptive ones.

- In response to the claim that aversion therapy is open to abuse, **covert sensitisation** is sometimes used instead. People are trained to punish themselves through **imagining** ('covert') the aversive consequences of some undesirable behaviour ('sensitisation'). This method can help to control excessive drinking, overeating and smoking.

- While therapies based on classical conditioning usually involve **emotional responses** as well as **observable behaviours**, those based on operant conditioning are aimed **directly** at observable behaviours. Once the undesirable/maladaptive behaviour has been identified, the next step is to identify the reinforcers that maintain such behaviour. The final step is to restructure the environment so that the maladaptive behaviour is no longer reinforced.

- Undesirable behaviours can be **extinguished** by **removing** the reinforcers that maintain them; alternatively, aversive stimuli can be used to **punish** voluntary maladaptive behaviours. Operant conditioning can also be used to increase desirable behaviours through making **positive reinforcement contingent** on the voluntary manifestation of the behaviour.

- According to the behavioural model, people can learn to behave in abnormal ways when they are unintentionally reinforced by others for doing so, as when parental attention is given when a child shouts. Equally, abnormal behaviours can be eliminated through deliberately failing to reinforce them.

- Aversive stimuli can be used to **punish** voluntary maladaptive behaviours, as in the use of electric shocks to stop self-mutilating behaviour. However, such methods are not as effective as those using positive reinforcement, partly because of the tendency for punished behaviour to be **overgeneralised**. Punishment also tends to produce only temporary suppression of undesirable behaviour which will resurface unless substituted by a behaviour that is reinforced. The use of punishment also raises ethical issues, particularly when used with very young children.

- The case of a male schizophrenic who had not spoken to anyone for 19 years demonstrates the use of **behaviour shaping** to change behaviour based on **positive reinforcement**. Behaviour shaping has been used most notably with the chronically disturbed and mentally retarded, who are extremely difficult to communicate with, as well as with anorectics.

- Ayllon and Haughton observed that hospital staff were inadvertently reinforcing the uncooperative behaviour of withdrawn schizophrenic patients by giving them increased attention. They decided that the rules should be changed so that uncooperative behaviour was no longer reinforced. Socially appropriate **target behaviours** began to increase when they were reinforced with pennies.

- Based on this approach, Ayllon and Azrin devised the **token economy system**, in which individuals are given tokens in exchange for desirable behaviour. In turn, the tokens (conditioned reinforcers) can be exchanged for 'privileges'. The tokens were effective in eliciting and maintaining desired behaviours, and the use of token economies also improved both staff and patient morale. Token economies have also been used successfully with children with conduct disorders.

- Individuals must be gradually 'weaned off' the tokens to be replaced by social reinforcers, both in the therapeutic setting and in community facilities such as 'half-way houses'. But this transfer is often unsuccessful and re-hospitalisation rates are high. Token economies can also lead to 'token learning' which can be unproductive outside the immediate therapeutic setting.

- A general criticism of therapies based on the behavioural model is that by focusing on the observable aspects of a disorder (the disorder is 'cured' when the behaviour is changed), they fail to identify the underlying causes. One consequence of this is **symptom substitution**.
- A second criticism is that behaviours changed in one context do not generalise to different contexts. To avoid this problem, behaviour therapists try to work in environments which are as representative of real life as possible; they also encourage people to avoid environments which elicit maladaptive behaviours and to have follow-up treatment.
- The most serious criticism of behavioural methods of treatment, especially those involving punishment, is ethical. Behaviour therapists are seen as manipulating people, depriving them of their freedom, dehumanising and controlling them. In their own defence, behaviour therapists argue that they always obtain consent and that they are only doing in a more systematic/consistent way what we all do in our everyday lives.

11

THERAPIES BASED ON THE COGNITIVE MODEL

Introduction and overview

The cognitive model's view of abnormality (see Chapter 2) sees mental disorders as resulting from distortions in people's cognitions and thoughts. The aim of therapies based on the cognitive model is to demonstrate to people seeking treatment that their distorted or irrational thoughts are the main contributors to their difficulties. If the faulty modes of thinking can be *modified* or *changed*, then disorders can be alleviated.

The goal of therapies based on the cognitive model, then, is to change maladaptive behaviour by changing the way people think. Some psychologists believe cognitive therapies to be a collection of techniques that really belong to the domain of the behavioural model (and thus the term *cognitive-behavioural therapies* is sometimes used to describe them). In some cases, the dividing line between a therapy based on the behavioural model and one based on the cognitive model can be very fine and arbitrary. Indeed, therapists who identify their orientation as primarily *behavioural* or primarily *cognitive* may actually be doing the same thing.

Supporters of the cognitive model, however, believe that when behaviour changes, it does so as a result of changes in cognitive processes, and hence it is possible to separate cognitively based therapies from behavioural ones. Like therapies based on the psychodynamic model, cognitive therapies aim to produce *insight*. However, rather than focusing on the past, therapies based on the cognitive model try to produce insight into *current cognitions*. We will begin this chapter by looking at some of the therapeutic approaches devised by Albert Bandura who, whilst often considered a *behaviour therapist*, attempts to change behaviour by altering thoughts and perceptions. After this, we will look at Albert Ellis' *rational-emotive therapy*, Aaron Beck's *cognitive therapy for depression*, *attributional therapy*, Donald Meichenbaum's *stress inoculation therapy* and some of the more recent cognitively based applications to therapy.

Albert Bandura's approaches to therapy

Many behaviour therapists incorporate cognitive processes into their theoretical outlook and cognitive procedures into their methodology (Wilson, 1982). Techniques like systematic desensitisation and covert sensitisation, for example, use *visual imagery*. The interface between behavioural methods and the cognitive model has been termed *cognitive behaviour therapy*, and one of the leading researchers is Albert Bandura.

As we noted in Chapter 2 (see page 16), certain kinds of learning cannot be *solely* explained in terms of classical or operant conditioning. According to Bandura (1969) and other *social learning theorists*, humans and some other animals can learn directly *without* experiencing some event, and can acquire new forms of behaviour from others simply by observing them (a process called *observational learning*). Moreover, whether we see people being rewarded or punished can strengthen or reduce our own inhibitions against behaving in similar ways. If we see someone receiving a positive outcome for a behaviour, our restraint against performing that behaviour is lowered (*response disinhibition*). However, if we see someone experiencing a negative outcome for a behaviour, our restraint is heightened (*response inhibition*).

Bandura argues that a person's maladaptive behaviours can be altered by exposing those demonstrating such behaviours to appropriate *models*, that is, others performing actions the person is afraid to perform. As well as changing behaviour, this approach to therapy aims to change thoughts and perceptions as well. Box 11.1 illustrates the application of *modelling* to the treatment of a phobia, an application which Bandura (1971) reports eliminated fear in over 90% of those who underwent it (see Figure 11.1 overleaf).

Box 11.1   An application of modelling

The therapist performed the fearless behaviour at each step and gradually led participants into touching, stroking and then holding the snake's body with gloved and bare hands while the experimenter held the snake securely by the head and tail. If a participant was unable to touch the snake following ample demonstration, she was then asked to place her hands on the experimenter's and to move her hand down gradually until it touched the snake's body. After the participants no longer felt any apprehension about touching the snake under these conditions, anxieties about contact with the snake's head area and entwining tail were extinguished.

The therapist again performed the tasks fearlessly, and then the experimenter and the participant performed the responses jointly; as participants became less fearful, the experimenter gradually reduced his participation and control over the snake, until eventually participants were able to hold the snake in their laps without assistance, to let the snake loose in the room and retrieve it, and to let it crawl freely over their

bodies. Progress through the graded approach tasks was paced according to the participants' apprehensiveness. When they reported being able to perform one activity with little or no fear, they were eased into a more difficult interaction.

(Bandura, 1971)

Box 11.1 illustrates what is known as *participant modelling* and involves the individual observing the therapist's behaviour and then imitating it. This method seems to be more effective than having people watch filmed or video-taped models (a method known as *symbolic modelling*). Modelling has been successfully used with a variety of phobias and, as well as eliminating undesirable behaviours, has also been used to establish new and more appropriate behaviours.

In *assertiveness training*, for example, people who experience difficulty in asserting themselves in interpersonal situations are required to perform in the presence of a group who provide feedback about the adequacy of performance. Then, the therapist assumes the individual's role and models the appropriate assertive behaviour. The individual is asked to try again, this time imitating the therapist. The alternation between *behavioural rehearsal* and modelling continues until the assertive role has been mastered. When this occurs, the skills are tried out in real-life situations. This approach has also been widely used in *social skills training*, in which people who lack the ability to function effectively in certain situations observe others performing the desired behaviours and then attempt to imitate them.

Bandura (1977) believes that one reason for modelling's effectiveness is the development of a cognitive concept he calls *self-efficacy*. Being able to perform a behaviour that was previously impossible is held to raise a person's evaluation of the degree to which he or she can cope with difficult situations. According to Bandura, when people encounter new situations in which they have difficulty, they are much more willing to engage in behaviours that were previously avoided.

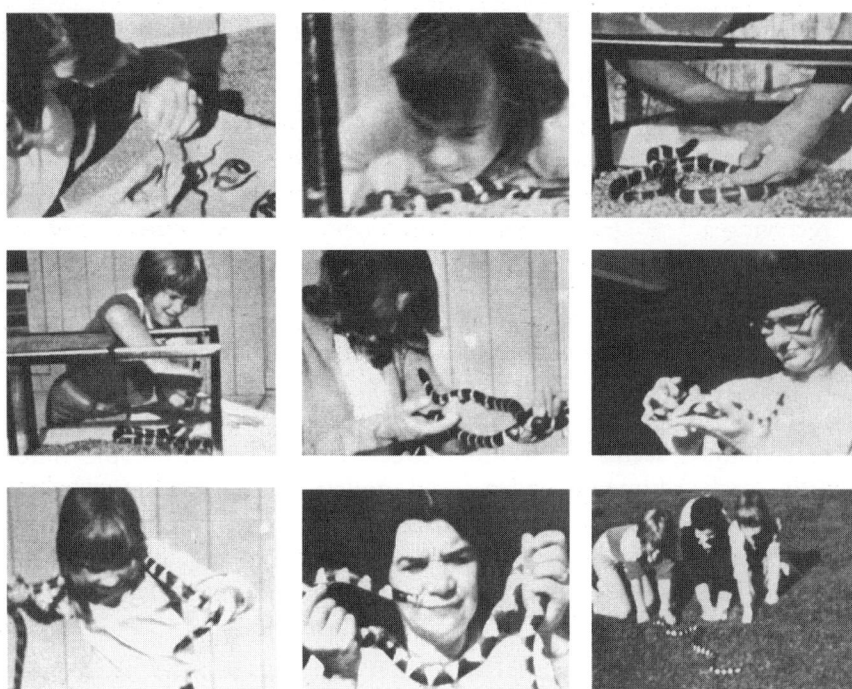

Figure 11.1 As this sequence of photographs shows, modelling can be an effective way of treating phobias

Albert Ellis' rational-emotive therapy (RET)

Another cognitively based approach to treatment is *rational-emotive therapy* (RET) which was developed in the 1950s by Albert Ellis. After becoming dissatisfied with what he termed the 'passivity of psychoanalysis', Ellis, a trained psychoanalyst, began to develop his own therapeutic approach. For several years, Ellis' approach to therapy was regarded as being on the periphery. However, RET is now practised by a large number of therapists, particularly in the United States.

Ellis (1958, 1962) argues that many of the emotional difficulties experienced by people are due to the *irrational beliefs* they bring to bear on their experiences and the reinforcement these irrational beliefs receive through being repeated. For Ellis (1991), these irrational beliefs can be understood as part of what he terms the *A–B–C model*. According to this, a significant activating event (A) is followed by a highly charged emotional consequence (C). However, to say that A is the cause of C is not *always* correct, even though it may be appear to be as far as a person is concerned. Rather, Ellis sees C as occurring because of a person's belief system (B). Inappropriate emotions, such as depression and guilt, can only be abolished if a change occurs in a person's beliefs and perceptions.

To illustrate this, suppose a person rings up several friends to invite them out for a drink, but finds that none is able to accept the invitation. This activating event (A) might produce the emotional consequence (C) that the person feels depressed, isolated and worthless. For Ellis, C occurs because of the person's belief system (B) which holds that because no one has accepted the invitation, it must mean that no one likes him or her.

The aim of RET is to try and help people find flaws in their thinking and, to use Ellis' term, 'to make mincemeat' of these maladaptive cognitions by creating D, a *dispute belief system* which has no severe emotional consequences. In the example we used above, D might run along the lines of 'people have already made plans to go out and just because they can't accept my invitation doesn't mean they don't like me'.

Ellis has suggested that two of the most common mal-adaptive cognitions people hold are (1) that they are worthless unless they are perfectly competent at everything they try and (2) that they must be approved of and loved by everyone they meet. Because such beliefs make impossible demands on people who hold them, Ellis believes that they lead to feelings of anxiety, failure and, frequently, abnormal behaviour. Some other irrational beliefs frequently encountered by therapists are shown in Box 11.2.

Box 11.2   Some common irrational beliefs encountered in RET

- Certain people I must deal with are thoroughly bad and should be severely blamed and punished for it.
- It is awful and upsetting when things are not the way I would very much like them to be.
- My unhappiness is always caused by external events; I cannot control my emotional reactions.
- If something unpleasant might happen, I should keep dwelling on it.
- It is easier to avoid difficulties and responsibilities than to face them.
- I should depend on others who are stronger than I am.
- Because something once strongly affected my life, it will do so indefinitely.
- There is always a perfect solution to human problems, and it is awful if this solution is not found.

(based on Rohsenow & Smith, 1982)

Once the irrational beliefs a person holds have been identified, therapy continues by guiding him or her to substitute more logical or realistic thoughts for the maladaptive ones, a task which Ellis believes can be accomplished 'by any therapist worth his or her salt'. Ellis sees the rational-emotive therapist as an *exposing and nonsense-annihilating scientist*. Therapists claim that the universe is logical and rational, and the appropriate means of understanding it is the scientific method of controlled observation. Ellis and his followers see people as having the *capacity* for rational understanding

and the *resources* for personal growth. However, people also have the capacity to delude themselves and accept irrational beliefs.

As we noted earlier, the first stage in therapy is for the individual to recognise and question their irrational beliefs. Rather than remaining 'anonymous', as a classical psychoanalyst would do, and occasionally offering some form of interpretation, the rational-emotive therapist will show the person how to ask questions like '*where* is the evidence that I am a worthless person if I am not universally approved?', '*who* says I must be perfect?' and '*why* must things go exactly the way I would like them to go?'

Once people have recognised and analysed their beliefs, they are taught to substitute more realistic alternatives in an attempt to engender *full acceptance*. Rather than measuring themselves against an impossible standard, a rational-emotive therapist emphasises that failures should not be seen as 'disastrous', confirming a lack of self-worth, but merely as 'unfortunate' events. Lange & Jakubowski (1976) have presented some rational alternatives to the beliefs therapists frequently encounter. These are shown in Box 11.3.

Box 11.3   Some rational alternatives to irrational beliefs

Irrational belief: I *must* prove myself to be thoroughly competent, adequate and achieiving, or I *must* at least have real competence or talent at something important.

Rational alternative belief: What I do doesn't have to be perfect to be good. I will be happier if I achieve at a realistic level rather than strive for perfection.

Irrational belief: I *have* to view life as awful, terrible, horrible, or catastrophic when things do not go the way I would like them to go.

Rational alternative belief: If I can't change the situation, it may be unfortunate but not catastrophic. I can make plans for my life to be as enjoyable as possible.

Irrational belief: I *must* have sincere love and approval almost all the time from all the people who are significant to me.

Rational alternative belief: I would *like* to be approved, but I do not *need* such approval.

Ellis and his colleagues use a variety of approaches to try and minimise people's self-defeating beliefs. Rather than focussing on people's histories, rational-emotive therapists focus on the 'here and now'. As Ellis (1984) has put it:

> 'Therapists do not spend a great deal of time ... encouraging long tales of woe, sympathetically getting in tune with emotionalising or carefully and incisively reflecting feelings.'

Ellis is not interested in what he calls 'long-winded dialogues', which he sees as 'indulgent'. Rather, RET aims to help people *get* better rather than *feel* better during a therapy session and to accept reality 'even when it is pretty grim'.

Indeed, by providing people with warmth, support, attention and caring, their need for love (which is usually the central core of their circumstances: Elkins, 1980) is reinforced. There is also the possibility that people become dependent on the therapy and the therapist. The direct approach used in RET is illustrated in Box 11.4, in which Ellis discusses the problems experienced by a 25-year-old female.

Box 11.4   RET in action

Therapist: The same crap! It's always the same crap. Now, if you would look at the crap – instead of 'Oh, how stupid I am! He hates me! I think I'll kill myself!' – then you'd get better right away.

Person: You've been listening! (laughs)

Therapist: Listening to what?

Person: (*laughs*) Those wild statements in my mind, like that, that I make.

Therapist: That's right! Because I know that you have to make those statements – because I have a good theory. And according to my theory, people couldn't get upset unless they made those nutty statements to themselves ... Even if I loved you madly, the next person you talk to is likely to hate you. So I like brown eyes and he likes blue eyes, or something. So then you're dead! Because you really think: 'I've got to be accepted! I've got to act intelligently!' Well, why?

Person: (*very soberly and reflectively*) True.

Therapist: You see?

Person: Yes.

Therapist: Now, if you will learn that lesson, then you've had a very valuable session. Because you don't have to upset yourself. As I said before: if I thought you were the worst [*expletive deleted*] who ever existed, well that's my *opinion*. And I'm entitled to it. But does that make you a turd?

Person: (*reflective silence*)

Therapist: *Does* it?

Person: No.

Therapist: What makes you a turd?

Person: *Thinking* that you are.

Therapist: That's right! Your *belief* that you are. That's the only thing that could ever do it. And you never have to believe that. See? You control your thinking. I control my thinking – *my* belief about you. But you don't have to be affected by that. You *always* control what you think.

(taken from Ellis, 1984)

Emmelkamp *et al.* (1978) have reported that RET seems to be effective for at least some types of psychological disorder. However, Haaga & Davison (1993) have reported that for other types of disorder (such as agoraphobia), RET is less effective than therapies derived from other models. Quite clearly, RET is an active and directive therapeutic approach, and one in which the therapist's personal beliefs and values are an inevitable part of what goes on during therapy. However, Ellis' (1984) view that 'no one and nothing is supreme', that 'self-gratification' should be encouraged and that 'unequivocal love, commitment, service and ... fidelity to any interpersonal commitment, especially marriage, leads to harmful consequences' have been disputed (e.g. Bergin, 1980).

The argumentative approach to therapy, in which the therapist attacks those beliefs which are regarded to be foolish and illogical, has also been questioned, particularly by those who stress the importance of *empathy* in therapy (see Chapter 12). For example, Fancher (1995) believes that all cognitive therapies rely on a common-sense view of cognition and falsely assume that therapists are capable of identifying 'faulty thinking': what is foolish and illogical to the therapist may not be foolish and illogical in terms of the individual's own experiences.

Brandsma *et al.* (1978) have reported that RET is effective in producing behaviour change amongst those who are self-demanding and who feel guilty for not living up to their own standards of perfection. For people with severe thought disorders (as is the case in schizophrenia), however, the therapy is clearly ineffective, since people with such disorders are highly unlikely to respond to an Ellis-type analysis of their problems (Ellis, 1993).

Aaron Beck's cognitive restructuring therapy

Like Ellis, Beck (1967) was originally trained as a psychoanalyst. As with RET, Beck's therapy assumes that psychological disorders stem primarily from irrational beliefs that cause people to behave in maladaptive ways. Beck's approach to therapy is specifically designed to treat *depressed* people. According to Beck and his colleagues, depression arises through implicit assumptions people make about themselves. Beck *et al.* (1979) believe that depressed people suffer from a *cognitive triad* of negative beliefs about themselves, their future and their experiences. Beck sees such beliefs as arising from faulty information-processing and faulty logic.

We identified several types of faulty thinking that can contribute to people's depression in Chapter 2 (see pages 17–18). As we noted in Chapter 2, the aim of Beck's therapy is to identify the implicit and self-defeating assumptions depressed people make about themselves, change their validity and substitute more adaptive assumptions. Box 11.5 illustrates an exchange between a therapist using Beck's cognitive approach and a student who believed that she would not get into the college she had applied to.

Box 11.5	Beck's approach to therapy in action
Therapist:	Why do you think you won't be able to get into the university of your choice?
Student:	Because my grades were not really so hot.
Therapist:	Well, what was your grade average?
Student:	Well, pretty good up until the last semester in high school.
Therapist:	What was your grade average in general?
Student:	As and Bs.
Therapist:	Well, how many of each?
Student:	Well, I guess, almost all of my grades were As but I got terrible grades my last semester.
Therapist:	What were your grades then?
Student:	I got two As and two Bs.
Therapist:	Since your grade average would seem to come out to almost all As, why do you think you won't be able to get into the university?
Student:	Because of competition being so tough.
Therapist:	Have you found out what the average grades are for admissions to the college?
Student:	Well, somebody told me that a B+ average would suffice.
Therapist:	Isn't your average better than that?
Student:	I guess so.
(taken from Beck *et al.* 1979)	

Notice how the therapist attempts to reverse the 'catastrophising beliefs' held by the student concerning herself, her situation and her future. Note also how the therapist takes a gentler, less confrontational and more experiential approach to the student than would be the case with RET.

Box 11.5 illustrates the strategy of identifying a person's self-impressions which, although not recognised as such, are misguided. As Williams (1992) has noted, once the self-impressions have been identified, the therapist's role is to attempt to disprove rather than confirm the person's negative self-image. By sharing his or her knowledge of the cognitive model, the person undergoing therapy may then understand the origins of the disorder and ultimately develop skills to apply effective interventions independently.

Given its original purpose, it is hardly surprising that studies indicate that Beck's approach to therapy is most successful in treating depression (Andrews, 1991). However, Fairburn *et al.* (1993) have shown that the therapy can also be used successfully with eating disorders. Whether Beck's approach can be applied to other disorders like schizophrenia and the personality disorders is currently receiving much attention (Beck & Freeman, 1990; Tarrier *et al.*, 1993).

Attributional therapy

Attibutional therapy is a relatively recent cognitive approach to the treatment of depression which derives from the research we described in Chapter 5 concerning the revised theory of learned helplessness (see page 54). As we noted in Chapter 5, attributions are our beliefs about the causes of our own and other people's behaviours. Attributional therapists hold that, in some cases, depressed people make unrealistic or faulty attributions concerning their own behaviour and that these can cause considerable distress. When asked to explain a successful outcome (such as passing an examination), most people make what are called *dispositional* (or *internal*) attributions, that is, success is explained in terms of something about the person (such as 'natural ability' or 'all the hard work I did'). However, when asked to explain an unsuccessful outcome (such as failing an examination), we tend to make *situational* (or *external*) attributions and explain failure in terms of factors outside of us and perhaps beyond our control (such as 'an unfair examination' or 'poor teaching'). This tendency to take credit for success and deny responsibility for failure is called the *self-serving bias* and is empirically well-established (Miller & Ross, 1975).

For depressed people, however, failures tend to be attributed to internal causes even when there is no evidence to support such an attribution. Successful outcomes, by contrast, tend to be attributed to external causes. For example, a depressed individual who passes an examination may attribute the success to 'an easy examination paper that anybody could have passed', when in fact it was the individual's own ability that produced the positive outcome.

Attributional therapists attempt to break down the vicious circle that people low in self-esteem experience. This involves training them to perceive successes as resulting from internal factors and at least some failures from external factors which are beyond their control. According to Brockner & Guare (1983), changing attributions can result in increased self-esteem, greater confidence and better performance. Moreover, Brockner and Guare report that beneficial changes can occur after only a small number of therapy sessions, which is clearly advantageous.

A good illustration of this was provided by Rabin *et al.* (1986). 235 depressed adults were given a ten-session programme that initially explained the advantages of interpreting events in the way that non-depressed people do. After this, the depressed adults were trained to reform their habitually negative patterns of thinking and labelling by, for example, being given 'homework assignments' in which they recorded each day's positive events and the contributions they had made to them. As compared with a group of depressed people given no programme, the group that received the ten-session programme reported experiencing significantly less depression.

Donald Meichenbaum's stress inoculation therapy

Meichenbaum's (1976) *stress inoculation therapy* assumes that people sometimes find situations stressful because of their *misperceptions* about them. The aim of stress inoculation therapy is to train people to cope more effectively with potentially stressful situations. The therapy consists of three stages. The first, *cognitive preparation*, involves the therapist and person exploring the way in which stressful situations are thought about by the person. Typically, people react to stress by offering negative self-statements, such as 'I can't handle this'. This makes an already stressful situation even more stressful. The second stage, *skill acquisition and practice*, attempts to develop more adaptive self-statements in the face of stress. These are then learned and practised. Meichenbaum (1976) has described some of the self-statements that would be used to help a person preparing for a stressful situation to confront and handle a stressful situation and to cope with the feeling of being overwhelmed. These are shown in Box 11.6, along with some reinforcing self-statements.

Box 11.6   Some coping self-statements used in stress inoculation therapy

Preparing for a stressful situation

- What is it you have to do?
- You can develop a plan to deal with it.
- Just think about what you can do about it; that's better than getting anxious.
- No negative self-statements; just think rationally.
- Don't worry; worry won't help anything.
- Maybe what you think is anxiety is eagerness to confront it.

Confronting and handling a stressful situation

- Just 'psych' yourself up – you can meet this challenge.
- One step at a time; you can handle the situation.
- Don't think about fear; just think about what you have to do. Stay relevant.
- This anxiety is what the therapist said you would feel. It's a reminder to use your coping exercises.
- This tenseness can be an ally, a cue to cope.
- Relax; you're in control. Take a slow deep breath.
- Ah, good.

Coping with the feeling of being overwhelmed

- When fear comes, just pause.
- Keep the focus on the present; what is it that you have to do?
- Label your fear from 0 to 10 and watch it change.
- You should expect your fear to rise.
- Don't try to eliminate fear totally; just keep it manageable.
- You can convince yourself to do it. You can reason fear away.

- It will be over shortly.
- It's not the worst thing that can happen.
- Just think about something else.
- Do something that will prevent you from thinking about fear.
- Describe what is around you. That way you won't think about worrying.

Reinforcing self-statements

- It worked; you did it.
- Wait until you tell your therapist about this.
- It wasn't as bad as you expected.
- You made more out of the fear than it was worth.
- Your damn ideas – that's the problem. When you control them, you control your fear.
- It's getting better each time you use the procedures.
- You can be pleased with the progress you're making.
- You did it!

(Meichenbaum, 1976)

The final stage of therapy, *application and practice*, involves the person applying the strategies that have been rehearsed in actual stress-producing situations. Initially, the person is placed in a situation that is moderately easy to cope with. Once this has been mastered, a situation that is more difficult to cope with is presented. According to Meichenbaum *et al.* (1982), the 'power of positive thinking' approach advocated by stress inoculation therapy can be quite successful in bringing about effective behaviour change particularly in relation to anxiety and pain.

Some other applications of therapies derived from the cognitive model

Like other therapies, therapies based on the cognitive model have received considerable scrutiny as to their worth (see, for example, Andrews, 1993). Recent research has shown that cognitively based therapies can be particularly helpful in the treatment of *panic disorder*. As we noted in Chapter 6, Clark (1993) has argued that the core disturbance in this disorder is an abnormality in thinking in which people interpret normal bodily signs and symptoms as indications of an impending mental or physical catastrophe (such as a heart attack). Because of their fears, people become *hypervigilant* and repeatedly scan their body for signs of danger which results in them noticing sensations which other people would not be aware of. Additionally, subtle *avoidance behaviours* prevent people from disconfirming their negative beliefs. For example, people convinced that they are suffering from cardiac disease may avoid exercise and rest whenever a palpitation occurs in the belief that this will avoid a fatal heart attack.

Studies conducted by Clark *et al.* (1994) and Shear *et al.* (1994) have shown that cognitively based therapies can be highly effective in changing the cognitions and behaviour of 90% of those treated. However, whether therapies derived from the cognitive model can and should be used with other disorders is less clear-cut.

For example, in a review of research findings concerning obsessive-compulsive disorder, James & Blackburn (1995) have shown that, of the few well-controlled studies examining the effectiveness of cognitively based therapies, there is little evidence to suggest that they bring about an improvement.

Conclusions

The goal of therapies based on the cognitive model is to change maladaptive behaviour by changing the way people think. There are several types of therapy based on the cognitive model. These have been used to treat a number of types of mental disorder, particularly depression. Although cognitively based therapies have been shown to be useful in the treatment of this disorder, their usefulness in the treatment of other disorders is less well established.

SUMMARY

- The aim of therapies based on the cognitive model is to show people that their distorted/irrational thoughts are the main contributors to their disorders; if the faulty thinking can be **modified/changed**, then disorders can be alleviated.
- Sometimes the term **cognitive-behavioural therapies** is used to refer to therapies based on the cognitive model, implying that they really belong to the behavioural model. It is often difficult to distinguish between them, and therapists who identify their orientation as primarily 'behavioural' or 'cognitive' may actually be doing the same thing.
- However, cognitive therapists believe that behavioural changes occur as a result of cognitive changes. They try to produce **insight** into **current cognitions**.
- Bandura is a leading figure in **cognitive-behaviour therapy**, which represents the interface between behavioural methods and the cognitive model. As a **social learning theorist**, he believes that conditioning is not a sufficient explanation for certain kinds of learning; humans and some non-human animals can acquire new forms of behaviour simply by observing others' behaviour (**observational learning**). Further, if we see

someone receiving a positive outcome for a behaviour, this will produce **response disinhibition**, while a negative outcome will produce **response inhibition**.
- According to Bandura, maladaptive behaviours can be altered by exposing the person to appropriate **models**, as in the treatment of a snake phobia, where the therapist demonstrates fearless behaviour and encourages the phobic person to gradually do the same through imitation (**participant modelling**). This seems to be more effective than **symbolic modelling**.
- As well as changing behaviour, **modelling** aims to change thoughts and perceptions. It has been successfully used with a variety of phobias and is also used to establish new/more appropriate behaviours, as in **assertiveness training**, in which the therapist models appropriately assertive behaviour which is imitated by the individual (**behavioural rehearsal**). When the assertive role has eventually been mastered, the skills are tried out in real-life situations. This approach has also been widely used in **social skills training**.
- One reason for the effectiveness of modelling is the development of **self-efficacy**. This enables

people, when confronting difficult situations, to engage in behaviours that were previously avoided.

- Ellis developed **rational-emotive therapy (RET)** in the 1950s after becoming dissatisfied with the 'passivity of psychoanalysis'. He argues that many emotional difficulties are due to people's 'irrational beliefs', which can be understood as part of the **A–B–C model**. A (a significant activating event) might seem to be the cause of C (a highly charged emotional consequence), but C is in fact caused by B (a person's belief system). Inappropriate emotions, such as depression and guilt, can only be removed if there is a change in a person's beliefs/perceptions.
- RET aims to help people find flaws in their thinking by creating D (a **dispute belief system**) which has no severe emotional consequences. Maladaptive cognitions make impossible demands on the people who hold them, producing anxiety, feelings of failure and, often, abnormal behaviour.
- Once a person's irrational beliefs have been identified, therapy involves guiding him/her to substitute them with more logical/realistic ones and to produce **full acceptance**. The therapist challenges the person's irrational beliefs, presenting the universe as logical/rational; the scientific method of controlled observation is the appropriate means of understanding it. People have the **capacity** for rational understanding but are also capable of deluding themselves and thinking irrationally.
- RET seems to be effective for at least some types of disorder but less so for others (such as agoraphobia) compared with therapies based on other models. It is effective in changing behaviour amongst people who are self-demanding and feel guilty for not living up to their own standards of perfection. However, it is clearly ineffective for those, like schizophrenics, with severe thought disorders.
- RET is an active, directive and, indeed, argumentative approach, which has been questioned by those who stress the importance of **empathy** in therapy.
- Beck's **cognitive restructuring therapy** assumes, like RET, that mental disorders stem primarily from irrational beliefs that lead to maladaptive behaviour. Beck's approach is specifically designed to treat **depressed** people, who suffer from a **cognitive triad** of negative beliefs about themselves, their future, and their experiences.

These beliefs arise from faulty information-processing and logic.

- The aim of Beck's therapy is to identify the implicit and self-defeating assumptions of depressed people. The therapist takes a gentler, less confrontational, and more experiential approach than would occur with RET. Not surprisingly, Beck's approach is most successful in treating depression, although it has also been used successfully with eating disorders.
- **Attributional therapy** is an approach to the treatment of depression derived from the revised theory of learned helplessness, according to which depressed people make unrealistic/faulty attributions about their own behaviour, which can cause great distress.
- Depressed people tend to display the reverse of the normal **self-serving bias**, such that they attribute their failures to **internal/dispositional** factors and their successes to **external/situational** factors. Attributional therapists try to break down the vicious circle experienced by people of low self-esteem, and beneficial changes have been reported after only a few sessions. Therapy may involve 'homework assignments' in which each day's positive events and the person's contributions to them are recorded.
- Meichenbaum's **stress inoculation therapy** assumes that people sometimes find situations stressful because of their **misperceptions** about them. Therapy aims to train people to cope more effectively with potentially stressful situations, through **cognitive preparation**, **skill acquisition and practice**, and **application and practice**, in which the person applies the strategies that have been rehearsed in actual stress-producing situations.
- Some categories of **coping self-statements** used in stress inoculation therapy include **preparing for a stressful situation/confronting and handling a stressful situation/coping with the feeling of being overwhelmed/reinforcing self-statements.**
- Cognitively based therapies can be particularly helpful in treating **panic disorder**, central to which is the interpretation of normal bodily signs and symptoms as indicating an impending mental/physical catastrophe. This induces **hypervigilance** in relation to bodily sensations. In addition, subtle **avoidance behaviours** prevent people from disconfirming their negative beliefs. The effectiveness of cognitive therapies with other disorders is far less certain.

12

THERAPIES BASED ON THE HUMANISTIC

Introduction and overview

We noted in Chapter 2 that the humanistic model sees people as *sets of potentials* who are basically 'good' and who strive for growth, dignity and self-determination. Mental disorders are seen as arising when external factors somehow block the potential for personal growth. The goal of therapies based on the humanistic model is to remove such blocks and to put people 'in touch' with their true self. Our aim in this chapter is to examine some of the therapeutic approaches that have been devised by those who subscribe to the humanistic model. We will consider Carl Rogers' client- (or person-) centred therapy and the Gestalt therapy of Frederick Perls. We will also look at some of the humanistic approaches to group therapy.

Carl Rogers' client- (or person-) centred therapy

Humanistic therapy was first introduced in the 1940s by Carl Rogers. Rogers originally called his approach *client-centred therapy*. However, in 1974, he and his colleagues changed the name to *person-centred therapy* in order to focus more clearly on the human values the approach emphasises (Meador & Rogers, 1984). The

therapy is also called *non-directive therapy* because Rogers refused to tell people what to do or what to think (but see also page 19). Instead of directing therapy, the Rogerian approach is to clarify feelings by rephrasing what people say and repeatedly asking what they really believe and feel. Rather than looking at earlier parts of life, Rogers believed in focusing on the present.

For many people, it is unusual that a therapist should refuse to offer expert advice. In a film made by Rogers in 1964, a woman who sought advice on what to tell her daughter about her relationships with men was repeatedly asked by Rogers what *she* thought. After several direct questions, Rogers replied:

> 'I feel this is the kind of very private thing that I couldn't possibly answer for you, but I sure as anything will try to help you work towards your own answer' (Meador & Rogers, 1973).

In Rogers' own words, the central premise of person-centred therapy is that:

> 'the individual has within him or herself, vast resources of self-understanding, for altering his or her self-concept, attitudes and self-directing behaviour, and that these resources can be tapped if only a definable climate of facilitative psychological attitudes can be provided' (Rogers, 1986).

Figure 12.1   Carl Rogers (1902–87), founder of client-centred/person-centred therapy

There are three major elements in the 'definable climate' or 'therapeutic atmosphere' which Rogers believed would encourage personal growth in his clients. These are *genuineness, unconditional positive regard*, and *empathy*.

ENCOURAGING PERSONAL GROWTH

Genuineness

Genuineness (which is also known as *authenticity* or *congruence*) refers to a real human relationship in which therapists honestly express their own feelings. According to Rogers, it would be harmful to clients if a therapist could not be 'dependably real', that is, truly accept and like them, even though their values might differ from those of the therapist. Therapists who tried to manufacture a fake concern or hide their own beliefs would actually *impede* true personal growth in their clients. As Bennett (1985) has observed, Rogers admitted that he sometimes had negative feelings about some clients. The most common feeling was boredom, and

Rogers expressed this rather than holding it in. If the therapist says one thing, but somehow communicates a different feeling, then the client will pick this up and believe the therapist cannot be trusted. Genuineness is the most important of the three elements and Rogers' views on genuineness are shown in Box 12.1.

> **Box 12.1   Genuineness**
>
> Sometimes (in therapy) a feeling 'rises up in me' which seems to have no particular relationship to what is going on. Yet I have learned to accept and trust this feeling in my awareness and to try to communicate it to my client. For example, a client is talking to me, and I suddenly feel an image of him as a pleading little boy, folding his hands in supplication, saying 'Please let me have this, please let me have this'. I have learned that if I can be real in the relationship with him and express this feeling that has occurred in me, it is very likely to strike some deep note in him and advance our relationship.
>
> (Rogers, 1980)

Unconditional positive regard

Unconditional positive regard means respecting clients as important human beings with values and goals and accepting people for what they are without reservation. Rogers believed that therapists should not judge clients' worth by their behaviour. Rather, they should provide clients with a sense of security that encourages them to follow their own feelings and recognise the essential dignity of each person. Clients must therefore be convinced that therapists actually like and respect them and that the positive regard they give does not depend on what the client says or does.

Empathy

Empathy (or *empathic understanding*) is the process of perceiving the world from the client's perspective and understanding what he or she is experiencing. It is not to be confused with sympathy. For example, a therapist who says, 'I'm sorry you feel insecure', may be genuine in what he or she says, but may not be empathic because empathy involves an attempt to 'get inside the client's head' and to try and fully understand why the client lacks security. In other words, the client must be convinced that he or she is understood by the therapist. In the absence of such understanding, a client might think, 'Sure, this therapist says he likes me and respects me, but that's because he really doesn't know me. If he really knew me, he wouldn't like me'.

TECHNIQUES USED IN ROGERIAN THERAPY

One way in which empathic understanding can be achieved is through a technique known as *active listening* in which the therapist attempts to grasp both the *content* of what the client is saying and the *feeling* behind it. To communicate empathy, the therapist uses *reflection*, summarising the client's message (in terms of its content and feeling) and feeding this back to the client. Although empathy requires a great deal of skill, Rogers (1986) sees active listening as 'one of the most potent forces for change that I know'. As well as helping clients understand or clarify their feelings, active listening also lets them know that the therapist both understands and accepts what is being said. According to Thorne (1984), empathy is the most 'trainable' of the three major elements, but is at the same time remarkably rare. As we noted earlier on, therapists do not offer direct advice or interpretations, but may ask for clarifications now and again. Box 12.2 illustrates a therapist showing empathic understanding of a client.

Box 12.2	Empathic understanding
Client:	I was thinking about this business of standards. I somehow developed a sort of knack, I guess, of, well, habit, of trying to make people feel at ease around me, or to make things go along smoothly.
Therapist:	In other words, what you did was always in the direction of trying to keep things smooth and to make other people feel better and to smooth the situation.
Client:	Yes. I think that's what it was. Now the reason why I did it probably was – I mean, not that I was a good little Samaritan going around making other people happy, but that was probably the role that felt easiest for me to play. I'd been doing it around the home so much. I just didn't stand up for my own convictions, until I don't know whether I have any convictions to stand up for.
Therapist:	You feel that for a long time you've

been playing the role of kind of smoothing out the frictions or differences or what not . . .

Client:	Mm-hmm.
Therapist:	Rather than having any opinion or reaction of your own in the situation. Is that it?
Client:	That's it. Or that I haven't been really honestly being myself, or actually knowing what my real self is, and that I've been playing a sort of false role. Whatever role no one else was playing, and that needed to be played at the time, I'd try to fill it in.

(Rogers, 1951)

Genuineness, unconditional positive regard and empathy are interconnected. Changes in a client's moment-to-moment feelings require that the therapist accepts and values the client, that is, shows both empathy and unconditional positive regard. As we noted, genuineness is the most important of all, because a meaningful relationship demands that empathy and unconditional positive regard are honest and real.

Typically, Rogerian therapy sessions are held once a week with the client and therapist facing each other. A client who says, for example, 'I'm depressed', might have the therapist respond with, 'Sounds like you're really down', an approach known as *reflection*. Through this process, the client comes to feel heard and understood. The passive reflection by the therapist is gradually replaced by *active interpretation*. By going beyond the overt content of what the client says, the therapist responds to what he or she senses to be the client's true feelings. The therapist starts to confront the client with inconsistencies in what he or she is saying, and may, for example, point out that the client is failing to take responsibility for personal actions.

So, in an atmosphere where anything that is felt may be expressed, the focus is more on *present feelings* than on past feelings. During therapy, clients begin to realise that, perhaps for the first time, someone is listening to them, and they become more and more aware of long-denied feelings and thoughts, and learn to accept these and incorporate them into their self-concept. In

Rogers' own words, clients 'get it together' and experience *congruence*.

APPLICATION AND EVALUATION OF ROGERIAN THERAPY

Rogerian therapy has been applied not only to individuals, but also in human-relations training for professionals of all kinds, including nurses, crisis workers and counsellors. In universities, for example, the approach has been used with students who have not yet made career choices. The therapy helps decision-making by providing an encouraging atmosphere in which clients can explore various choices and paths. As we have noted, Rogerian therapists do not tell clients what to do. Instead, they help them to arrive at their own decisions. Box 12.3 illustrates an interaction between a Rogerian therapist and a client.

Box 12.3   Client-centred therapy in action

Client: I guess I do have problems at school ... You see, I'm the chairman of the Science department, so you can imagine what kind of a department it is.

Therapist: You sort of feel that if *you're* in something that it can't be too good. Is that ...?

Client: Well, it's not that I ... It's just that I'm ... I don't think that I could run it.

Therapist: You don't have any confidence in yourself?

Client: No confidence, no confidence in myself. I never had any confidence in myself. I – like I told you that – like when even when I was a kid, I didn't feel I was capable and I always wanted to get back with the intellectual group.

Therapist: This has been a long-term thing, then. It's gone on a long time.

Client: Yeah, the *feeling* is – even though I know it isn't, it's the feeling that I have, that I haven't got it, that ... that ... that ... people will find out that I'm dumb or ... or ...

Therapist: Masquerade ...

Client: Superficial, I'm just superficial.

There's nothing below the surface. Just superficial generalities, that ...

Therapist: There's nothing really deep and meaningful to you.

Client: No – they don't know it, and ...

Therapist: And you're terrified they're going to find out.

Client: My wife has a friend, and – and she and the friend got together so we could go out together with her and my wife and her husband ... And the guy, he's an engineer and he's, you know – he's got it, you know; and I don't want to go, I don't want to go because ... because if ... if we get together he's liable to start to ... to talk about something I don't know, and I'll ... I won't know about that.

Therapist: You're terribly frightened in this sort of thing.

Client: I ... I'm afraid to be around people who ... who I feel are my peers. Even in pool ... now I ... I play pool very well and ... if I'm playing with some guy that I ... I know I can beat, *psychologically*, I can run 50, but ... but if I start playing with somebody that's my level, I'm done. I'm done. I ... I ... I'll miss a ball every time.

Therapist: So the ... the fear of what's going on just immobilises you, keeps you from doing a good job.

(based on Hersher, 1970)

Rogers was not afraid to have his therapy evaluated through research publications. For example, Rogers & Dymond (1954) published studies detailing the success of the therapy. Unlike supporters of some other therapies who rely on their own judgements, Rogers recorded therapeutic sessions so that the various techniques he employed could be evaluated. In one study, for example, Truax (1966) obtained permission from Rogers and his clients to record therapy sessions in order to determine their effectiveness. Truax found that only those clients who showed progress were regularly followed by a positive response from Rogers, and that during their therapy, clients made more statements indicating progress. What this would seem to suggest is that social reinforcement is very powerful. This is not meant to discredit client-centred therapy, but shows that Rogers was very effective in adopting a strategy for altering a person's behaviour. Although the term *non-directive* was initially used to describe Rogerian therapy, when Rogers realised he was reinforcing positive statements, he stopped referring to it as non-directive because it quite clearly was not.

One way in which Rogers attempted to validate client-centred therapy empirically was through a method called *Q-sort*. This consists of a number of cards with statements relating to the self, such as 'I am a domineering person'. Clients are required to arrange the cards in a series of ten piles ranging from 'very characteristic of me' to 'not at all characteristic of me' to describe their self-image. The process is then repeated to describe the 'ideal self'. After this, the two Q-sorts are correlated to determine the discrepancy between the self-image as it is and the ideal self-image. During the course of therapy, the procedure is repeated several times, the idea being that if the therapy is having a beneficial effect, the discrepancy between the self-image and the ideal self-image should narrow (and the correlation between them increase).

Other critics of Rogerian therapy, such as Bandura (1969), have objected to Rogerian methods on the grounds that they treat people in the same way irrespective of their disorder (a comment which applies to other therapies as well!). It has also been suggested that providing people with unconditional positive regard might actually be harmful, because they might leave therapy with the unrealistic expectation that anything they do will meet with the approval of society. The therapy is also limited in terms of the disorders that it can be applied to. Like psychoanalysis, Rogerian therapy is not appropriate for disorders such as schizophrenia. It seems that Rogerian therapy is most effective for people who want to change and who are intelligent enough to gain some sort of insight concerning their problems.

Other critics have argued that the humanistic model is simply wrong in viewing humans as being basically 'good' (see Chapter 2). Whether a person who has exhibited signs of antisocial personality disorder should be provided with unconditional positive regard is debatable. The therapy is, however, much more affordable and much less time-consuming than, say, psycho-

dynamic therapies. Perhaps cynically, those neurotic individuals who are 'decent' might actually enjoy and profit from talking about their problems with a person as sympathetic as Rogers.

Frederick Perls' Gestalt therapy

Gestalt therapy was devised by a German-born psychiatrist, Frederick (Fritz) Perls. Like Rogers' person-centred approach, Perls believed that therapy should aim to help people integrate conflicting parts of their personality. Perls was dissatisfied with psychoanalysis and called it 'a disease that pretends to be a cure'. However, whilst Perls agreed with Rogers that people are free to make choices and to direct their growth, Gestalt therapy is highly *directive*, and the therapist leads the client through *planned experiences*. Despite his dissatisfaction with psychoanalysis, Perls agreed with Freud that mental disorders result from unconscious conflicts and, like Freud, Perls stressed the importance of dream analysis. However, whereas Freud saw dreams as the 'royal road to the unconscious', Perls saw dreams as 'disowned parts of the personality'. Another difference between Freud and Perls was that Perls believed current problems (the 'here and now') could be focused on, and that people have responsibility for the direction of their own lives (which is, of course, consistent with the humanistic model we outlined in Chapter 2).

Perls called his therapy Gestalt therapy, referring to the German word that means 'pattern' or 'organised whole', because he believed that when therapy was complete, a person became 'whole' and could resume normal growth. The approach was particularly influential in the 1960s, especially in the United States. According to Gestalt therapists, psychologically healthy people are *aware* of themselves so fully that they can detect whatever requires their attention. Mental disorders occur as a result of a blockage of awareness. Perls saw awareness as being critical, because if people are unaware of what they want or feel at any time or moment, then they have limited control over their feelings and behaviour. At times, we act out of habit rather than choice, and the habits may become self-defeating.

Gestalt therapists, then, see mental disorders as being

Figure 12.2   Frederick (Fritz) Perls (1893–1970), founder of Gestalt therapy

due to the inability to integrate various aspects of the personality (such as thoughts, feelings and actions) into a healthy, well-organised whole. The aim of therapy is therefore to help a person to bring together the 'alienated fragments' of the self into an integrated, unified whole (the sense of wholeness being termed *organismic self-regulation*). By achieving a sense of wholeness, Gestalt therapists believe that people can relate more fully to others and live more spontaneous lives.

The development of awareness allows an individual to confront and make choices, the assumption being that when allowed to make choices, people choose self-enhancing and growthful options instead of self-defeating ones that have been used before. So, by being aware of inner conflicts, people can accept the reality of them, rather than denying them and keeping them repressed. This can help them make productive choices despite misgivings and fear.

The primary focus of Gestalt therapy is on the moment-to-moment *awareness* of the self. The therapist's role is that of an *active co-explorer* with clients,

encouraging them to break through whatever defences are preventing them from fully experiencing their feelings and thoughts. The relationship between the client and therapist has been likened to that between an apprentice and master (Kempler, 1973). The skill the master teaches to the apprentice is, of course, that of awareness. As the relationship between them develops, the therapist uses awareness to enhance growth in the client.

Perls did not believe there was any set formula for achieving this. However, Levitsky & Perls (1970) provided guidelines for therapists. In many ways, Gestalt therapists behave like psychoanalysts by, for example, directing clients' attentions to conflicts and dreams. But as we noted, Gestalt therapists interpret dreams differently. For them, fragments of dreams are aspects of personality, and the aim is to help clients piece together dream fragments as they relate to current problems.

Typically, therapy is conducted in a *group setting* with the focus on one person at a time. Various techniques are used to help people become aware of who they are and what they are feeling and of personal responsibility. According to Gestalt therapists, any action implies a choice, and with choice goes responsibility. On some occasions, a therapist will deliberately frustrate clients, especially if clients are trying to lean on the therapist when support is not really necessary. The therapist's job is to emphasise awareness on the part of the client and this can be achieved in a variety of ways. Some of these are described in Box 12.4.

Box 12.4   Some techniques used in Gestalt therapy

The following techniques or 'directed experiments' are usually carried out in a consulting room or a group setting.

Role playing: A person who is angry at his mother, say, first plays himself talking to his mother and then reverses the roles and becomes the mother. Perls believed that by acting out both sides to a conflict, a person would complete *unfinished business*, that is, become aware of unexpressed feelings that had been carried around for many years. This allows a sense of completion to be gained which frees the individual to deal with present-day problems rather than those from the past (and note how different this

---

is to Rogers' therapy). Indeed, unlike a Rogerian, a Gestalt therapist might even become involved and join in the role playing. In the *empty chair exercise*, the client moves back and forth between two chairs. In one of the chairs the client first plays him- or herself talking to his or her mother. The client then moves to the other chair and assumes the role of the mother.

Amplification: The therapist asks the client to exaggerate some behaviour or feeling in order to become more aware of it. A man who responds to a question about his wife, for example, might talk favourably about her, but draw his fingers towards his palm slightly. When asked to exaggerate this, the client might make a fist, strike the table and offer revealing comments about his wife.

Dialogue: In this, the client undertakes verbal confrontations between opposing wishes and ideas. One example of clashing personality elements is *underdog* and *top dog*. The former, and its suggestions of 'don't take chances' is confronted with the latter and its suggestions that 'you'll never progress if you don't take chances'. A heightened awareness of the elements of conflict can clear the path towards resolution, perhaps through compromise.

Speaking in the first person: This approach helps people recognise and take responsibility for their own actions. A person who says 'sometimes people are afraid to take the first step in initiating a relationship for fear of being rejected' is encouraged to restate this in the first person: '*I* am afraid to take the first step . . . because *I* fear being rejected'.

- Stop imagining. Experience the real.
- Stop unnecessary thinking. Rather, taste and see.
- Express rather than manipulate, explain, justify or judge.
- Give in to unpleasantness and pain just as to pleasure. Do not restrict your awareness.
- Accept no 'should' or 'ought' other than your own. Adore no graven image.
- Take full responsibility for your actions, feelings and thoughts.
- Surrender to being as you are.

Perhaps one way of evaluating the effectiveness and appropriateness of Gestalt therapy is in terms of the number of people who have adopted the approach. Proponents of the therapy argue that its growth is one indicator of its effectiveness. However, according to Rimm & Masters (1979), there have been few controlled studies to validate the therapy, and therefore we do not know if it is effective or not. In response to this, Gestalt therapists argue that controlled research is not necessary because the direct experiences of those who have received the therapy is overwhelming evidence that it works. Moreover, because the therapy is so individualised, it cannot be evaluated in the same way as other therapies (a point to which we will return in the following chapter). There is, however, evidence to suggest that techniques like amplification can be effective (Simkin & Yontef, 1984), though clearly Gestalt therapy, like other therapies, is going to be more effective with some populations than others.

The ultimate aim of therapy is not just to make people aware of their problems, but to teach them *how* to become aware so that they can do this independently. When this has been achieved, therapy is complete. The *moral injunctions* of Gestalt therapy are presented in Box 12.5.

Box 12.5   The moral injunctions of Gestalt therapy

- Live now. Be concerned with the present rather than the past or future.
- Live here. Deal with what is present rather than what is absent.

Humanistic approaches to group therapy

Although we described group approaches to therapy when we considered therapies based on the psychodynamic model, it is the humanistic model that has contributed most to the group therapy movement. The major therapeutic gains of a group approach are held to be the development of intimacy and cooperation by virtue of being part of a mutually supportive group, and finding out about oneself through candid interactions with others.

The earliest form of humanistic group therapy, which laboured under the generic term *human potential movement* was the *encounter group*, which was very much part of the American (and, in particular, Californian) culture of the 1960s and 1970s. Encounter groups were originally developed by Rogers as what Graham (1986) has called:

> 'a means whereby people can break through the barriers erected by themselves and others in order to react openly and freely with one another'.

Participants (rather than *clients*) are encouraged to act out their emotions, rather than just talk about them, through bodily contact and structured 'games'. The group leader (or *facilitator*) attempts to create an atmosphere of mutual trust in which group members, who usually number between eight and eighteen, feel free to express their feelings irrespective of whether these are positive or negative. According to Rogers (1973), this expression reduces defensiveness and promotes self-actualisation.

Sensitivity training groups (or *T-groups*) were first introduced in the late 1940s with the intention of helping group leaders improve the functioning of groups by democratic methods. Later, the approach was used to help business executives improve their relations with co-workers. Unlike encounter groups, in which feelings are expressed by yelling, weeping, touching exercises, and other unrestrained displays of emotion, T-groups were originally limited to 'subtler' emotional expressions. However, whether such groups can bring about change is questionable, and some have warned against the dangers of such groups. It has been claimed, for example, that such groups can precipitate, if not cause, various sorts of psychological disturbances. Aggressive,

highly charismatic and authoritarian leaders were the most likely to have 'casualties', that is, people who suffered a severe psychological disturbance that endured up to six months after the group experience. One of the destructive characteristics is the pressure to have some ecstatic, or what Maslow (1968) would call *peak*, experience which is viewed as being necessary for continuing mental health. Maslow himself, however, would argue that such experiences are relatively uncommon and certainly cannot be produced 'on demand'.

We noted on page 133 that Gestalt therapy is typically conducted in a group setting with the focus on one person at a time. However, in its pure group form, participants in Gestalt therapy *help one another* work through their emotional crises. Unlike T-groups, but like encounter groups, unrestrained emotional outpouring is encouraged, with the emphasis being placed on the participants' present experiences. For Perls (1967), such group approaches are helpful because:

> 'in the safe emergency of the therapeutic situation, the (individual) discovers that the world does not fall to pieces if he or she gets angry, sexy, jealous or mournful'.

Conclusions

The present chapter has examined some of the therapies which are based on the humanistic model of abnormality. These therapies, which aim to put people in touch with their true self, have attracted considerable interest, and there is evidence to suggest that in some cases, they can be effective in the treatment of certain types of mental disorder.

SUMMARY

- According to the humanistic model, mental disorders arise when external factors block the individual's potential for personal growth. Humanistic therapies aim to remove such blocks and to put people 'in touch' with their true self.
- Humanistic therapy was first introduced in the 1940s by Carl Rogers (**client-centred therapy**); this was renamed **person-centred** therapy in

order to focus more on the human values emphasised by this approach. It is also called **non-directive therapy**. The approach involves clarifying feelings by rephrasing what people say and repeatedly asking what they really believe/feel **in the present**. No expert advice is offered.
- There are three major elements in the 'definable climate'/'therapeutic atmosphere' which Rogers

believed would encourage personal growth, namely **genuineness**, **unconditional positive regard** and **empathy**.

- **Genuineness (authenticity/congruence)** is the most important of the three elements and refers to a real human relationship in which therapists honestly express their own feelings. Trying to fake concern or hide their own beliefs/values would actually **impede** true personal growth in clients. If the therapist says one thing, but communicates something different, the client will detect this and see the therapist as untrustworthy.

- **Unconditional positive regard** means respecting clients as important human beings with values/goals and accepting them for what they are without reservation. Clients' worth shouldn't be judged by their behaviour but they should be given a sense of security that encourages them to follow their own feelings. Clients must be convinced that therapists actually like/respect them and that this positive regard is not dependent on what they say/do.

- **Empathy (empathic understanding)** is the process of perceiving the world from the client's perspective by trying to 'get inside the client's head'. The client must be convinced that he/she is understood by the therapist. This can be achieved through **active listening**, in which the therapist tries to grasp both the **content** of what the client is saying and the **feeling** behind it. To communicate empathy, the therapist uses **reflection**, through which the client comes to feel heard and understood.

- Although empathy requires considerable skill, Rogers saw it as a major means of achieving change. It is the most 'trainable' of his three elements but is also remarkably rare. The three elements are interconnected.

- Typically, Rogerian therapy involves a once-weekly session with client and therapist facing each other. Passive reflection is gradually replaced by **active interpretation**, in which the therapist goes beyond the overt content of what the client says and responds to what seems to be the client's true feelings. The therapist points out inconsistencies in what is said and may point out that the client is failing to take responsibility for personal actions. Clients become more and more aware of long denied feelings/thoughts which they gradually accept and incorporate into their self-concept (**congruence**).

- Rogerian therapy has been used not only with individuals, but also in human-relations training for nurses, crisis workers and counsellors. It helps people to make their own decisions (e.g. about careers) by providing an encouraging atmosphere in which options can be explored.

- Rogers attempted to evaluate his therapy through research publications, rather than relying on his own judgements. One method of evaluation is to record therapy sessions. Truax's study suggested that social reinforcement is a very powerful strategy for changing people's behaviour. While this does not discredit client-centred therapy, it does imply that it is not 'non-directive' after all.

- Another method of validating client-centred therapy used by Rogers was the **Q-sort**, which can be used to describe the self-image, the ideal self, and the discrepancy between them. The procedure is repeated several times during the course of therapy: if therapy is having a beneficial effect, the discrepancy should narrow.

- One criticism of Rogerian therapy is that all clients are treated in the same way regardless of their disorder. Another is that unconditional positive regard may actually be detrimental because clients might come to expect, unrealistically, that anything they do will be accepted by society; it is also debatable whether someone with antisocial personality should be given unconditional positive regard.

- Like psychoanalysis, client-centred therapy is not suitable for disorders such as schizophrenia, but is most effective for people who want to change and who are capable of gaining insight into their problems. It is much more affordable and less time-consuming than psychodynamic therapies.

- Like Rogers' person-centred approach, Fritz Perls' **Gestalt therapy** is aimed at helping people integrate conflicting parts of their personality. But unlike Rogers' approach, Gestalt therapy is highly **directive** and the therapist leads the client through 'planned experiences'.

- Despite his dissatisfaction with psychoanalysis, Perls, like Freud, believed that mental disorders stem from unconscious conflicts and stressed the importance of dream analysis. However, Perls saw dreams as 'disowned parts of the personality' and focused on the 'here and now'; people are also responsible for the direction of their own lives.

- **Gestalt** is the German word for 'pattern'/'organised whole'. Mental disorders are due to a blockage of **awareness**, an inability to integrate various aspects of the personality (thoughts/feelings/actions) into a healthy, well-organised whole. The aim of therapy is to help the person to bring together the 'alienated fragments' of the self into an integrated, unified whole (**organismic self-regulation**).

- The development of awareness allows the individual to confront and make self-enhancing and growthful choices, instead of self-defeating ones that are made when awareness is blocked.
- The therapist's role is that of an **active co-explorer** with clients, encouraging them to break through whatever defences are preventing them from fully experiencing their thoughts/feelings. The therapist has also been likened to a master who teaches the skill of awareness to the apprentice/client.
- While there is no set formula for achieving awareness, therapists direct clients' attention to conflicts and dreams; dream fragments are aspects of personality and the aim is to help clients piece them together as they relate to current problems. This usually takes place in a **group setting** with the focus on one person at a time. Various techniques ('directed experiments') may be used, including **role playing**, which helps the person to complete **unfinished business** and may include the **empty chair exercise**, **amplification**, **dialogue**, and **speaking in the first person**.
- The ultimate aim of therapy is to teach people **how** to become aware of their problems, so that they can do this independently. Gestalt therapy involves a number of **moral injunctions**; these are 'rules' to live one's life by.
- Despite the growth in popularity of Gestalt therapy, there have been few controlled studies to evaluate its effectiveness. Its supporters argue that the direct experiences of clients are overwhelming evidence that it works, and that its individualised nature makes it impossible to evaluate in the same way as other therapies.
- The humanistic model has contributed more than any other to **group therapy** (the **human potential movement**). Mutually supportive groups can provide intimacy and cooperation and the chance to learn about oneself through frank interactions with others.
- The earliest form of humanistic group therapy was the **encounter group**, originally developed by Rogers, in which 'participants' are encouraged to act out their emotions, both positive and negative, through bodily contact and structured 'games'. The 'facilitator' tries to create an atmosphere of mutual trust.
- **Sensitivity training groups (T-groups)** were originally intended to help group leaders improve group functioning by democratic methods. Later, they were used to help business executives improve their relations with co-workers. Compared with encounter groups, emotional expression was originally much more restrained/subtle. However, their effectiveness in producing change has been questioned and some critics claim that they may actually precipitate/cause psychological disturbances. One destructive characteristic is the pressure to have some ecstatic/'peak' experience, but according to Maslow, these cannot be produced 'on demand'.
- In its pure form, participants in **Gestalt** therapy **help one another** work through their emotional crises. Unrestrained emotional expression is encouraged. Such group approaches are helpful, says Perls, because the individual discovers that it is safe to get angry/jealous etc.

13

ASSESSING THE EFFECTIVENESS OF THERAPIES

Introduction and overview

In the previous five chapters, we have described some of the forms of therapy that either have been or are currently being used to treat mental disorders. Although we looked at the procedures involved in the various therapies and the sorts of disorders they are used to treat, we did not consider in any detail whether the therapies are effective and if some types of therapy are more effective than others. Our aim in this chapter is to look at some of the attempts that have been made to assess the effectiveness of the various therapies we have described. As we do this, we will consider some of the major issues that surround such attempts.

Early attempts at assessing the effectiveness of therapy

The first systematic attempt at evaluating the effectiveness of therapy was made by Hans Eysenck (1952). Eysenck examined psychoanalysis and *eclectic* psychotherapy (that is, psychotherapy incorporating a variety of approaches rather than the single approach used in psychoanalysis). Prior to the publication of Eysenck's findings, the value and effectiveness of psychotherapeutic approaches had not been seriously questioned since, at least as far as the therapists were concerned, many of those seeking treatment improved and reported themselves satisfied with their course of therapy.

According to Eysenck, however, Freudian therapeutic approaches were 'unsupported by any scientifically acceptable evidence'. Looking at studies conducted between 1920 and 1951, Eysenck discovered that in only 44% of cases treated using psychoanalysis could the person be considered 'cured', 'much improved' or 'improved'. Using the same criteria to assess people treated by means of eclectic psychotherapy, the figure was higher, at 64%.

Eysenck argued that many people with psychological problems actually improve without any professional treatment, a phenomenon known as *spontaneous recovery* or *spontaneous remission*. In order to assess the effectiveness of the two psychotherapies, it was necessary for Eysenck to compare the figures he had obtained with a *control group* of people who had similar problems to those who received therapy, but did not themselves receive any form of professional treatment (by, for example, being treated only custodially in an institution). Eysenck located two such studies that had been carried out and found that 66% satisfied the 'cured', 'much improved' or 'improved' criteria. On the basis of these data, Eysenck concluded that:

'There thus appears to be an inverse correlation between recovery and psychotherapy: the more psychotherapy, the smaller the recovery rate'.

The claim that no treatment is at least as effective, if not more effective, than professional treatment was not greeted enthusiastically by those who practised psychoanalysis or eclectic psychotherapy. Nor, we should note, was Eysenck's additional claim that it was unethical for therapists to charge people for their services, when the evidence seemed to suggest that they were paying for nothing.

In the years that followed the publication of Eysenck's controversial article, a number of critiques were made of the conclusions he drew and a large amount of research was conducted on assessing the effectiveness of therapy. For example, some researchers questioned Eysenck's inclusion as 'failures' those people who 'dropped out' of therapy, on the grounds that somebody who leaves therapy cannot necessarily be counted as 'not cured'. When the figures reported by Eysenck were reanalysed to take this into account, the figure of 44% for psychoanalysis rose to a considerably higher 66%.

Other researchers (such as Bergin, 1971) argued that the success rate for psychoanalysis could be raised to 83%, if 'improvement' was measured in a different way. Yet other researchers argued that the people in Eysenck's 'control' group differed in important ways from those who received treatment (a point acknowledged by Eysenck). Malan *et al.* (1975), for example, noted that 'untreated' individuals actually had one assessment interview which some of them perceived as a powerful impetus for *self-induced change*. Since the interview clearly influenced at least some people, they could hardly be considered to have 'spontaneously' recovered. Even the author of one of the articles from which Eysenck arrived at his figure for spontaneous recovery noted that there were differences between those who received therapy and those who did not.

The issue of measurement in evaluations of effectiveness

In order to evaluate a therapy, it is clearly necessary to have some way of *measuring* its effectiveness, that is, there should be what Crooks & Stein (1991) term a *criterion of success*. Unfortunately, it is not easy to determine what the most appropriate criterion should be. Some therapists would argue that the most appropriate and straightforward measurement of effectiveness is an observable change in behaviour. After all, if a person has a phobia before a course of therapy begins but does not have one after it has ended, then the therapy has surely been successful (Guscott & Taylor, 1994).

Those who use therapies based on the behavioural model (see Chapter 10) define their therapeutic goals in such terms and would certainly want observable change to be used as the criterion of success. However, in the case of some other therapies, this criterion would be considered inappropriate. As Krebs and Blackman (1988) have pointed out, psychoanalysts would argue that for therapy to be effective, unconscious conflicts must be resolved and a restructuring of personality produced (see Chapter 9). Since these cannot be directly measured, psychoanalysts would argue that an observable change in behaviour cannot be the *only* criterion of success.

Even if such a measure were appropriate, there is a further problem in deciding *who* will determine whether or not a behaviour change has occurred. To use the therapist him- or herself would surely be a mistake. What therapist, who has seen a person over a long period of time (and who in all probability has been receiving payment), would conclude that a treatment has been ineffective? Therapists clearly have a stake in believing that their therapy is positive and they cannot be unbiased, no matter how hard they try.

Being unable to directly measure outcomes, psychoanalysts would argue that we must rely on the reports of those who have received therapy. However, this approach assumes that people are always excellent judges of their own behaviour, an assumption which is unlikely to be true. Moreover, since the insights gained in psychoanalysis are, by their nature, unique, it is impossible to measure objectively how much insight has been gained.

Another possibilty, that of using the family and friends of the person who has received treatment, is also problematic, since in at least some cases, family members and/or friends may actually be the *cause* of a person's problems! Consider, for example, a woman who has sought therapy in order to be more assertive and who is married to an overbearing husband. As Krebs and Blackman (1988) have noted, we would hardly expect the husband to approve of his previously submissive wife's increased assertiveness.

Perhaps the most objective assessors would be therapists who were not involved in the treatment of an individual and who would, presumably, be unlikely to be biased in their judgements. This approach to assessing effectiveness was used by Sloane and his colleagues (1975) in a study designed to compare the effectiveness of psychotherapy, behaviour therapy and no therapy at all. The participants were 90 people suffering from various anxiety and personality disorders. They were carefully matched according to age, sex and their mental disorder, and then randomly assigned to a course of psychotherapy, behaviour therapy or were placed on a waiting list for therapy but did not actually receive any treatment. Highly experienced clinicians, who were experts in either psychotherapy or behaviour therapy, interviewed the participants before the study began and, without knowing which group the participants had been assigned to, at various times later on. The results showed that after four months of therapy, 80% of those treated using behaviour therapy *or* psychotherapy had either improved or recovered. For the control group, the figure was 48%, suggesting that contrary to the claim made by Eysenck (1952), psychotherapy *did* have a significant effect as compared with no treatment at all.

When the participants were assessed one year after therapy, those treated with psychotherapy or behaviour therapy had maintained their improvement, whereas those in the control group had made small but significant gains towards the levels of the two treatment groups. Sloane and his colleagues concluded that whilst spontaneous remission may occur (as Eysenck had claimed), both of the therapeutic techniques used were still better than no treatment at all. Some important issues surrounding the study conducted by Sloane *et al.* are considered in Box 13.1.

which extended over a lengthy period of time, such as ten years. Should we keep those in the 'control' group, who might (for example) be suicidal, free from treatment for that period of time? What if a person specifically sought out a particular therapy, but was assigned to either an alternative therapy or the control group?

In an ideal experiment, a person would be 'blind' as to the form of therapy he or she was receiving in order to control for any expectations about the treatment he or she might have. Even if this could be done, would we really want to do it? Would it be ethical to deceive a person into thinking that another form of therapy was the same thing as the therapy that was being given?

Whilst carefully controlled research is essential, there are, as we're sure you'll appreciate, many questions that can be asked about this sort of research whose importance should not be neglected.

More recently Durham, *et al.* (1994) compared cognitive therapy, analytic psychotherapy and anxiety management training for generalised anxiety disorder (see Chapter 7) using an *assessor* who was 'blind' to the individual's therapist and treatment condition. Individuals were rated according to *symptom change*, a criterion devised by Jacobson *et al.* (1984) for determining the proportion of outpatients returning to normal functioning. The results showed cognitive therapy to be significantly more effective than analytic psychotherapy, with anxiety management training falling in between these two.

As well as an observable change in behaviour, there are many other measures that could be used to assess the effectiveness of therapy. These include scores obtained on psychometric tests, and what are known as *recidivism rates*, that is, whether or not a person is readmitted for therapy or seeks additional therapy in a period of time after an initial course of therapy has ended. Using these measures, Luborsky *et al.* (1975), for example, claimed that improvements that followed a course of psychotherapy were significantly higher than was observed in people who received no treatment at all. Additionally, Luborsky and his colleagues reported that the outcome was better the more sessions that were undertaken (an observation that has been termed the

Box 13.1   Experimental studies of the effectiveness of therapy – some important questions

Although the study conducted by Sloane *et al.* (1975) was methodologically sound, it does raise a number of important questions. As we noted in the text, the participants were assigned to one of two therapeutic groups or a 'control' group. Suppose a similar study was to be conducted *dose-effect relationship*: see Chapter 6). We should remember, however, that because a greater number of treatments requires more *time*, the possibility that the passage of time itself contributes to improvement cannot be ruled out.

Meta-analytic studies of effectiveness

One way of overcoming the possibility that certain types of measurement may 'favour' certain types of therapy is to look at *all* types of measurement that have been used by researchers. This approach was taken by Smith and her associates (1980), who examined 475 different studies concerned with the effectiveness of therapy. Some of these studies compared differences between therapies with respect to their effectiveness, whilst other compared the effectiveness of a therapy against no treatment at all. Because researchers sometimes used more than one *criterion of success*, Smith and her associates actually had 1,776 *outcome measures* which varied from being highly subjective (as when the outcome measures were supplied by therapists) to much more objective (as when physiological measures were used).

The researchers used a statistical method called *meta-analysis* to analyse the results of the 475 studies. Meta-analysis allows researchers to *combine* the results from all of the studies conducted and produce what might be described as an 'average estimate' of the size of effect of whatever is being investigated (in this case, the effectiveness of therapy). The researchers found that, as far as therapies derived from the psychodynamic model were concerned, those receiving therapy scored significantly higher on a large number of criteria for success as compared with those who received no treatment, although as Figure 13.1 shows, there was considerable overlap in the outcomes for treated and untreated (or control) individuals.

On the basis of their findings, Smith *et al.* concluded that the evidence overwhelmingly supported the view that psychodynamic therapies are effective and that such therapies:

'benefit people of all ages as reliably as schooling educates them, medicine cures them or business turns a profit. The average person who receives

therapy is better off at the end of it than 80% of persons who do not'.

However, the researchers also acknowledged that the case for psychotherapy's effectiveness was far from proven. As they noted:

'This does not mean that everyone who receives psychotherapy improves. The evidence suggests that some people do not improve, and a small number [Smith *et al.* report a figure of 9%] get worse'.

The conclusions reached by Smith and her associates were a far cry from Eysenck's (1965) remark that 'current psychotherapeutic procedures have not lived up to the hopes which greeted their emergence 50 years ago'. However, the way in which Smith *et al.* had conducted their meta-analysis attracted considerable criticism. For example, Shapiro & Shapiro (1982) expressed concern that over half of the people receiving treatment in the 475 studies were *students*, who are hardly representative of the population in general. Shapiro and Shapiro also pointed out that in at least some of the studies, the psychological problems being treated were not particularly serious including as they did smoking, overeating and performance anxieties.

Perhaps more important was the fact that the meta-analysis included studies which were seriously methodologically flawed. In a reanalysis of the original meta-analysis, Prioleau *et al.* (1983) found only 32 studies that could be considered to be free from methodological defects and sound in all other respects. Analysis of these studies led Prioleau and her colleagues

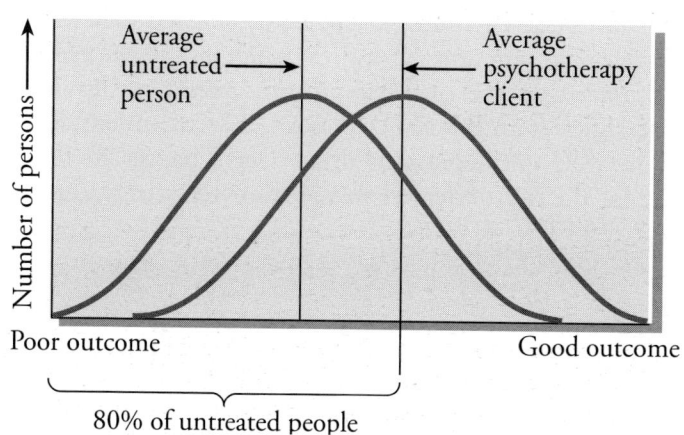

Figure 13.1   Normal distribution curves showing improvement by those treated with psychotherapy as compared with untreated people (based on Smith, *et al.,* **1980)**

to a different conclusion from that reached by Smith *et al.*:

'Thirty years after Eysenck first raised the issue of the effectiveness of psychotherapy ... and after about 500 outcome studies have been reviewed, we are still not aware of a single convincing demonstration [of] the benefits of psychotherapy.'

The journal in which Prioleau and her colleagues' study was reported (*Behavioural and Brain Sciences*) invited several of those who had been involved in the debate about psychotherapy's effectiveness, including Eysenck and Smith, to comment on the findings reported by Prioleau and her colleagues. The only thing that seemed to be agreed about psychotherapy's effectiveness was that no agreement could be reached! The debate about the effectiveness of psychotherapy has yet to be resolved. Some evidence (e.g. NIMH, 1987) suggests that psychotherapy can be at least as effective as chemotherapy in the treatment of certain disorders. Andrews (1993), on the other hand, has argued that dynamic psychotherapy is no better than routine clinical care. In Andrews' view:

'The lack of evidence for efficacy despite considerable research, the real possibility of harm and the high cost all make dynamic psychotherapy unlikely to be a preferred option of the health service'.

Meta-analyses of research concerning the effectiveness of other therapies have also been conducted. In one recent study, Piccinelli and his colleagues (1995) looked at the effectiveness of chemotherapy (see Chapter 8) in the treatment of obsessive-compulsive disorder (see Chapter 7). The study showed that with a variety of outcome measures (such as *global clinical improvement* and *psychosocial adjustment*), drugs were far superior to *placebo* (see Box 13.2) treatment, with non-SSRI antidepressant drugs (see Chapter 8) being by far the most effective in the short-term treatment of the disorder.

Comparing the relative effectiveness of therapies

We have already encountered several studies which, at least in part, aimed to compare the effectiveness of various types of therapy. Another example of this sort of investigation is a study conducted by May (1975), who assigned schizophrenics who had not previously been hospitalised to one of five groups. One group received individual psychoanalytic-type psychotherapy, whilst a second was given *phenothiazine* drugs alone. The third group was given a combination of psychotherapy and drugs, and the fourth ECT. The fifth group received *milieu therapy*, which is a form of treatment that attempts to make the total environment of a disturbed person (including all personnel and other individuals) a *therapeutic community*.

The criteria of success used by May were assessments of the improvement as made by nurses and clinicians, measures of 'release' rates and the duration of hospitalisation. The results showed that the drugs alone, and psychotherapy plus drugs, were the two most effective forms of treatment. Since the results also showed that these two forms of treatment did not differ from one another, May concluded that psychotherapy had little or no tangible effects.

Faced with these findings, it is tempting to conclude that some types of therapy *are* more effective than others. Despite methodological problems relating to their meta-analysis, Smith *et al.* (1980) argued that whilst all therapies produced beneficial changes, no particular type of therapy was significantly better than any other. A similar conclusion had been reached by Luborsky *et al.* (1975) some years before the publication of Smith *et al.*'s meta-analysis. Borrowing from Lewis Carroll's *Alice in Wonderland*, Luborsky and his colleagues suggested that as far as effectiveness was concerned, 'everybody has won and all must have prizes'.

Explaining the different conclusions reached by researchers as to the relative effectiveness of therapies is difficult. However, one potential explanation is in terms of the measurements taken. As we noted earlier, different therapies have different goals and therefore define 'improvement' in different ways. When an observable change in behaviour is used as the criterion of success, behaviour therapy (which, as we saw in Chapter 10, focuses on overt behaviour) emerges as being far superior to psychodynamic therapies (Shapiro & Shapiro, 1982). It could be argued that it would be much 'fairer' to examine the extent to which a therapy satisfies its *own* goals, but then we are faced with the problem of whether everybody would consider the goals set by a therapeutic approach to be satisfactory ones.

Kiesler (1966) anticipated the problems outlined above in an article in which he argued that the question, 'which type of therapy is better?', is actually an inappropriate one. According to Kiesler, a much better question to ask is, 'what type of treatment by what type of therapist is most effective in dealing with specific problems among specific persons?'. Kiesler's question may be a more appropriate one, since it avoids the pitfalls of using *general outcome measures* which may mask difficulties between therapies, but it is also a much more difficult one to answer.

Do therapists affect a therapy's effectiveness?

Although they may practise the same therapeutic procedure, the evidence suggests that not all therapists are equally effective which, as Wolpe (1985) has suggested, would imply that any benefits cannot be solely attributable to the therapy itself. Research conducted by Russell (1981) has shown that, irrespective of the therapy they use, experienced therapists are generally (but not always) more effective than novice therapists. As Carlson (1988) has remarked, this finding itself suggests that therapists have something to learn, which must mean that therapeutic processes are not entirely futile! One reason for the effectiveness of experienced therapists is their willingness to embrace what Beitman *et al.* (1989) have termed *technical eclecticism* or *multimodal therapy*, in which techniques are borrowed from different therapies in order to tailor treatment to a specific individual.

Experience alone, however, does not seem to be sufficient. Research has consistently found that, as far as psychotherapy is concerned, the most effective therapists are those who genuinely care about those they treat and who aim to establish a relationship which is empathic and fosters respect and trust. By contrast, a lack of these qualities seems to be associated with *client deterioration*. As Truax & Carkhuff (1964) have observed:

'[People] whose therapists offered a high level of unconditional positive warmth, self-congruence or genuineness, and empathic understanding showed significant positive personality and behaviour changes on a wide variety of indices, and ... [people] whose therapists offered relatively low levels of these conditions during therapy exhibited significant deterioration in personality and behaviour functioning' (see also Chapter 12).

The qualities described by Truax and Carkhuff are not, of course, exclusive to therapists. In a study conducted by Strupp & Hadley (1979), university professors who were not professionally trained in psychotherapy, but were known to be warm, trustworthy and empathic were asked to 'treat' students experiencing depression and anxiety. Despite their lack of professional training, the professors were able to bring about a significant improvement in at least some of the students, and the improvement was just as great as that produced in other students by professional therapists.

Luborsky (1984) has termed the ability to establish a warm and understanding relationship, in which the person seeking treatment and the person providing it believe they are working together, a *therapeutic alliance*. On the basis of Strupp and Hadley's findings, it seems reasonable to suggest that it is the therapeutic alliance rather than a knowledge of mental disorders and their treatment that is most important at least for some types of disorder. The possibility that a treatment effect can be attributable solely to a therapist suggests, as many researchers have argued, that the effectiveness of a method may have little more value than the *placebo effect*. The placebo effect is discussed in detail in Box 13.2.

Box 13.2   The placebo effect

According to London (1964):

'Whatever is new and enthusiastically introduced and pursued seems, for the time, to work better than what previously did, whether or not it is more valid scientifically. Eventually, these novelties too join the Establishment of Techniques and turn out [to be] nothing more than went before.'

London was commenting on the fact that, in some cases, the mere belief or expectation that a treatment will be effective can be sufficient to convince a person that he or she has been helped and to thus show signs of improvement. Shapiro (1971), for example, has described the apparently successful use by faith healers and physicians several centuries ago of drugs made from crocodile dung, human perspiration and pigs' teeth to treat illnesses they did not understand with ingredients that had no medicinal value.

Today, the media are constantly hailing new treatments as 'wonder cures' and it is possible that the therapeutic benefits associated with such cures are derived simply from the media attention they are given. In order to try and assess the therapeutic power of a treatment and overcome the placebo effect, researchers use a technique known as *double blind control*. In this, the person administering the treatment and the person receiving it are kept in ignorance as to the exact nature of the treatment being studied. Since neither knows what has actually been given, the expectations of both are minimised.

In studies assessing the effectiveness of drugs, the placebo treatment is an inert pill or injection. In psychotherapy, a person receiving a placebo is given relaxation therapy without any attempt being made to address the psychological problem. Achieving satisfactory double blind control is not always straightforward. For example, in studies of psychotherapeutic drugs, people can sometimes tell if they are receiving a placebo because of the *absence* of side-effects (see Chapter 8). However, this problem can be overcome by using what Fisher and Greenberg (1980) have termed *active placebos* which mimic a drug's side-effects but exert no other effect.

The meta-analytic study conducted by Smith and her colleagues (1980) revealed that there was a significant placebo effect in therapy, confirming that when people *believe* they are receiving therapeutic attention, they tend to show some sort of improvement.

Does the type of disorder affect a therapy's effectiveness?

It certainly seems that some types of therapy are more effective for certain types of disorder. For example, Pines (1982) has noted that the use of drugs is essential in the treatment of schizophrenia, whereas psychodynamically based forms of therapy 'contribute little additional benefit'. Behavioural treatments have been shown to be significantly better than other approaches for the treatment of agoraphobia (Berman and Norton, 1985). However, even within a therapeutic approach, differences have been observed. Recall, for example, that in Chapter 10 we noted that one type of behaviour therapy (flooding) is more effective than others (systematic desensitisation and implosion therapy) in the treatment of some types of phobia.

The meta-analytic studies we described earlier on also support the view that all therapies are not equally effective with different types of disorder. Amongst other things, Smith *et al.* (1980) found that whilst therapies derived from the psychodynamic model are effective, they are much more effective with anxiety disorders than with schizophrenia (see above). We should also note that the rate of spontaneous remission has been shown to vary considerably depending on the disorder. Bergin and Lambert (1978), for example, discovered that people experiencing depression and generalised anxiety disorders are much more likely to spontaneously recover than those experiencing phobic or obsessive-compulsive disorders.

Does the type of person receiving therapy affect its effectiveness?

As Carlson (1988) has remarked, at least some people have a choice about the sort of therapy they would prefer to undergo. To put this another way, in at least some cases people *self-select* a particular type of therapy. This means that it is very difficult to assess therapies, because some people will either change therapists or leave their therapy completely. As well as making it difficult to assess the effectiveness of a particular therapy, it makes comparisons between therapies difficult, since in both cases we are left with the evaluation *only* of those people who remain.

In spite of the above, there are some research findings that should be mentioned. In a review of the relevant literature, Garfield (1980) reported that therapies derived from the psychodynamic model are most effective with well-educated, articulate, strongly motivated and confident people experiencing light to moderate depression, anxiety disorders or interpersonal problems. Researchers use the term the *YAVIS effect* to describe the people with whom psychodynamically oriented therapies are likely to be successful. Such people tend to be **y**oung, **a**ttractive, **v**erbal, **i**ntelligent and **s**uccessful.

It is also worth noting that, since no two people will ever present *exactly* the same set of problems, no two people will ever receive precisely the same treatment. As Vallis *et al.* (1986) have remarked, precisely what will happen in a given therapeutic session is very hard to specify or assess even in those therapies (such as behaviour therapy) where the therapist operates much more to a 'script' as far as the therapeutic session is concerned.

Finally, we should be aware that at least some types of therapy *must* take into account the fact that people seeking treatment will come from diverse cultural or ethnic backgrounds. Rogler and his associates (1987), for example, have suggested that psychoanalysis or other forms of therapy requiring high levels of verbal skills would be inappropriate for a person who came from a community in which the members had completed little formal education. In Hispanic societies, the views concerning the roles of men and women are different from the views held by most members of Western societies. A therapeutic approach which did not take into account the established values and traditions within other cultures would lack what Baron (1989) has termed *cultural sensitivity* and would be unlikely to be of benefit to a person seeking help. Similarly, Linn *et al.* (1991) have shown that, as compared with American schizophrenics, Asian schizophrenics require significantly smaller amounts of neuroleptics for optimal treatment. The reason for this is not clear, but it is likely that differences in metabolic rates, body fat and cultural practices (in, for example, eating) might be responsible.

Conclusions

Assessing the effectiveness of therapies and comparing their relative effectiveness is much more difficult than it might at first sight appear to be. The principal difficulty lies in terms of measurement. Since there is no *criterion of success* which satisifes everybody, it is impossible to make judgements about effectiveness with which everyone would agree.

SUMMARY

- The first systematic attempt to evaluate the effectiveness of therapy was Eysenck's 1952 assessment of psychoanalysis and **eclectic** psychotherapy. The percentage of cases in which cure/improvement was reported was 44 and 64 respectively, compared with a **spontaneous recovery/remission rate** of 66%; the latter was based on a 'control group' of people with similar problems to those who received therapy but who did not themselves receive any.
- Eysenck concluded that the more psychotherapy, the smaller the recovery rate, i.e. no treatment is at least as effective, if not more so, than professional treatment. He also claimed that it is unethical for therapists to charge people for their services when they seem to be paying for nothing.
- Eysenck's evaluation caused great controversy and his study was criticised by several researchers. For example, Eysenck included as 'failures' those who dropped out of therapy; when his figures are reanalysed taking this into account, the success rate for psychoanalysis rises to 66%. Also, Eysenck himself acknowledged that people in his 'control' group differed in important ways from those who received treatment, and these 'untreated' individuals actually had one assessment interview which some of them perceived as encouraging **self-induced change**, i.e. they could hardly be categorised as having 'spontaneously' recovered.
- It is difficult to determine what the most appropriate **criterion of success** should be when trying to **measure** the effectiveness of therapy. Those who subscribe to the behavioural model define their therapeutic goals in terms of observable changes in behaviour, while psychoanalysts would argue that for therapy to be effective, unconscious conflicts must be resolved and a restructuring of personality achieved; since these

cannot be directly measured, observable changes in behaviour cannot be the **only** criterion of success.

- A further problem is deciding **who** will determine that a behaviour change has occurred. Therapists themselves cannot be unbiased, since they have a stake in believing that their therapy is effective. Those who have received therapy may not always be the best judges of their own behaviour, and it is impossible to measure objectively how much insight has been gained in psychoanalysis since this is by its nature unique.
- Using friends and family of the person who has received treatment is also problematic, since one/more of these may be the **cause** of a person's problems.
- Perhaps the most objective assessors would be therapists not involved in the actual treatment being assessed. This method was used in Sloane *et al.*'s comparison of psychotherapy, behaviour therapy, and no therapy at all (placed on a waiting list); matched participants were randomly assigned to one of the three groups. Experts in one or other form of therapy interviewed the participants before the study began and at various points later on, without knowing which group they had been assigned to.
- After four months of therapy, 80% of those treated by behaviour therapy **or** psychotherapy had either improved/recovered, compared with 48% of the control group. These improvements were maintained one year after therapy. While spontaneous remission may occur, both therapeutic techniques used were still better than no treatment at all. As methodologically sound as the Sloane *et al.* study may be, it raises some crucial ethical issues.
- Using the criterion of 'symptom change', Durham *et al.* compared cognitive therapy, analytic psychotherapy, and anxiety management training for generalised anxiety disorder. Cognitive therapy was significantly more effective than analytic psychotherapy, with anxiety management training falling in between these two.
- Other ways of assessing therapeutic effectiveness include scores on psychometric tests and **recidivism rates**. Luborsky *et al.* used these measures, claiming that improvements following psychotherapy were significantly higher compared with no treatment at all. They also found evidence for the **dose-effect relationship**, but it is possible that the mere passage of **time** contributes to improvement.
- If certain types of measurement may 'favour' cer-

tain types of therapy, a solution is to look at **all** types of measurement researchers have used. Smith *et al.* examined 475 studies in which more than one criterion of success was used, both subjective and objective, producing 1776 **outcome measures**. They used **meta-analysis** to analyse the combined results of all the studies, providing an 'average estimate' of the size of the effectiveness of therapy.

- Smith *et al.* found that psychodynamic therapies proved beneficial on a large number of criteria for success, compared with no-treatment controls. The average person who receives therapy is better off after therapy than 80% of those who do not. They concluded that these findings show overwhelmingly that psychodynamic therapies are effective, although some people show no improvement, while 9% actually get worse.
- The Smith *et al.* meta-analysis has itself been criticised. For example, over half of those receiving treatment in the 475 studies were **students**, and in at least some studies the problems being treated were fairly minor (e.g. smoking and overeating). More seriously, some of the studies included were methodologically flawed; when Prioleau *et al.* excluded these, leaving 32, they confirmed Eysenck's original claim that there is no convincing evidence that psychotherapy is beneficial.
- There has been continued debate about the effectiveness of psychotherapy and agreement still cannot be reached. There have also been meta-analytic studies of the effectiveness of other therapies. For example, Piccinelli *et al.* found that, using a variety of outcome measures, drugs were far superior to **placebos** in the treatment of obsessive-compulsive disorder, especially non-SSRI antidepressant drugs.
- A study by May assigned previously non-hospitalised schizophrenics to one of five groups: psychoanalytic-type psychotherapy, **phenothiazine** drugs alone, a combination of psychotherapy and drugs, ECT, and **milieu therapy** ('therapeutic community'). The criteria of success were nurse and clinician assessments, measures of 'release' rates, and the duration of hospitalisation. The drugs alone, and psychotherapy plus drugs, proved to be the most effective, but there was no difference between the two, suggesting that psychotherapy had little/no tangible effects.
- Smith *et al.* had argued that, while all therapies are beneficial, no particular type of therapy is significantly better than any other. This supported the conclusions of an earlier study by Luborsky *et al.*

- One reason for different researchers reaching different conclusions is that different therapies define 'improvement' in different ways. When an observable change in behaviour is used as the criterion of success, behaviour therapy emerges as far superior to psychodynamic therapies.
- To ask which type of therapy is better is inappropriate since it assumes 'general outcome measures' which may mask differences between therapies. Kiesler prefers to ask about the effectiveness of different therapies in relation to different therapists, different disorders and different individuals. This is a much more complex question.
- Despite practising the same therapeutic procedures, not all therapists are equally effective, implying that any benefits cannot be solely attributable to the therapy itself. Experienced therapists are usually more effective than novices, partly because the former are wlling to embrace **technical eclecticism/multi-modal therapy**.
- As far as psychotherapy is concerned, the most effective therapists are those who genuinely care about their clients, aim to establish an empathic relationship, and are warm and trustworthy; a lack of these qualities seems to be associated with 'client deterioration'. There is evidence that people who possess these qualities can produce therapeutic benefits even if they have not been professionally trained.
- It may be the **therapeutic alliance** rather than a knowledge of mental disorders and their treatment that is most important, at least for some types of disorder. The possibility that a treatment may be effective solely because of the therapist suggests that the effectiveness of a method may have little more value than the **placebo effect**.
- In order to assess the therapeutic power of a treatment and overcome the placebo effect, researchers use **double blind control**. This is not always straightforward in the case of psychotherapeutic drug research, compared with (non-psychotherapeutic) drug research, in which the placebo is an inert pill/injection. One solution is the use of **active placebos**.

- Smith *et al.* revealed a significant placebo effect in therapy, confirming that when people **believe** they are receiving therapeutic attention, they usually **expect** to improve and tend to show some improvement.
- Some types of treatment seem to be more effective for certain types of disorder. For example, drugs are essential in the treatment of schizophrenia, whereas psychodynamic therapy has little effect. Behavioural treatments are significantly better than other approaches in the treatment of agoraphobia, but flooding is more effective than systematic desensitisation and implosion therapy in the treatment of some types of phobia.
- Smith *et al.*'s meta-analytic study found that while psychodynamic therapies are effective, they are much more effective with anxiety disorders than with schizophrenia. The rate of spontaneous remission varies between different disorders, with depression and generalised anxiety disorders showing much higher rates than phobic or obsessive-compulsive disorders.
- In at least some cases, people **self-select** a particular type of therapy, making it very difficult to assess the effectiveness of a particular therapy or the relative effectiveness of different therapies. However, evidence suggests that psychodynamic therapies are most effective with well-educated, articulate, highly motivated/confident people with non-severe depression, anxiety disorders or interpersonal problems. This overlaps with the 'YAVIS effect'.
- No two people will ever present **identical** problems or receive identical treatment, even in those therapies (such as behaviour therapy) where there is a 'script'. Some types of therapy **must** take into account the diversity of cultural/ethnic backgrounds of the clients, such as language, gender roles, values and traditions, i.e. they must display **cultural sensitivity** to be of any benefit. Biological factors related to culture, such as differences in metabolic rate, body fat, and eating habits, might also be important in relation to drug treatment.

REFERENCES

ABRAHAM, K. (1911) Notes on the psychoanalytical investigation and treatment of manic-depressive insanity and allied conditions. Originally written in 1911 and later published in E. Jones (Ed.) *Selected Papers of Karl Abraham, MD.* London: The Hogarth Press.

ABRAMSON, L.Y., SELIGMAN, M.E.P. & TEASDALE, J.D. (1978) Learned helplessness in humans: Critique and reformulation. *Journal of Abnormal Psychology*, 87, 49–74.

ADAMS, H.E., TOLLISON, C.S. & CARSON, T.P. (1981) Behaviour therapy with sexual preventative medicine. In S.M. Turner, K.S. Calhoun & H.E. Adams (Eds.) *Handbook of Clinical Behaviour Therapy.* New York: Wiley.

ALEXANDER, F. (1946) Individual psychotherapy. *Psychosomatic Medicine*, 8, 110–115.

ALLEN, M. (1976) Twin studies of affective illness. *Archives of General Psychiatry*, 33, 1476–1478.

AMERICAN PSYCHIATRIC ASSOCIATION (1952) *Diagnostic and Statistical Manual of Mental Disorders.* Washington: American Psychiatric Association.

AMERICAN PSYCHIATRIC ASSOCIATION (1994) *Diagnostic and Statistical Manual of Mental Disorders* (4th edition). Washington: American Psychiatric Association.

ANDREWS, G. (1991) The evaluation of psychotherapy. *Current Opinions of Psychotherapy*, 4, 379–383.

ANDREWS, G. (1993) The essential psychotherapies. *British Journal of Psychiatry*, 162, 447–451.

ARLOW, J. (1984) Psychoanalysis. In R. Corsini (Ed.) *Current Psychotherapies* (3rd edition). Itasca, ILL: Peacock.

ASKEVOLD, F. & HEIBERG, A. (1979) Anorexia nervosa: Two cases in discordant MZ twins. *Psychological Monographs*, 70, 1–70.

ATKINSON, R.L., ATKINSON, R.C., SMITH, E.E. & BEM, D.J. (1993) *Introduction to Psychology* (11th edition). London: Harcourt Brace Jovanovich.

AYLLON, T. & HAUGHTON, E. (1962) Control of the behaviour of schizophrenic patients by food. *Journal of the Experimental Analysis of Behaviour*, 5, 343–352.

AYLLON, T. & AZRIN, N.H. (1968) *The Token Economy: A Motivational System for Therapy and Rehabilitation.* New York: Appleton Century Crofts.

BACHRACH, A., ERWIN, W. & MOHN, J. (1965) The control of eating behaviour in an anorexic by operant conditioning. In L. Ullman & L. Krasner (Eds.) *Case Studies in Behaviour Modification.* New York: Holt, Rinehart & Winston.

BADDELEY, A.D. (1990) *Human Memory.* Hove: Lawrence Erlbaum Associates.

BAILEY, C.L. (1979) Mental illness – a logical misrepresentation? *Nursing Times*, May, 761–762.

BALON, R., JORDAN, M., PHOL, R. & YERAGNI, V. (1989) Family history of anxiety disorders in control subjects with lactate-induced panic attacks. *American Journal of Psychiatry*, 146, 1304–1306.

BANDURA, A. (1969) *Principles of Behaviour Modification.* New York: Holt Rinehart & Winston.

BANDURA, A. (1971) *Social Learning Theory.* Morristown, NJ: General Learning Press.

BANDURA, A. (1977) *Social Learning Theory* (2nd edition). Englewood Cliffs, NJ: Prentice-Hall.

BANNISTER, D., SALMON, P. & LIEBERMAN, D.M. (1964) Diagnosis–treatment relationships in psychiatry: A statistical analysis. *British Journal of Psychiatry*, 110, 726–732.

BANYARD, P.E. (1996) *Applying Psychology to Health.* London: Hodder & Stoughton.

BARNETT, P. & GOTTLIB, I. (1988) Psychosocial functioning and depression: Distinguishing among antecedents, concomitants and consequences. *Psychological Bulletin*, 104, 97–126.

BARON, M., RISCH, N., HAMBURGER, R., MANDEL, B., KUSHNER, S., NEWMAN, M., DRUMER, D. & BELMAKER, R. (1987) Genetic linkage between X-chromosome markers and bipolar affective illness. *Nature*, 326, 289–292.

BARON, R.A. (1989) *Psychology: The Essential Science.* London: Allyn & Bacon.

BARR, C.E., MEDNICK, S.A. & MUNK-JORGENSON, P. (1990) Exposure to influenza epidemics during gestation and adult schizophrenia: A forty-year study. *Archives of General Psychiatry*, 47, 869–874.

BATESON, G., JACKSON, D., HALEY, J. & WEAKLAND, J. (1956) Toward a theory of schizophrenia. *Behavioural Science*, 1, 251–264.

BECK, A.T. (1967) *Depression: Causes and Treatment.* Philadelphia: University of Philadelphia Press.

BECK, A.T. (1974) The development of depression: A cognitive model. In R.J. Friedman & M.M. Katz (Eds.) *The Psychology of Depression: Contemporary Theory and Research.* New York: Wiley.

BECK, A.T. & FREEMAN, A. (1990) *Cognitive Therapy of Personality Disorders.* New York: Guilford Press.

BECK, A.T. & WEISHAAR, M.E. (1989) Cognitive therapy. In R.J. Corsini & D. Wedding (Eds.) *Current Psychotherapies.* Itasca, ILL: Peacock.

BECK, A.T. & YOUNG, J.E. (1978) College blues. *Psychology Today*, September, 80–92.

BECK, A.T., RUSH, A.J., SHAW, B.F. & EMORY, G. (1979) *Cognitive Therapy of Depression.* New York: Guilford Press.

BEE, H.L. (1992) *The Developing Child.* New York: HarperCollins.

BEITMAN, B., GOLDFRIED, M. & NORCROSS, J. (1989) The movement toward integrating the psychotherapies: An overview. *American Journal of Psychiatry*, 146, 138–147.

BELFER, P.L. & GLASS, C.R. (1992) Agoraphobic anxiety and fear of fear: Test of a cognitive–attentional model. *Journal of Anxiety Disorders*, 6, 133–146.

BEMIS, K.M. (1978) Current approaches to the aetiology and treatment of anorexia nervosa. *Psychological Bulletin*, 85, 593–617.

BENDER, M. (1995) The war goes on. *The Psychologist*, 8, 78–79.

BENNETT, D. (1985) Rogers: More intuition than therapy. *APA Monitor*, 16, 3.

BENTALL, R. (1996) The illness that defies diagnosis. *The Times*, May 20, 14.

BERGIN, A.E. (1971) The evaluation of therapeutic outcomes. In A.E. Bergin & S.L. Garfield (Eds.) *Handbook of Psychotherapy and Behaviour Change: An Empirical Analysis.* New York: Wiley.

BERGIN, A.E. (1980) Psychotherapy and religious values. *Journal of Consulting and Clinical Psychology*, 48, 642–645.

BERGIN, A.E. & LAMBERT, M.J. (1978) The evaluation of therapeutic outcomes. In S.A. Garfield & A.E. Bergin (Eds.) *Handbook of Psychotherapy and Behaviour Change: An Empirical Analysis* (2nd edition). New York: Wiley.

BERMAN, J.S. & NORTON, N.C. (1985) Does professional training make a therapist more effective? *Psychological Bulletin*, 98, 401–407.

BERNE, E. (1964) *Games People Play: The Psychology of Human Relationships.* New York: Grove Press.

BERNE, E. (1976) *Beyond Games and Scripts.* New York: Grove Press.

BICK, P.A. & KINSBOURNE, M. (1987) Auditory hallucinations and subvocal speech in schizophrenic patients. *American Journal of Psychiatry*, 32, 297–306.

BINI, L. (1938) Experimental researches on epileptic attacks induced by electric current. *American Journal of Psychiatry*, Supplement 94, 172–183.

BION, W.R. (1961) *Experiences in Groups.* London: Tavistock.

BLANEY, P. (1975) Implications of the medical model and its alternatives. *American Journal of Psychiatry*, 132, 911–914.

BLEULER, E. (1911) *Dementia Praecox or the Group of Schizophrenias.* New York: International University Press.

BLEULER, M.E. (1978) The long-term course of schizophrenic psychoses. In L.C. Wynne, R.L. Cromwell & S. Mathyse (Eds.) *The Nature of Schizophrenia: New Approaches to Research and Treatment.* New York: Wiley.

BLISS, E.W. & BRANCH, C.H. (1960) *Anorexia Nervosa: Its History, Psychology and Biology.* New York: Hoeber Medical Book.

BOOTZIN, R.R. & ACOCELLA, J.R. (1984) *Abnormal Psychology: Current Perspectives.* New York: Random House.

BRACHA, H.S., TORREY, E.F., BIGELOW, L.B., LOHR, J.B. & LININGTON, B.B. (1991) Subtle signs of prenatal maldevelopment of the head ectoderm in schizophrenia: A preliminary monozygotic twin study. *Biological Psychiatry*, 30, 719–725.

BRANDSMA, J.M., MAULTSBY, M.C. & WELSH, R. (1978) Self-help techniques in the treatment of alcoholism. Unpublished manuscript cited in G.T. Wilson & K.D. O'Leary *Principles of Behaviour Therapy.* Englewood Cliffs, NJ: Prentice-Hall.

BREGGIN, P. (1979) *Electroshock: Its Brain Disabling Effects.* New York: Springer.

BROCKNER, J. & GUARE, J. (1983) Improving the performance of low self-esteem individuals: An attributional approach. *Academy of Management Journal,* 29, 373–384.

BROOKE, S. (1996) The anorexic man. *The Sunday Times (Style Section),* Feb 11, 17.

BROWN D. & ZINKIN, L. (1994) *The Psyche and the Social World: Developments in Group-Analytic Theory.* London: Routledge.

BROWN, G.W. & HARRIS, T.O. (1978) *Social Origins of Depression: A Study of Psychiatric Disorder in Women.* London: Tavistock.

BRUCH, H. (1978) *Eating Disorders: Obesity, Anorexia Nervosa and the Person Within.* New York: Basic Books.

BUNNEY, W., GOODWIN, F. & MURPHY, D. (1972) The 'switch process' in manic-depressive illness. *Archives of General Psychiatry,* 27, 312–317.

BUSS, A.H. (1966) *Psychopathology.* New York: Wiley.

CALLAGHAN, P. & O'CARROLL, M. (1993) Making women mad. *Nursing Times,* 89, 26–29.

CARLSON, N.R. (1988) *Discovering Psychology.* London: Allyn & Bacon.

CARSON, R. (1989) Personality. *Annual Review of Psychology,* 40, 227–248.

CAUTELA, J.R. (1967) Covert sensitisation. *Psychology Reports,* 20, 459–468.

CHANCE, P. (1984) I'm OK, you're a little odd. *Psychology Today,* 18–19.

CHUA, S.E. & McKENNA, P.J. (1995) Schizophrenia – a brain disease? A critical review of structural and functional cerebral abnormality in the disorder. *British Journal of Psychiatry,* 166, 563–582.

CLARIDGE, G. (1987) The continuum of psychosis and the gene. *British Journal of Psychiatry,* 150, 129–133 (correspondence).

CLARK, D.M. (1993) Treating panic attacks. *The Psychologist,* 6, 73–74.

CLARK, D.M., SALKOVSKIS, P.M., HACKMANN, A., MIDDLETON, H., ANASTASIADES, P. & GELDER, M. (1994) A comparison of cognitive therapy, applied relaxation and imipramine in the treatment of panic disorder. *British Journal of Psychiatry,* 164, 759–769.

COCHRANE, R. (1983) *The social creation of mental illness.* London: Longman.

COCHRANE, R. (1995) Women and depression. *Psychology Review,* 2, 20–24.

COHN, H.W. (1994) What is existential psychotherapy? *British Journal of Psychiatry,* 165, 699–701.

COLMAN, A.M. (1987) *What is Psychology? The Inside Story.* London: Hutchinson.

COMINGS, D.E. & COMINGS, B.G. (1987) Hereditary agoraphobia and obsessive-compulsive behaviour in relatives of patients with Gilles de la Tourette's syndrome. *British Journal of Psychiatry,* 151, 195–199.

COOPER, J.E. (1995) On the publication of the Diagnostic and Statistical Manual of Mental Disorders (4th edition). *British Journal of Psychiatry,* 166, 4–8.

COOPER, J.E., KENDELL, R.E., GURLAND, B.J., SHARPE, L., COPELAND, J.R.M. & SIMON, R. (1972) *Psychiatric Diagnosis in New York and London.* Oxford: Oxford University Press.

COOPER, P.J. (1995) Eating disorders. In A.A. Lazarus & A.M. Colman (Eds.) *Abnormal Psychology.* London: Longman.

COOPER, P.J., CAMPBELL, E.A., DAY, A., KENNERLEY, H. & BOND, A. (1988) Non-psychotic psychiatric disorder after childbirth: A prospective study of prevalence, incidence, course and nature. *British Journal of Psychiatry,* 152, 799–806.

COREY, G. (1991) *Theory and Practice of Counselling and Psychotherapy.* Pacific Groves, CA: Brooks/Cole.

COWART, J. & WHALEY, D.L. (1971) Punishment of self-mutilation behaviour. Cited in D.L. Whaley & R.W. Malott *Elementary Principles of Behaviour.* New York: Appleton Century Crofts.

CRISP, A.H. (1967) Anorexia nervosa. *Hospital Medicine,* 1, 713–718.

CROOK, T. & ELIOT, J. (1980) Parental death during childhood and adult depression: A critical review of the literature. *Psychological Bulletin,* 87, 252–259.

CROOKS, R.L. & STEIN, J. (1991) *Psychology: Science, Behaviour and Life* (2nd edition). London: Harcourt Brace Jovanovich.

CROW, T.J., CROSS, A.G., JOHNSTONE, E.C. & OWEN, F. (1982) Two syndromes in schizophrenia and their pathogenesis. In F.A. Henn & G.A. Nasrallah (Eds.) *Schizophrenia as a Brain Disease.* New York: Oxford University Press.

CROW, T.J. & DONE, D.J. (1992) Prenatal exposure to influenza does not cause schizophrenia. *British Journal of Psychiatry,* 161, 390–393.

CUTTS, T.F. & BARRIOS, B.A. (1986) Fear of weight gain among bulimic and non-disturbed females. *Behaviour Therapy,* 17, 626–636.

DAVID, A.S. (1994) Frontal lobology: Psychiatry's new pseudoscience. *British Journal of Psychiatry,* 161, 244–248.

DAVIDSON, J. (1992) Drug therapy of post-traumatic stress disorder. *British Journal of Psychiatry,* 160, 309–314.

DAVIES, T. (1994) Bless his cotton socks. *The Daily Telegraph,* September 17, 42.

DAVIS, J.M. (1974) A two-factor theory of schizophrenia. *Journal of Psychiatric Research,* 11, 25–30.

DAVISON, G. & NEALE, J. (1990) *Abnormal Psychology* (5th edition). New York: Wiley.

DAVISON, G. & NEALE, J. (1994) *Abnormal Psychology* (6th edition). New York: Wiley.

DEIN, S. (1994) Cross-cultural psychiatry. *British Journal of Psychiatry,* 165, 561–564.

DETERA-WADLEIGH, S., BERRETTINI, W., GOLDIN, L., BOORMAN, D., ANDERSON, S. & GERSHON, E. (1987) Close linkage if c–Harvey–ras–I and the insulin gene to affective disorder is ruled out in three North American pedigrees. *Nature*, 325, 806–807.

DILSAVER, J. (1989) Panic disorder. *American Family Physician*, 39, 167–173.

DIXON, P., REHLING, G. & SHINWACH, R. (1993) Peripheral victims of the Herald of Free Enterprise disaster. *British Journal of Medical Psychology*, 66, 193–202.

DOANE, J.A., FALLOON, I.R.H., GOLDSTEIN, M.J. & MINTZ, J. (1985) Parental affective style and the treatment of schizophrenia: Predicting course of illness and social functioning. *Archives of General Psychiatry*, 42, 34–42.

DOBSON, R. (1996) Confront your phobias in virtual reality. *The Sunday Times*, January 21, 14.

DURHAM, R.C., MURPHY, J., ALLAN, T., RICHARD, K., TRELIVING, L.R. & FENTON, G.W. (1994) Cognitive therapy, analytic psychotherapy and anxiety management training for generalised anxiety disorder. *British Journal of Psychiatry*, 165, 315–323.

EAGLES, J.M. (1991) The relationship between schizophrenia and immigration: Are there alternatives to psychosocial hypotheses? *British Journal of Psychiatry*, 159, 783–789.

EGELAND, J., GERHARD, D., PAULS, D., SUSSEX, J., KIDD, K., ALLEN, C., HOSTETTER, A. & HOUSEMAN, D. (1987) Bipolar affective disorder linked to DNA markers on chromosome 11. *Nature*, 325, 783–787.

EISENBERG, I. (1995) The social construction of the human brain. *American Journal of Psychiatry*, 152, 1563–1575.

ELKINS, R.L. (1980) Covert sensitisation treatment of alcoholism. *Addictive Behaviours*, 5, 67–89.

ELLIS, A. (1958) *Rational Psychotherapy*. California: Institute for Rational Emotive Therapy.

ELLIS, A. (1962) *Reason and Emotion in Psychotherapy*. Secaucus, NJ: Lyle Stuart (Citadel Press).

ELLIS, A. (1984) Rational–emotive therapy. In R. Corsini (Ed.) *Current Psychotherapies* (3rd edition). Itasca, Il: Peacock.

ELLIS, A. (1991) The revised ABC of rational–emotive therapy. *Journal of Rational Emotive and Cognitive Behaviour Therapy*, 9, 139–192.

ELLIS, A. (1993) Reflections on rational–emotive therapy. *Journal of Consulting and Clinical Psychology*, 61, 199–201.

EMMELKAMP, P.M.G. & WESSELS, H. (1975) Flooding in imagination versus flooding *in vivo*: A comparison with agoraphobics. *Behaviour Research and Therapy*, 13, 7–15.

EMMELKAMP, P.M.G., KUIPERS, A.C.M. & EGGERAAT, J.B. (1978) Cognitive modification versus prolonged exposure *in vivo*: A comparison with agoraphobics as subjects. *Behaviour Research and Therapy*, 16, 33–42.

EYSENCK, H.J. (1952) The effects of psychotherapy: An evaluation. *Journal of Consulting Psychology*, 16, 319–324.

EYSENCK, H.J. (1965) The effects of psychotherapy. *International Journal of Psychiatry*, 1, 97–142.

EYSENCK, H.J. (1967) *The Biological Basis of Personality*. Springfield, ILL: Charles C. Thomas.

FAIRBURN, C.G., JONES, R. & PEVELER, R.C. (1993) Psychotherapy and bulimia nervosa: The longer-term effects of interpersonal psychotherapy, behaviour therapy and cognitive behaviour therapy. *Archives of General Psychiatry*, 50, 419–428.

FALEK, A. & MOSER, H.M. (1975) Classification in schizophrenia. *Archives of General Psychiatry*, 32, 59–67.

FANCHER, R.T. (1995) *Cultures of Healing*. New York: W.H. Freeman.

FARINA, A. (1982) The stigma of mental disorders. In A.G. Miller (Ed.) *In the Eye of the Beholder*. New York: Praeger.

FERSTER, C. (1965) Classification of behaviour pathology. In L. Krasner & L. Ullman (Eds.) *Research in Behaviour Modification*. New York: Holt, Rinehart & Winston.

FINK, M. (1984) Meduna and the origins of convulsive therapy in suicidal patients. *American Journal of Psychiatry*, 141, 1034–1041.

FISHER, S. & GREENBERG, R. (Eds.) (1980) *A Critical Appraisal of Biological Treatments for Psychological Distress: Comparisons with Psychotherapy and Placebo*. Hillsdale, NJ: Erlbaum.

FLEISCHMAN, P.R. (1973) Letter to the editor. *Science*, 180, 356.

FOMBONNE, E. (1995) Anorexia nervosa: No evidence of an increase. *British Journal of Psychiatry*, 166, 462–471.

FORD, D.H. & URBAN, H.B. (1963) *Systems of Psychotherapy: A Comparative Study*. New York: Wiley.

FREEMAN, C. (Ed.) (1995) *The ECT Handbook*. London: Gaskell.

FREUD, S. (1894) The defence neuropsychoses. In J. Strachey (Ed.) *The Standard Edition of the Complete Psychological Works of Sigmund Freud*. (Volume 1). London: The Hogarth Press, 1953.

FREUD, S. (1909) *Analysis of a Phobia in a Five-Year-Old Boy*. London: The Hogarth Press.

FREUD, S. (1915) A case of paranoia running counter to the psychoanalytical theory of the disease. In *Collected Papers* Volume 2. London: The Hogarth Press.

FREUD, S. (1917) *Mourning and Melancholia*. London: The Hogarth Press.

FROMM-REICHMAN, F. (1948) Notes on the

development of treatment of schizophrenics by psychoanalytic psychotherapy. *Psychiatry*, 11, 263–273.

GAINES, A. (1992) *Ethnopsychiatry: The Cultural Construction of Professional and Folk Psychiatries.* New York: New York State University.

GARFIELD, S.L. (1980) *Psychotherapy: An Eclectic Approach.* New York: Wiley.

GARFIELD, S. & BERGIN, A. (1994) Introduction and historical overview. In A. Bergin & S. Garfield (Eds.) *Handbook of Psychotherapy and Behaviour Change.* Chichester: Wiley.

GARFINKEL, P.E. & GARNER, D.M. (1982) *Anorexia Nervosa: A Multidimensional Perspective.* New York: Basic Books.

GARNER, D.M. (1986) Cognitive–behavioural therapy for eating disorders. *The Clinical Psychologist*, 39, 36–39.

GARNER, D.M., GARFINKEL, P.E., SCHWARZ, D. & THOMPSON, M. (1980) Cultural expectations of thinness in women. *Psychological Reports*, 47, 483–491.

GARROD, A.B. (1859) *The Nature and Treatment of Gout and Rheumatic Gout.* London: Walton & Maberly.

GELDER, M., GATH, D. & MAYON, R. (1989) *The Oxford Textbook of Psychiatry* (2nd edition). Oxford: Oxford University Press.

GEORGE, M.S. & BALLENGER, J.C. (1992) The neuropsychology of panic disorder: The emerging role of the right parahippocampal region. *Journal of Anxiety Disorders*, 6, 181–188.

GIBSON, H.B. (1967) Self-reported delinquency among schoolboys and their attitudes towards the police. *British Journal of Social and Clinical Psychology*, 6, 168–173.

GOLDSTEIN, M. & PALMER, J. (1975) *The Experience of Anxiety: A Casebook* (2nd edition). New York: Oxford University Press.

GOTTESMAN, I.I. & SHIELDS, J. (1972) *Schizophrenia and Genetics: A Twin Study Vantage Point.* New York: Academic Press.

GRAHAM, H. (1986) *The Human Face of Psychology.* Milton Keynes: Open University Press.

GREEN, B.L. (1994) Psychosocial research in traumatic stress: An update. *Journal of Traumatic Stress*, 7, 341–363.

GRIER, W. & COBBS, P. (1968) *Black Rage.* New York: Basic Books.

GROSS, R.D. (1995) *Themes, Issues and Debates in Psychology.* London: Hodder & Stoughton.

GUSCOTT, R. & TAYLOR, L. (1994) Lithium prophylaxis in recurrent affective illness: Efficacy, effectiveness and efficiency. *British Journal of Psychiatry*, 164, 741–746.

HAAGA, D.A. & BECK, A.T. (1992) Cognitive Therapy. In S. Pakyel (Ed.) *Handbook of Affective Disorders* (2nd edition). Cambridge: Cambridge University Press.

HAAGA, D.A. & DAVISON, G.C. (1993) An appraisal of rational-emotive therapy. *Journal of Consulting and Clinical Psychology*, 61, 215–220.

HAMMEN, C.L. (1985) Predicting depression: A cognitive-behavioural perspective. In P. Kendall (Ed.) *Advances in Cognitive-Behavioural Research and Therapy* (Volume 4). New York: Academic Press.

HARRISON, P. (1995) Schizophrenia: A misunderstood disease. *Psychology Review*, 2, 2–6.

HASSETT, J. & WHITE, K.M. (1989) *Psychology in Perspective.* Cambridge: Harper & Row.

HAY, P., SACHDEV, P. & CUMMING, S. (1993) Treatment of obsessive–compulsive disorder by psychosurgery. *Acta Psychiatrica Scandinavia*, 87, 197–207.

HEATHER, N. (1976) *Radical Perspectives in Psychology.* London: Methuen.

HENDERSON, A.S., JABLENSKY, A. & SARTORIUS, N. (1994) ICD-10: A neuropsychiatrist's nightmare? *British Journal of Psychiatry*, 165, 273–275.

HERSHER, L. (Ed.) (1970) *Four Psychotherapies.* New York: Appleton-Century-Crofts.

HESTON, L.L. (1966) Psychiatric disorders in foster-home-reared children of schizophrenic mothers. *British Journal of Psychiatry*, 122, 819–825.

HESTON, L.L. (1970) The genetics of schizophrenia and schizoid disease. *Science*, 167, 249–256.

HIGHFIELD, R. (1993a) Hunt closes in on schizophrenia gene. *The Daily Telegraph*, September 6, 28.

HIGHFIELD, R. (1993b) Brain chemical holds clue to schizophrenia. *The Daily Telegraph*, September 30, 9.

HIGHFIELD, R. (1995) Revealed: the source of those voices we hear. *The Daily Telegraph*, June 28, 18.

HODGKINSON, S., SHERRINGTON, R., GURLING, H., MARCHBANKS, R., REEDERS, S., MALLET, J., McINNIN, H., PETERSSON, H. & BRYNJOLFSSON, J. (1987) Molecular genetic advantage for heterogeneity in manic depression. *Nature*, 325, 805–806.

HODGSON, R.J. & RACHMAN, S. (1972) The effects of contamination and washing in obsessional patients. *Behaviour Research and Therapy*, 10, 111–117.

HOLLAND, A.J., HALL, A., MURRAY, R., RUSSELL, G.F.M. & CRISP, A.H. (1984) Anorexia nervosa: A study of 34 twin pairs and one set of triplets. *British Journal of Psychiatry*, 145, 414–418.

HOLMES, D.S. (1994) *Abnormal Psychology* (2nd edition). New York: HarperCollins.

HOLMES, J. (1996) Psychoanalysis – An endangered species? *Psychiatric Bulletin*, 20, 321–322.

HOUSTON, J.P., HAMMEN, C., PADILLA, A. & BEE, H. (1991) *Introduction to Psychology* (3rd edition). London: Harcourt Brace Jovanovich.

HSU, L.K. (1990) *Eating disorders.* New York: Guilford.

HUGDAHL, K. & ÖHMAN, A. (1977) Effects of

instruction on acquisition of electrodermal response to fear relevant stimuli. *Journal of Experimental Psychology*, 3, 608–618.

HUNT, L. (1995) Why a fear of spiders is all in the genes. *The Independent*, December 20, 17.

ILLMAN, J. & TAYLOR, B. (1995) Dangerous obsessions. *The Guardian*, October 31, 14.

ISAACS, W., THOMAS, J. & GOLDIAMOND, I. (1960) Application of operant conditioning to reinstate verbal behaviour in psychotics. *Journal of Speech and Hearing Disorders*, 25, 8–12.

IVERSEN, L.L. (1979) The chemistry of the brain. *Scientific American*, 241, 134–149.

JACOBSON, N.S., FOLLETTE, W.C. & REVENSTORF, D. (1984) Psychotherapy outcome research: Methods for reporting variability and evaluating clinical significance. *Behaviour Therapy*, 15, 336–352.

JAHODA, M. (1958) *Current Concepts of Mental Health*. New York: Basic Books.

JAMES, I.A. & BLACKBURN, I.-M. (1995) Cognitive therapy with obsessive-compulsive disorder. *British Journal of Psychiatry*, 166, 144–150.

JAMISON, K. (1989) Mood disorders and patterns of creativity in British writers and artists. *Psychiatry*, 52, 125–134.

JOHNSON, D. (1989) Schizophrenia as a brain disease. *American Psychologist*, 44, 553–555.

JONES, M. C. (1924) The elimination of children's fears. *Journal of Experimental Psychology*, 7, 382–390.

JONES, M.C. (1925) A laboratory study of fear: The case of Peter. *Pedagogical Seminary*, 31, 308–315.

JOSEPH, S., YULE, W., WILLIAMS, R. & HODGKSINSON, P. (1993) Increased substance use in survivors of the Herald of Free Enterprise. *British Journal of Medical Psychology*, 66, 185–192.

KALINOWSKY, L. (1975) Psychosurgery. In A. Freedman, H. Kaplan & B. Sadock (Eds.) *Comprehensive Textbook of Psychiatry*. Baltimore: Williams & Wilkins.

KAPLAN, A. & WOODSIDE, D. (1987) Biological aspects of anorexia nervosa and bulimia nervosa. *Journal of Consulting and Clinical Psychology*, 55, 645–653.

KAY, R.W. (1994) Geomagnetic storms: Association with incidence of depression as measured by hospital admission. *British Journal of Psychiatry*, 164, 403–409.

KELSOE, J.R., GINNS, E.I., EGELAND, J.A. & GERHARD, D.S. (1989) Re-evaluation of the linkage relationship between chromosome 11 loci and the gene for bipolar disorder in the Old Order Amish. *Nature*, 342, 238–243.

KEMPLER, W. (1973) Gestalt therapy. In R. Corsini (Ed.) *Current Psychotherapies*. Itasca, ILL: Peacock.

KENDELL, R.E. (1975) *The Role of Diagnosis in Psychiatry*. Oxford: Blackwell.

KENDLER, K.S., McLEAN, C., NEALE, M., KESSLER, R., HEATH, A. & EAVES, L. (1991) The genetic epidemiology of bulimia nervosa. *American Journal of Psychiatry*, 148, 1627–1637.

KETY, S.S. (1974) From rationalisation to reason. *American Journal of Psychiatry*, 131, 957–963.

KETY, S.S. (1975) Biochemistry of the major psychoses. In A. Freedman, H. Kaplan & B. Sadock (Eds.) *Comprehensive Textbook of Psychiatry*. Baltimore: Williams & Wilkins.

KETY, S.S., ROSENTHAL, D., WENDER, P.H. & SCHULSINGER, F. (1968) The types and prevalence of mental illness in the biological and adoptive families of adopted schizophrenics. In D. Rosenthal & S.S. Kety (Eds.) *The Transmission of Schizophrenia*. Elmsford, NY: Pergamon Press.

KIESLER, D.J. (1966) Some myths of psychotherapy research and the search for a paradigm. *Psychological Bulletin*, 65, 110–136.

KIMBLE, D.P. (1988) *Biological Psychology*. New York: Holt, Rinehart & Winston.

KIPPER, D. (1992) Psychodrama: Group therapy through role playing. *International Journal of Group Psychotherapy*, 42, 495–521.

KLANING, U., MORTENSEN, P.B. & KYVIK, K.D. (1996) Increased occurrence of schizophrenia and other psychiatric illnesses among twins. *British Journal of Psychiatry*, 168, 688–692.

KLEBANOFF, L.D. (1959) A comparison of parental attitudes of mothers of schizophrenics, brain injured and normal children. *American Journal of Psychiatry*, 24, 445–454.

KLEIN, D.F. & RABKIN, J. (Eds.) (1981) *Anxiety: New Research and Changing Concepts*. New York: Raven Press.

KOLB, L.C. (1987) A neuropsychological hypothesis explaining post-traumatic stress disorders. *American Journal of Psychiatry*, 144, 989–995.

KOVEL, J. (1978) *A Complete Guide to Therapy*. Harmondsworth: Penguin.

KRAEPELIN, E. (1913) *Clinical Psychiatry: A Textbook for Physicians* (translated by A. Diffendorf). New York: Macmillan.

KREBS, D. & BLACKMAN, R. (1988) *Psychology: A First Encounter*. London: Harcourt Brace Jovanovich.

KRYSTAL, J.H., KOSTEN, T.R. & SOUTHWICK, S. (1989) Neurobiological aspects of PTSD: A review of clinical and preclinical studies. *Behaviour Therapy*, 20, 177–198.

LANGE, A.J. & JAKUBOWSKI, P. (1976) *Responsible Assertive Behaviour: Cognitive/Behavioural Procedures for Trainers*. Champaign, ILL: Research Press.

LASK, B. & BRYANT-WAUGH, R. (1992) Childhood onset of anorexia nervosa and related eating disorders. *Journal of Child Psychology and Psychiatry*, 3, 281–300.

LAUGHLIN, H.P. (1967) *The Neuroses*. Washington, DC: Butterworth.

LAURANCE, J. (1993) Is psychotherapy all in the mind? *The Times*, April 15, 7.

LEE, S., HSU, L.K.G. & WING, Y.K. (1992) Bulimia nervosa in Hong Kong Chinese patients. *British Journal of Psychiatry*, 161, 545–551.

LEON, G.R. (1990) *Case Histories of Psychopathology*. Boston: Allyn & Bacon.

LEVITSKY, A. & PERLS, F.S. (1970) The rules and games of Gestalt therapy. In J. Fagan & I. Shephard (Eds.) *Gestalt Therapy Now*. Palo Alto, CA: Science and Behaviour Books.

LEWINSOHN, P.M. (1974) A behavioural approach to depression. In R. Friedman & M. Katz (Eds.) *The Psychology of Depression: Contemporary Theory and Research*. Washington, DC: Winston/Wiley.

LEWINSOHN, P.M. & HOBERMAN, H.M. (1982) Depression. In A.S. Bellack, M. Hersen & A.E. Kazdin (Eds.) *International Handbook of Behaviour Modification and Therapy*. New York: Plenum.

LEWINSOHN, P.M., HOPS, H. & ROBERTS, R.E. (1993) Adolescent psychopathology: I. Prevalence and incidence of depression and other DSM-3-R disorders in high school students. *Journal of Abnormal Psychology*, 102, 133–144.

LEWIS, A.J. (1975) The survival of hysteria. *Psychological Medicine*, 5, 9–12.

LEWIS, S. (1994) ICD-10: A neuropsychiatrist's nightmare? *British Journal of Psychiatry*, 164, 157–158.

LIDZ, T. (1973) Commentary on 'A critical review of recent adoption, twin and family studies of schizophrenia: Behavioural genetics perspectives'. *Schizophrenia Bulletin*, 2, 402–412.

LINN, K.-M., MILLER, M.H., POLAND, R.E., NUCCIO, I. & YAMAGUCHI, M. (1991) Ethnicity and family involvement in the treatment of schizophrenic patients. *Journal of Nervous and Mental Disorder*, 179, 631–633.

LITTLEWOOD, R. (1992) Psychiatric diagnosis and racial bias: Empirical and interpretive approaches. *Social Science and Medicine*, 34, 141–149.

LITTLEWOOD, R. & LIPSEDGE, M. (1989) *Aliens and Alienists: Ethnic Minorities and Psychiatry*. London: Unwin Hyman.

LONDON, P. (1964) *The Modes and Morals of Psychotherapy*. New York: Holt, Rinehart & Winston.

LUBORSKY, L. (1984) *Principles of Psychoanalytic Psychotherapies: A Manual for Supportive–Expressive Treatment*. New York: Basic Books.

LUBORSKY, L., SINGER, B. & LUBORSKY, L. (1975) Comparative studies of psychotherapies: Is it true that 'everyone has won and all must have prizes'? *Archives of General Psychiatry*, 32, 49–62.

LYDIARD, R.B., BREWERTON, T.D., FOSSEY, M.D., LARAIA, M.T., STUART, G., BEINFIELD, M.C. & BALLENGER, J.C. (1993) CSF cholecystokinin octapeptide in patients with bulimia nervosa and in comparison with normal subjects. *American Journal of Psychiatry*, 150, 1099–1101.

MacPHILLAMY, D. & LEWINSOHN, P.M. (1974) Depression as a function of levels of desired and obtained pleasure. *Journal of Abnormal Psychology*, 83, 651–657.

MACKAY, D. (1975) *Clinical Psychology: Theory and Therapy*. London: Methuen.

MAHER, B. (1968) The shattered language of schizophrenia. *Psychology Today*, 30ff.

MALAN, D.H., HEATH, E.S., BACAL, H.A. & BALFOUR, F.H.G. (1975) Psychodynamic changes in untreated neurotic patients. *Archives of General Psychiatry*, 32, 110–126.

MALINOWSKI, B. (1929) *The Sexual Life of Savages*. New York: Harcourt Brace Jovanovich.

MARKS, I. (1987) *Fears, Phobias and Rituals*. New York: Oxford University Press.

MASLOW, A. (1968) *Towards a Psychology of Being* (2nd edition). Princeton, NJ: Van Nostrand Reinhold.

MAY, P.R. (1975) A follow-up study of the treatment of schizophrenia. In R.L. Spitzer & D.F. Klein (Eds.) *Evaluation of Psychological Therapies*. Baltimore: The Johns Hopkins University Press.

McGUIRE, P.K., BENCH, C.J., FRITH, C.D., MARKS, I.M., FRACKOWIAK, R.S.J. & DOLAN, R.J. (1994) Functional asymmetry of obsessive–compulsive phenomena. *British Journal of Psychiatry*, 164, 459–468.

McILVEEN, R.J., LONG, M. & CURTIS, A. (1994) *Talking Points in Psychology*. London: Hodder & Stoughton.

McILVEEN, R.J. & GROSS, R.D. (1996) *Biopsychology*. London: Hodder & Stoughton.

MEAD, M. (1935) *Sex and Temperament in Three Primitive Societies*. New York: Dell.

MEADOR, B.D. & ROGERS, C.R. (1973) Person-centred therapy. In R. Corsini (Ed.) *Current Psychotherapies*. Itasca, ILL: Peacock.

MEADOR, B.D. & ROGERS, C.R. (1984) Person-centred therapy. In R. Corsini (Ed.) *Current Psychotherapies* (3rd edition) Itasca, ILL: Peacock.

MEDNICK, S. (1958) A learning theory approach to schizophrenia. *Psychological Bulletin*, 55, 316–327.

MEICHENBAUM, D.H. (1976) Towards a cognitive therapy of self-control. In G. Schawrtz & D. Shapiro (Eds.) *Consciousness and Self-Regulation: Advances in Research*. New York: Plenum Publishing Co.

MEICHENBAUM, D.H., HENSHAW, D. & HIMMEL, N. (1982) Coping with stress as a problem-solving process. In W. Krohne & L. Laux (Eds.) *Achievement, Stress and Anxiety* . Washington, DC: Hemisphere.

MENNINGER, W.W. (Ed.) (1995) *Fear of Humiliation – Integrated Treatment of Social Phobia and Comorbid Conditions.* New Jersey: Jason Aronson.

MILLER, D.T. & ROSS, M. (1975) Self-serving biases in the attribution of causality: Fact or fiction? *Psychological Bulletin*, 82, 213–225.

MILLER, E. & MORLEY, S. (1986) *Investigating Abnormal Behaviour.* London: Erlbaum.

MILLER, J. (1983) *States of Mind.* New Tork: Pantheon.

MILLER, W.R., ROSELLINI, R.A. & SELIGMAN, M.E.P. (1977) Learned helplessness and depression. In J.D. Maser & M.E.P. Seligman (Eds.) *Psychopathology: Experimental Models.* San Francisco: W.H. Freeman.

MORENO, J.L. (1946) *Psychodrama.* New York: Beacon.

MOWRER, O.H. (1947) On the dual nature of learning – a reinterpretation of 'conditioning' and 'problem-solving'. *Harvard Educational Review*, 17, 102–148.

MURRAY, E.J. & FOOTE, F. (1979) The origins of fear of snakes. *Behaviour Research and Therapy*, 17, 489–493.

MURRAY, J. (1995) *Prevention of Anxiety and Depression in Vulnerable Groups.* London: Gaskell.

MURRAY, R., OON, M., RODNIGHT, R., BIRLEY, J. & SMITH, A. (1979) Increased excretion of dimethyltryptamine and certain features of psychosis. *Archives of General Psychiatry*, 36, 644–649.

NIMH (1987) *The Switch Process in Manic-Depressive Illness* (DHHS Publication No. ADM 81–108). Washington, DC: Government Printing Office.

NSF (1994) *National Schizophrenia Fellowship: A Guide to the Types of Drugs Available to Treat Schizophrenia.* London: National Schizophrenia Fellowship.

NUECHTERLEIN, K.H. & DAWSON, M.E. (1984) A heuristic vulnerability/stress model of schizophrenic episodes. *Schizophrenia Bulletin*, 10, 300–311.

O'CALLAGHAN, E., SHAM, P.C., TAKEI, N., MURRAY, G.K., HARE, E.H. & MURRAY, R.M. (1991) Schizophrenia following prenatal exposure to influenza epidemics between 1939 and 1960. *British Journal of Psychiatry*, 160, 461–466.

O'CALLAGHAN, E., SHAM, P.C. & TAKEI, N. (1993) Schizophrenia after prenatal exposure to 1957 A2 influenza epidemic. *The Lancet*, 337, 1248–1250.

O'CALLAGHAN, E., SHAM, P.C., TAKEI, N., MURRAY, G.K., GLOVER, G., HARE, E.H. & MURRAY, R.M. (1994) The relationship of schizophrenic births to sixteen infectious diseases. *British Journal of Psychiatry*, 165, 353–356.

OGILVIE, A.D., BATTERSBY, S., BUBB, V.J., FINK, G., HARMAR, A.J., GOODWIN, G.M. & SMITH, C.A.D. (1996) Polymorphism in the serotonin transporter gene associated with susceptibility to major depression. *The Lancet*, 347, 731–733.

OKASHA, A., SADEK, A., AL-HADDAD, M.K. & ABDEL,–MAWGOUD, M. (1993) Diagnostic agreement in psychiatry: A comparative study between ICD-9, ICD-10 and DSM-III-R. *British Journal of Psychiatry*, 162, 621–626.

O'LEARY, K.D. & WILSON, G.T. (1975) *Behaviour Therapy: Application and Outcome.* Englewood Cliffs, NJ: Prentice-Hall.

OSMOND, H. & SMYTHIES, J. (1953) Schizophrenia: A new approach. *The Journal of Mental Science*, 98, 309–315.

PAPP, L.A., KLEIN, D.F., MARTINEZ, J., SCHNEIER, F., COLE, R., LIEBOWITZ, M.R., HOLLANDER, E., FYER, A.J., JORDAN, F. & GORMAN, J.M. (1993) Diagnostic and substance specificity of recent life-stress experience. *Journal of Consulting and Clinical Psychology*, 51, 467–469.

PARK, R.J., LAWRIE, J.M. & FREEMAN, C.P. (1995) Post-viral onset of anorexia nervosa. *British Journal of Psychology.* 166, 386–389.

PARKIN, J.R. & EAGLES, J.M. (1993) Blood-letting in anorexia nervosa. *British Journal of Psychiatry*, 162, 246–248.

PARRY-JONES, W.Ll. & PARRY-JONES, B. (1993) Self-mutilation in four historical cases of bulimia. *British Journal of Psychiatry*, 163, 394–402.

PARRY-JONES, W.Ll. & PARRY-JONES, B. (1994) Implications of historical evidence for the classification of eating disorders: A dimension overlooked in DSM-3-R and ICD-10. *British Journal of Psychiatry*, 165, 287–292.

PATON, D. (1992) Disaster research: The Scottish dimension. *The Psychologist*, 5, 535–538.

PERLBERG, M. (1979) Trauma at Tenerife: The psychic aftershocks of a jet disaster. *Human Behaviour*, 49–50.

PERLS, F.S. (1967) Group versus individual therapy. *ETC: A Review of General Semantics*, 34, 306–312.

PICCINELLI, M., PINI, S., BELLANTUONO, C. & WILKINSON, G. (1995) Efficacy of drug treatment in obsessive–compulsive disorder: A meta–analytic review. *British Journal of Psychiatry*, 166, 424–443.

PICKERING, J. (1981) Perception. In *Psychological Processes: Units 5 & 6–7.* Milton Keynes: The Open University Press.

PINES, M. (1982) Movement grows to create guidelines for mental therapy. *New York Times*, May 4, C1, C6.

PIRAN, N., KENNEDY, S., GARFINKEL, P.E. & OWENS, M. (1985) Affective disturbance in eating disorders. *Journal of Nervous and Mental Disease*, 173, 395–400.

POLIVY, J. & HERMAN, C.P. (1985) Dieting and bingeing: Causal analysis. *American Psychologist*, 40, 193–201.

PRIOLEAU, L., MURDOCK, M. & BRODY, N. (1983) An analysis of psychotherapy versus placebo studies. *Behaviour and Brain Sciences*, 6, 273–310.

PYNOOS, R.S., GOENIJIAN, A., TASHJIAN, M.,

KARAKASHIAN, M., MANJIKAN, R., MANOUKIAN, G., STEINBERG, A.M. & FAIRBANKS, L.A. (1993) Post–traumatic stress reactions in children after the 1988 Armenian earthquake. *British Journal of Psychiatry*, 163, 239–247.

RABIN, A.S., KASLOW, N.J. & REHM, L.P. (1986) Aggregate outcome and follow-up results following self-control therapy for depression. Paper presented at the American Psychological Convention.

RACHMAN, S. (1977) *Fear and Courage*. San Francisco: W.H. Freeman.

RACHMAN, S. (1984) Agoraphobia – a safety signal perspective. *Behaviour Research and Therapy*, 22, 59–70.

RAPPAPORT, Z.H. (1992) Psychosurgery in the modern era: Therapeutic and ethical aspects. *Medicine and Law*, 11, 449–453.

RIMM, D.C. (1976) Behaviour therapy: Some general comments and a review of selected papers. In R.L. Spitzer & D.F. Klein (Eds.) *Evaluation of Psychological Therapies*. Baltimore: Johns Hopkins University Press.

RIMM, D.C. & MASTERS, J.C. (1979) *Behaviour Therapy: Techniques and Empirical Findings* (2nd edition). New York: Academic Press.

ROBERTS, J.P. (1995) Group psychotherapy. *British Journal of Psychiatry*, 166, 124–129.

ROBINSON, A.J. (1984) Rock and roll delusions. *British Journal of Psychiatry*, 145 , 672.

ROGERS, C.R. (1951) *Client-Centred Therapy: Its Current Practice, Implications and Theory*. Boston: Houghton-Mifflin.

ROGERS, C.R. (1973) My philosophy of interpersonal relationships and how it grew. *Journal of Humanistic Psychology*, 13, 3–16.

ROGERS, C.R. (1980) *A Way of Being*. Boston: Houghton-Mifflin.

ROGERS, C.R. (1986) Client-centred therapy. In I. Kutash & A. Wolf (Eds.) *Psychotherapist's Casebook*. San Francisco: Jossey-Bass.

ROGERS, C.R. & DYMOND, R.F. (Eds.) (1954) *Psychotherapy and Personality Change*. Chicago: University of Chicago Press.

ROGLER, L.H., MALGADY, R.G., CONSTANTINO, G. & BLUMENTHAL, R. (1987) What do culturally sensitive mental health services mean? The case of Hispanics. *American Psychologist*, 42, 565–570.

ROHSENOW, D.J. & SMITH, R.E. (1982) Irrational beliefs as predictors of negative affective states. *Motivation and Emotion*, 6, 299–301.

ROSE, S., LEWONTIN, R.C. & KAMIN, L.J. (1984) *Not in our Genes*. Hardmondsworth: Penguin.

ROSENHAN, D.L. (1973) On being sane in insane places. *Science*, 179, 365–369.

ROSENHAN, D.L. & SELIGMAN, M.E. (1984) *Abnormal Psychology*. New York: Norton.

ROSENTHAL, D. (Ed.) (1963) *The Genain Quadruplets*. New York: Basic Books.

ROTH, A. & FONAGY, P. (1996) *Research on the efficacy and effectiveness of the psychotherapies: A report to the Department of Health*. London: HMSO.

ROY, A. (1981) Role of past loss in depression. *Archives of General Psychiatry*, 38, 301–302.

RUDERMAN, A.J. (1986) Dietary restraint: A theoretical and empirical review. *Psychological Bulletin*, 99, 247–262.

RUDOLPH, K., WIRZ-JUSTICE, A. & KRAUCHI, K. (1993) Static magnetic fields decrease nocturnal pineal cAMP in the rat. *Brain Research*, 446, 159–160.

RUSSELL, G.F.M. (1979) Bulimia nervosa: An ominous variant of anorexia nervosa. *Psychological Medicine*, 9, 429–448.

RUSSELL, R. (1981) Report on effective psychotherapy: Legislative testimony. Paper presented at a public hearing on the Regulation of Mental Health Practitioners, New York: March 5.

SAHAKIAN, B. (1987) Anorexia nervosa and bulimia nervosa. In R.L. Gregory (Ed.) *The Oxford Companion to the Mind*. Oxford: Oxford University Press.

SANAVIO, E. (1988) Obsessions and compulsions: The Padua Inventory. *Behaviour Research and Therapy*, 26, 169–177.

SANE (1993a) *Depression and Manic Depression: The Swings and Roundabouts of the Mind*. London: SANE Publications.

SANE (1993b) *Medical Methods of Treatment: A Guide to Psychiatric Drugs*. London: SANE Publications.

SARBIN, T.R. (1992) The social construction of schizophrenia. In W. Flack, D.R. Miller & M. Wiener (Eds.) *What is Schizophrenia?* New York: Springer-Verlag.

SARTORIUS, N., KAELBER, C.T. & COOPER, J.E. (1993) Progress toward achieving a common language in psychiatry. Results from the field trials accompanying the clinical guidelines of mental and behavioural disorders in ICD–10. *Archives of General Psychiatry*, 50, 115–124.

SCHEPER-HUGHES, N. (1991) *Death Without Weeping: The Violence of Everyday Life in Brazil*. Los Angeles: University of California Press.

SCHILDKRAUT, J. (1965) The catecholamine hypothesis of affective disorders: A review of supporting evidence. *American Journal of Psychiatry*, 122, 509–522.

SCHNEIDER, B.H. & BYRNE, B.M. (1987) Individualising social skills training for behaviour-disordered children. *Journal of Consulting and Clinical Psychology*, 55, 444–445.

SCHNEIDER, K. (1959) *Clinical Psychopathology*. New York: Grune & Stratton.

SCOTT, J. (1994) Cognitive therapy. *British Journal of Psychiatry*, 164, 126–130.

SELIGMAN, M.E.P. (1973) Fall into hopelessness. *Psychology Today*, 7, 43–47.

SELIGMAN, M.E.P. & MAIER, S.F. (1967) Failure to escape traumatic shock. *Journal of Experimental Psychology*, 74, 1–9.

SHAPIRO, A.K. (1971) Placebo effects in medicine, psychotherapy and psychoanalysis. In A.E. Bergin & S.L. Garfield (Eds.) *Handbook of Psychotherapy and Behaviour Change: An Empirical Analysis*. New York: Wiley.

SHAPIRO, D.A. & SHAPIRO, D. (1982) Meta-analysis of comparative therapy outcome studies: A replication and refinement. *Psychological Bulletin*, 92, 581–604.

SHARP, C.W. & FREEMAN, C.P.L. (1993) The medical complications of anorexia nervosa. *British Journal of Psychiatry*, 162, 452–462.

SHEAR, K.K., PILKONIS, P.A., CLOITRE, M. & LEON, A.C. (1994) Cognitive behavioural treatment compared with nonprescriptive treatment of panic disorders. *Archives of General Psychiatry*, 51, 395–401.

SILVERSTEIN, C. (1972) Behaviour modification and the gay community. Paper presented at the annual conference of the Association for the Advancement of Behaviour Therapy, New York.

SIMKIN, J.S. & YONTEF, G.M. (1984) Gestalt therapy. In R.J. Corsini (Ed.) *Current Psychotherapies* (3rd edition). Itasca, ILL: Peacock.

SKINNER, B.F. (1948) Superstition in the pigeon. *Journal of Experimental Psychology*, 38, 168–172.

SKINNER, B.F. (1990) Can psychology be a science of mind? *American Psychologist*, 45, 1206–1210.

SLATER, E. & ROTH, M. (1969) *Clinical Psychiatry* (3rd edition). Ballière-Tindall and Cassell.

SLATER, E. & SHIELDS, J. (1969) Genetic aspects of anxiety. In M. Lader (Ed.) *Studies of Anxiety*. Ashford, England: Headley Brothers.

SLOANE, R., STAPLES, F., CRISTOL, A., YORKSTON, N. & WHIPPLE, K. (1975) *Psychotherapy Versus Behaviour Therapy*. Cambridge, MA: Harvard University Press.

SMITH, D. (1982) Trends in counselling and psychotherapy. *American Psychologist*, 37, 802–809.

SMITH, M.L., GLASS, G.V. & MILLER, T.I. (1980) *The Benefits of Psychotherapy*. Baltimore: Johns Hopkins University Press.

SMYTHIES, J. (1976) Recent progress in schizophrenia research. *The Lancet*, 2, 136–139.

SNAITH, R.P. (1994) Psychosurgery: Controversy and enquiry. *British Journal of Psychiatry*, 161, 582–584.

SOLYOM, L., TURNBULL, I.M. & WILENSKY, M. (1987) A case of self-induced leucotomy. *British Journal of Psychiatry*, 151, 855–857.

SPITZER, R.L. (1975) On pseudoscience in science, logic in remission and psychiatric diagnosis: A critique of Rosenhan's 'On being sane in insane places'. *Journal of Abnormal Psychology*, 84, 442–452.

SPITZER, R.L., SKODAL, A.E., GIBBON, M. &

WILLIAMS, J.B.W. (Eds.) (1981) *DSM-III Case Book*. Washington, DC: American Psychiatric Association.

STEVENS, J.R. (1982) Neurology and neuropathology of schizophenia. In F.A. Henn & G.A. Nasrallah (Eds.) *Schizophrenia as a Brain Disease*. New York: Oxford University Press.

STROBER, M. & KATZ, J.L. (1987) Do eating disorders and affective disorders share a common aetiology? *International Journal of Eating Disorders*, 6, 171–180.

STRUPP. H.H. & HADLEY, S.W. (1977) *Psychotherapy for Better or Worse: An Analysis of the Problem of Negative Effects*. New York: Jason Aronson.

STRUPP, H.H. & HADLEY, S.W. (1979) Specific versus non-specific factors in psychotherapy: A controlled study of outcome. *Archives of General Psychiatry*, 36, 1125–1136.

SUE, D., SUE, D. & SUE, S. (1994) *Understanding Abnormal Behaviour* (4th edition). Boston: Houghton-Mifflin.

SUI–WAH, L. (1989) Anorexia nervosa and Chinese food. *British Journal of Psychiatry*, 155, 568.

SULSER, F. (1979) Pharmacology: New cellular mechanisms of anti-depressant drugs. In S. Fielding & R.C. Effland (Eds.) *New Frontiers in Psychotropic Drug Research*. Mount Kisco, NY: Futura.

SUNDAY, S.R. & HALMI, K.A. (1990) Taste perceptions and hedonics in eating disorders. *Physiology and Behaviour*, 48, 587–594.

SZASZ, T.S. (1960) The myth of mental illness. *American Psychologist*, 15, 113–118.

SZASZ, T.S. (1962) *The Myth of Mental Illness*. New York: Harper & Row.

SZASZ, T.S. (1974) *Ideology and Insanity*. Harmondsworth: Penguin.

SZASZ, T.S. (1994) *Cruel Compassion – Psychiatric Control of Society's Unwanted*. New York: Wiley.

TALLIS, F. (1994) Obsessive-compulsive disorder. *The Psychologist*, 7, 312.

TALLIS, R. (1996) Burying Freud. *The Lancet*, 347, 669–671.

TARRIER, N., BECKETT, R. & HARWOOD, S. (1993) A trial of two cognitive behavioural methods of treating drug-resistant residual psychotic symptoms in schizophrenic patients. *British Journal of Psychiatry*, 162, 524–532.

TEASDALE, J. (1988) Cognitive vulnerability to persistent depression. *Cognition and Emotion*, 2, 247–274.

TEUTING, P., ROSEN, S. & HIRSCHFELD, R. (1981) *Special Report on Depression Research*. Washington, DC: NIMH-DHHS Publication No. 81–1085.

THOMAS, K. (1990) Psychodynamics: The Freudian approach. In I. Roth (Ed.) *Introduction to Psychology*. Hove: Lawrence Erlbaum Associates Ltd.

THORNE, B. (1984) Person-centred therapy. In W.

Dryden (Ed.) *Individual Therapy in Britain*. London: Harper Row.

TORREY, E.F. (1988) *Surviving Schizophrenia* (revised edition). New York: Harper & Row.

TORREY, E.F., TORREY, B.B. & PETERSON, M.R. (1977) Seasonality of schizophrenic births in the United States. *Archives of General Psychiatry*, 34, 1065–1070.

TOUYZ, S.W., O'SULLIVAN, B.T., GERTLER, R. & BEAUMONT, P.J.V. (1988) Anorexia nervosa in a woman blind since birth. *British Journal of Psychiatry*, 153, 248–249.

TREASURE, J.L. & HOLLAND, A.J. (1991) Genes and the aetiology of eating disorders. In P. McGuffin & R. Murray (Eds.) *The New Genetics of Mental Illness*. Oxford: Butterworth.

TRUAX, C.B. (1966) Reinforcement and non-reinforcement in Rogerian therapy. *Journal of Abnormal Psychology*, 71, 1–9.

TRUAX, C.B. & CARKHUFF, R.R. (1964) Significant developments in psychotherapy research. In L.E. Abt & B.F. Reiss (Eds.) *Progress in Clinical Psychology*. New York: Grune & Stratton.

TUCKER, A. (1994) The surgeon who picked brains. *The Guardian*, December 10, 21.

ULLMAN, L.P. & KRASNER, L. (1969) *A Psychological Approach to Abnormal Behaviour*. Englewood Cliffs, NJ: Prentice-Hall.

VALENSTEIN, E.S. (1973) *Brain Control*. New York: Wiley.

VALENSTEIN, E.S. (1980) Rationale and psychosurgical procedures. In E.S. Valenstein (Ed.) *The Psychosurgery Debate*. San Francisco: W.H. Freeman.

VALENSTEIN, E.S. (1990) The prefrontal area and psychosurgery. *Progress in Brain Research*, 85, 539–554.

VALLIS, M., McCABE, S.B. & SHAW, B.F. (1986) The relationships between therapist skill in cognitive therapy and general therapy skill. Paper presented to the Society for Psychotherapy Research (June), Wellesley, MA.

VAN DER KOLK, B.A., PITMAN, R.K. & ORR, S.P. (1989) Endogenous opioids, stress-induced analgesia and post-traumatic stress disorder. *Psychopharmacology Bulletin*, 25, 108–112.

VERKAIK, R. (1995) The kindest cut of all? *The Sunday Times*, July 30, 18–19.

WADE, C. & TAVRIS, C. (1993) *Psychology* (3rd edition). London: HarperCollins.

WAKEFIELD, J.C. (1992) The concept of mental disorder. *American Psychologist*, 47, 373–388.

WALKER, S. (1984) *Learning Theory and Behaviour Modification*. London: Methuen.

WALLER, G. (1993) Sexual abuse and eating disorders. *British Journal of Psychiatry*, 162, 771–775.

WATSON, J.B. & RAYNER, R. (1920) Conditioned emotional responses. *Journal of Experimental Psychology*, 3, 1–14.

WEBSTER, R. (1995) *Why Freud was Wrong: Sin, Science and Psychoanalysis*. London: HarperCollins.

WEHR, T. & ROSENTHAL, N. (1989) Seasonality and affective illness. *American Journal of Psychiatry*, 146, 829–839.

WEISSMAN, M. (1987) Advances in psychiatric epidemiology: Rates and risks for major depression. *American Journal of Public Health*, 77, 445–451.

WEISSMAN, M. & PAYKEL, E. (1974) *The Depressed Woman*. Chicago: University of Chicago Press.

WENDER, P.H. & KLEIN, D.F. (1981) The promise of biological psychiatry. *Psychology Today*, 15, 25–41.

WENDER, P.H., KETY, S.S., ROSENTHAL, D., SCHULSINGER, F., ORTMANN, J. & LUNDE, I. (1986) Psychiatric disorders in the biological and adoptive families of individuals with affective disorders. *Archives of General Psychiatry*, 43, 923–929.

WESSELEY, S. (1993) Shocking treatment. *The Times*, November 18, 22.

WESSLER, R.L. (1986) Conceptualising cognitions in the cognitive-behavioural therapies. In W. Dryden & W. Golden (Eds.) *Cognitive-Behavioural Approaches to Psychotherapy*. London: Harper & Row.

WHITE, J., DAVISON, G.C. & WHITE, M. (1985) Cognitive distortions in the articulated thoughts of depressed patients. Unpublished manuscript, University of Southern California, Los Angeles.

WHITTELL, G. (1995) Spectacular northern lights linked to suicidal depression. *The Times*, April 15, 9.

WICK, A. (1996) Schizophrenia. *The Telegraph Magazine*, May 25, 49.

WILLIAMS, J.M.G. (1992) *The Psychological Treatment of Depression*. London: Routledge.

WILLIAMS, J.M.G. & HARGREAVES, I.R. (1995) Neuroses: Depressive and anxiety disorders. In A.A. Lazarus & A.M. Colman (Eds.) *Abnormal Psychology*. London: Longman.

WILSON, G.T. & O'LEARY, K.D. (1978) *Principles of Behaviour Therapy*. Englewood Cliffs, NJ: Prentice-Hall.

WILSON, P. (1982) Combined pharmacological and behavioural treatment of depression. *Behaviour Research and Therapy*, 20, 173–184.

WING, J.K., COOPER, J.E. & SARTORIUS, N. (1974) *Measurement and Classification of Psychiatric Symptoms*. Cambridge: Cambridge University Press.

WINNICOTT, D.W. (1958) *Through Paediatrics to Psychoanalysis*. London: The Hogarth Press.

WINTER, A. (1972) Depression and intractible pain treated by modified prefrontal lobotomy. *Journal of Medical Sociology*, 69, 757–759.

WOLPE, J. (1958) *Psychotherapy by Reciprocal Inhibition*. Stanford, CA: Stanford University Press.

WOLPE, J. (1969) For phobia: A hair of the hound. *Psychology Today*, 3, 34–37.

WOLPE, J. (1973) *The Practice of Behaviour Therapy*. New York: Pergamon Press.

WOLPE, J. (1985) Existential problems and behaviour therapy. *The Behaviour Therapist*, 8, 126–127.

WOLPE, J. & RACHMAN, S. (1960) Psychoanalytic evidence: A critique based on Freud's case of Little Hans. *Journal of Nervous and Mental Disease*, 131, 135–145.

WOLPE, J. & WOLPE, D. (1981) *Our Useless Years*. Boston: Houghton-Mifflin.

WOOLEY, S. & WOOLEY, O. (1983) Should obesity be treated at all? *Psychiatric Annals*, 13, 884–885.

WURTMAN, R. & WURTMAN, J. (1989) Carbohydrates and depression. *Scientific American*, 251, 68–75.

WYNNE, L.C., SINGER, M.T., BARTKO, J.J. & TOOHEY, M.L. (1977) Schizophrenics and their families: Recent research on parental communication. In J.M. Tanner (Ed.) *Developments in Psychiatric Research*. London: Hodder & Stoughton.

YAGER, J., HATTON, C.A. & LAWRENCE, M. (1986) Anorexia nervosa in a woman totally blind since the age of two. *British Journal of Psychiatry*, 149, 506–509.

YULE, W. (1993) Children's trauma from transport disasters. *The Psychologist*, 7, 318–319.

ZIGLER, E. & PHILLIPS, L. (1961) Psychiatric diagnosis and symptomatology. *Journal of Abnormal Psychology*, 63, 69–75.

ZILBOORG, G. & HENRY, G.W. (1941) *A History of Medical Psychology*. New York: Norton.

INDEX

Please note that page numbers in **bold** refer to definitions and (main) explanations of particular concepts.